THE INQUIRING MIND

In recent years, philosophers have grown increasingly aware that epistemic excellence has a *personal* dimension—that it involves, not merely the possession of well-functioning cognitive faculties like vision and memory, but also various intellectual *character* virtues like curiosity, reflectiveness, open-mindedness, fair-mindedness, and intellectual courage, honesty, carefulness, and rigor. This insight has spawned the field of 'responsibilist' or character-based virtue epistemology. Jason Baehr's *The Inquiring Mind* is a major and systematic contribution to this field, one that will capture the interest of a wide range of philosophers and students. The book contains an introduction to virtue epistemology and intellectual virtues, as well as an in-depth examination of how the concept of intellectual virtue figures—and *fails* to figure—in an adequate philosophical account of knowledge. Baehr also defends a 'personal worth' account of the nature and structure of an intellectual virtue that draws heavily from the literature in both virtue epistemology and virtue ethics. *The Inquiring Mind* is a comprehensive and groundbreaking treatment of an important cutting-edge field in philosophy.

THE INQUIRING MIND

On Intellectual Virtues and Virtue Epistemology

JASON BAEHR

OXFORD
UNIVERSITY PRESS

OXFORD
UNIVERSITY PRESS

Great Clarendon Street, Oxford OX2 6DP

Oxford University Press is a department of the University of Oxford.
It furthers the University's objective of excellence in research, scholarship,
and education by publishing worldwide. Oxford is a registered trade
mark of Oxford University Press in the UK and in certain other countries

Published in the United States
by Oxford University Press Inc., New York

First published 2011

First published in paperback 2012

British Library Cataloguing in Publication Data
Data available

Library of Congress Cataloging in Publication Data
Data available

ISBN 978–0–19–960407–4
ISBN 978–0–19–965929–6

Printed in the United Kingdom by
Lightning Source UK Ltd., Milton Keynes

For my parents,

with deep gratitude

Acknowledgments

This book has been in the works for about a decade. The initial seed for it was planted just prior to my first week in graduate school when I picked up a copy of Linda Zagzebski's recently published *Virtues of the Mind* (1996) and, after reading the first twenty pages or so, said to my wife, "Well, I've discovered my dissertation topic." The book brought together in an exhilarating way several of my prior philosophical interests in epistemology, virtue ethics, philosophy of mind, and ancient philosophy. My prediction turned out to be true, as I ended up writing a dissertation, under the direction of Larry BonJour at the University of Washington, that dealt with several key themes in Linda's book—themes which, by no accident, are also central to the present book.

Initial work on the book began in my last two years of graduate school and continued during the 2002–2003 academic year, which I spent on a generous postdoctoral fellowship at Baylor University. That year Bob Roberts and Jay Wood were writing an initial draft of their book *Intellectual Virtues: An Essay in Regulative Epistemology* (2007). While most of our conversations revolved around their work in virtue epistemology, our time together had an important influence on my own thinking, an influence that is clearly evident in the pages that follow. I am grateful to Bob and Jay, and to Baylor, for a lot of great conversation and support that year.

Work on the book began in earnest in the fall of 2006 during a pre-tenure sabbatical at Loyola Marymount University. I have been hard at work on it since, and am very grateful to LMU for considerable ongoing support of the project, which has included Summer Research Grants in 2004, 2005, and 2007 and a Bellarmine College of Liberal Arts College Fellowship during the fall of 2007.

While many people have influenced the ideas and arguments put forth here, the influence of Linda Zagzebski and Larry BonJour is difficult to overstate. I am grateful to Linda for doing the sort of work she does: always innovative and insightful. While I take issue with some of her main theoretical proposals in the pages that follow, Linda's work—perhaps second only to Aristotle's—makes me want to *do* philosophy. I am also grateful to Linda for her generous conversation, feedback, and friendship over the past decade. My debt to Larry is different. While Larry does not work in virtue epistemology, the exceptional clarity and rigor of his work in traditional epistemology, together with his uncompromising attention to philosophically substantive issues and argumentation, have shaped and inspired me as a philosopher in profound ways. I am also very grateful for his feedback and friendship over the years—especially for his role in my graduate training and dissertation. His influence on this book is obvious (to me, at any rate) at several points and less obvious but no less real at many others.

Several colleagues and friends have also played a role in the development and writing of the book. I have the good fortune of working in a very supportive and engaging department. Nearly every member of my department has provided helpful feedback about one or more of the ideas contained herein. I am grateful to Tim Shanahan and Brian Treanor for a number of spontaneous but in depth and helpful conversations. And I am especially grateful to Michael Pace, Steve Porter, and Dan Speak, who have listened attentively and patiently to several (often half-baked) points or arguments that in one form or another have made their way into the book. These conversations have significantly improved the quality of the book and helped make the writing of it an enjoyable and rewarding experience. Conversations with friend and historian Phil Dow have had a similar effect. Phil's enthusiasm about this material, and his incorporation of parts of it into his own writing and teaching, have been and continue to be a source of inspiration to me.

I also owe a debt of gratitude to several fellow virtue epistemologists. My thinking in this area has been shaped and enriched over several years by conversations and correspondence with Guy Axtell, Heather Battaly, John Greco, Stephen Grimm, Wayne Riggs, Bob Roberts, Ernie Sosa, Jay Wood, and Linda Zagzebski. These folks are fine interlocutors and fine people. They make virtue epistemology a pleasant and invigorating field in which to work. I also owe a very special debt of gratitude to Stephen Grimm, Bob Roberts, and John Turri, who read the entire manuscript with care and provided a great deal of very helpful feedback. I only regret that I have not done more to incorporate their suggestions and deal with all of their concerns.

I taught portions of the manuscript in an undergraduate course in the spring of 2008 and in graduate courses in the fall of 2007 and 2009. These were rewarding experiences for me, and I thank the students in those courses for reading the material carefully and providing feedback. I am particularly grateful to the students in the fall 2009 course for their energetic reading and conversation.

Portions of the book have appeared in print elsewhere. Chapter 3 is a substantially revised version of "Character in Epistemology," *Philosophical Studies* 128 (2006): 479–514. Chapter 4 is a revision of "Character, Reliability, and Virtue Epistemology," *The Philosophical Quarterly* 56 (2006): 193–212. Chapter 5 is a revision of "Evidentialism, Vice, and Virtue" *Philosophy and Phenomenological Research* 78 (2009): 545–67. Chapter 8 is a revision of "The Structure of Open-Mindedness," forthcoming (2011) in the *Canadian Journal of Philosophy*. And a portion of Chapter 7 is taken from "On the Reliability of Moral and Intellectual Virtues," *Metaphilosophy* 38 (2007): 457–71. I am grateful to the publishers of these journals for permission to reprint this material.

Finally, I owe an incomparable debt of gratitude to my family. Erinn, Brendan, Lily, and Oliver fill my days with joy, making my life a good one. My parents, Ted and Tori, are a source of ceaseless and generous love and support. This book is dedicated to them.

JASON BAEHR

Contents

Chapter 1

INTRODUCTION

One remarkable feature of our species is its propensity for inquiry. We humans are neither oblivious to nor indifferent about our surroundings. Nor is our interest in our surroundings purely practical. Rather, as beings that are both reflective and rational, we often find ourselves fascinated and puzzled by the world around us. We desire to know, to *understand* how things are, were, or might someday be. As a result, we make intentional and sustained efforts to figure things out. We inquire.

Yet inquiry can go well or it can go poorly. Sometimes the difference is attributable to a relatively mechanical factor, as when a person fails to reach the truth on account of a defective cognitive faculty, for example, poor vision, weak hearing, or a faulty memory. Often, however, the success or failure of an inquiry has a more personal source. This is due to the fact that inquiry has a robustly *active* dimension. It involves observing, imagining, reading, interpreting, reflecting, analyzing, assessing, formulating, and articulating. Success in these activities is hardly guaranteed by the possession of sharp vision, sensitive hearing, or an impeccable memory. Rather, it requires an exercise of certain intellectual *character* traits. It can require, for instance, that one engage in *attentive* observation, *thoughtful* or *open-minded* imagination, *patient* reflection, *careful* and *thorough* analysis, or *fair-minded* interpretation and assessment.[1] As this suggests, inquiry makes substantial personal demands on inquirers. It demands an exercise of a range of "intellectual character virtues."

Typically, when we think or speak of "character" or "virtues," we have something distinctively moral in mind. We think of a virtuous person as one who is appropriately moved or motivated by ends like social justice or the alleviation of human suffering. Such a person is fair, respectful, benevolent,

[1] See Hookway (2000; 2001; 2003) for more on the structure and demands of inquiry, and on the importance of intellectual virtues for meeting these demands.

compassionate, and generous. As we have just seen, however, and as we will explore in much greater detail in the pages that follow, personal character is not exhausted by moral character. It also has an epistemic or intellectual dimension: a fully or broadly virtuous person can also be counted on to care deeply about ends like truth, knowledge, evidence, rationality, and understanding;[2] and out of this fundamental concern will emerge other traits like inquisitiveness, attentiveness, carefulness and thoroughness in inquiry, fair-mindedness, open-mindedness, and *intellectual* patience, honesty, courage, humility, and rigor.[3]

These virtues are the central subject matter of the present book. One aim of the book is to provide a reasonably deep and illuminating account of what intellectual virtues amount to—of their underlying nature, structure, and role in the cognitive economy. A second aim is more abstract: it is to evaluate the role that reflection on intellectual virtues should play within epistemology, which (broadly construed) is the philosophical study of knowledge and related intellectual goods.[4] Accordingly, the book is intended as a contribution to the growing literature in "virtue epistemology," which is a recent collection of approaches to epistemology that give the concept of intellectual virtue a central and fundamental role.[5]

As this brief preview suggests, my objective in the book is largely theoretical in nature. It is not primarily to inspire change in the intellectual conduct or character of my readers; nor is it to specify the practical steps a person might take to become intellectually virtuous. Nevertheless, I hope it is not outrageous to suppose that something like the present inquiry might have at least a modest effect in this regard. For, as Aristotle noted long ago, one expedient to becoming good is getting clear on the nature and structure of the good itself.[6] And a major

[2] This dimension of personal character may still be part of "moral" character on a sufficiently broad conception of morality. For more on the distinction between the intellectual and moral realms, and for a corresponding distinction between intellectual and moral virtues, see the Appendix.

[3] "Intellectual," in the preceding sentence, is intended to modify, not just "patience," but also the immediately subsequent virtue terms. I employ this construction throughout the book so as to avoid repeated use of "intellectual" when referring to several of the traits in question (e.g. intellectual courage, intellectual honesty, intellectual integrity, intellectual rigor, and so on).

[4] This is a broad but apt conception of the field. See Alston (2005: 2–3) and Roberts and Wood (2007: 3) for more on this conception.

[5] For overviews of the field, see Wood (1998), Zagzebski (1998), my (2004) and (2008), and Battaly (2008), Greco and Turri (2009).

[6] Of the "chief good," Aristotle famously says: "Surely, then, knowledge of the good must be very important for our lives? And if, like archers, we have a target, are we not more likely to hit the

part of what I shall attempt to do here is uncover the nature and structure of one important dimension of personal worth.

In the remainder of this introductory chapter, I undertake three main tasks. First, I develop three extended illustrations of intellectual virtue so as to better "fix the referent" of the discussion. Second, I offer a brief account of the history and present landscape of virtue epistemology. Third, I offer an overview of the rest of the book.

1.1 *Intellectual virtue: some examples*

To get a better sense of what intellectual virtue amounts to, it is helpful to consider a few concrete instances of it.[7] The first example is taken from a recent account (Miller 2002) of Abraham Lincoln's well-known efforts at self-education:

> Lincoln's life would be punctuated by intense projects in self-education and research, starting with his "picking up" "somehow" reading and writing. Surely it is a little unusual for a twenty-three-year-old man, now on his own and making his way in the world, to go to some trouble to borrow a textbook on grammar—walking six miles to borrow it—and then on his own (asking for some assistance) to teach himself that rudimentary subject. Lincoln himself, in his longer autobiographical piece, included two of the more striking of his grown-up personal educational projects... The first of these was his studying grammar... The second of his remarkable projects in adult self-education—this one perhaps still more impressive—further along in life and reported now to the world by himself, was this: "He studied and nearly mastered the six books of Euclid, since he was a member of Congress"... Lincoln left out of his account his teaching himself surveying in order to take a job as a deputy surveyor. He had to learn the practical application of the principles of trigonometry, and got two

right mark? If so, we must try at least roughly to comprehend what it is..." (*NE* 2000, 1094a 22–30, trans. Crisp). A concern with inspiring intellectual change on the part of philosophical readers is not entirely foreign to epistemology. In his *Discourse on Method* (1968), for instance, Descartes extols a wide range of intellectual character traits with an eye toward improving the intellectual practices and habits of his reader (see especially Discourse II, pp. 35–44). A similar point bolds for certain segments of Locke's *Essay Concerning Human Understanding* (1996) (see especially BK. IV. chs. 12–20). For a recent philosophical treatment of intellectual virtues aimed explicitly at inspiring growth in these traits, see Roberts and Wood (2007: esp. ch. 1).

[7] Here and elsewhere I alternate between the use of "virtues" (plural) and "virtue" (singular). We can think of "virtue" as an overall state or condition of character consisting in the possession of several individual "virtues."

> books on the subject of surveying, and learned enough to do the job... More important, he studied the law. He borrowed books from John T. Stuart, read and studied Blackstone, taught himself to be a lawyer. (52)

This impression of Lincoln as an unrelenting autodidact is confirmed by the following account of his reading habits:

> [I]t would be quite a study to go through the available record to identify all the places, times, and postures in which those who had known Abraham in Indiana and in New Salem remembered him reading a book: reading while the horse rests at the end of a row, reading while walking on the street, reading under a tree, reading while others went to dances, reading with his legs up as high as his head, reading between customers in the post office, reading stretched at length on the counter of the store. In Lord Charnwood's classic biography an employer says: "I found him... cocked on a haystack with a book." (48)

A related example, also from nineteenth-century American history, is the self-education of Frederick Douglass. A Maryland slave, Douglass was prevented by his master from learning to read on the grounds that it would make him useless and unhappy. In his autobiography, Douglass explains that what was to his master "a great evil, to be carefully shunned, was to me a great good, to be diligently sought; and the argument which he so warmly urged, against my learning to read, only served to inspire me with a desire and determination to learn" (2001: 32). So Douglass took his education into his own hands:

> The plan which I adopted, and the one by which I was most successful, was that of making friends of all the little white boys whom I met in the street. As many of these as I could, I converted into teachers. With their kindly aid, obtained at different times and in different places, I finally succeeded in learning to read. When I was sent on errands, I always took my book with me, and by going on part of my errand quickly, I found time to get a lesson before my return. I used also to carry bread with me, enough of which was always in the house, and to which I was always welcome; for I was much better off in this regard than many of the poor white children in our neighborhood. This bread I used to bestow upon the hungry little urchins, who, in return, would give me that more valuable bread of knowledge. (34)

Douglass's plan was successful indeed, for within a couple of years he was voraciously consuming whatever literature he could get his hands on, from the Bible to newspapers to political treatises.

The cases of Lincoln and Douglass illustrate the point that intellectual virtue is fundamentally rooted in a deep and abiding desire for knowledge and understanding—a desire for "cognitive contact with reality," as Linda Zagzebski (1996) has described it. They also suggest that this fundamental motivation tends to spawn a range of more specific characteristics or virtues, including intellectual courage, diligence, determination, perseverance, ingenuity, and resourcefulness. Finally, the cases illustrate the fact that the aim or goal of intellectual virtue is relatively broad in scope, that is, that an intellectually virtuous person is characteristically curious about a rather wide range of ideas and subject matters.

A third and somewhat different example is drawn from C. P. Snow's 1934 novel *The Search*, which chronicles the rise and fall of a talented and ambitious young scientist named Arthur Miles. In the passage that follows, Miles describes his admiration for his good friend and colleague Constantine:

> [Constantine] recalled and concentrated all the ecstatic moments I had found in science. Here was a man of the greatest powers who spent his time doing rather dull experiments very accurately. He did not pretend that he would not like something more exciting; but that might come his way; meanwhile, he went happily on, doing his own work, reading everyone else's, fitting it all into a great cosmic scheme. His research was not as well-known as mine. He had not gone as far. He was content with it. He lived in something like poverty. He was the secretary of one or two international editorial bodies, which did valuable, humble, completely unrewarded work.
>
> I had met many other scientists who would have claimed to do what Constantine did, working with intelligent devotion, not caring over-much how knowledge was obtained as long as it duly came. But, in moments of doubt, I had never been satisfied with their intelligence or their devotion. To question either in Constantine's case would have not been worldly-wise but merely absurd. I did not know a more remarkable mind; nor anyone who wanted so little for himself. (174)

Like Lincoln and Douglass, Constantine is driven by a firm desire for knowledge and understanding—a desire that reveals something significant about his personal character or about who he is as a person. And here as well the desire in question gives rise to a range of other virtuous traits, for example, to intellectual carefulness, diligence, and perseverance. Finally, the passage suggests that intellectual virtues involve an "intelligent devotion" to epistemic goods that *overrides* or *outranks* various other desires and concerns. Constantine places greater value, for instance, on the advancement of scientific knowledge than he does on goods like professional status, honor, and wealth. In this respect, he also exemplifies virtues like intellectual humility and generosity.

Examples of better and worse intellectual character are legion in literature and real life.[8] I offer this small sampling mainly to illustrate the idea that there is in fact an intellectual or epistemically oriented dimension of personal character and to provide some indication of its substance. The examples also are intended to provide some sense of the underlying psychological structure of intellectual virtue, specifically, of the fact that individual intellectual virtues tend to "flow" from something like a desire for truth or knowledge—a desire that outweighs and subordinates various competing desires.

1.2 *Virtue epistemology*

With an initial idea of what intellectual virtues amount to before us, I turn now to a very brief history and overview of the field of virtue epistemology, which again is an approach to the philosophical study of knowledge and related intellectual goods that gives a central and fundamental role to the concept of intellectual virtue.

1.2.1 *A very brief history*

Aristotle is widely regarded as the first philosopher to identify a class of intellectual virtues distinct from the class of moral virtues and to give them a central role in an account of human knowing. He defined intellectual virtues as "states by virtue of which the soul possesses truth by way of affirmation or denial"; and he identified "art" (*techne*), "scientific knowledge" (*episteme*), "practical wisdom" (*phronesis*), "philosophic wisdom" (*sophia*), and "intuitive reason" (*nous*) as the five central intellectual virtues (*NE* 1139b). As this list suggests, Aristotle did not think of intellectual virtues as character traits, but rather as cognitive capacities or powers.[9]

In the centuries following Aristotle, a limited number of philosophers (most notably Thomas Aquinas) continued to focus on intellectual virtues in their discussions of knowledge. By the modern period, however, the attention of philosophers writing about knowledge began to shift away from the characteristics of excellent cognitive *agents* and onto the status and properties of certain

[8] For discussions of some intellectual *vices*, see Frankfurt (1988), Battaly (2010), and my (2010).

[9] See Montmarquet (1993: 19–20). The character model of intellectual virtue that I am concerned with here instead resembles Aristotle's account of *moral* virtue (see Zagzebski 1996: 137–57 for a helpful discussion of Aristotle's distinction between moral and intellectual virtues).

beliefs (e.g. belief in an external or material world).[10] As a result, ensuing centuries witnessed increasingly fewer treatments of intellectual virtue; and by the middle of the twentieth century, talk of intellectual virtue had all but vanished from mainstream philosophical discussions of knowledge.[11]

The modern period also witnessed a general philosophical drift from an ancient and medieval preoccupation with *moral* virtue. Virtue-oriented accounts of the moral life began to give way—owing largely to the influence of Immanuel Kant and John Stuart Mill—to discussions about the nature of morally right action, for example, about whether a morally right action is better understood as one that conforms to the moral law (Kant) or one that "maximizes utility" (Mill). Here as well the notions of virtue and character began to fade into the background.

By the middle of the twentieth century, however, a number of moral philosophers, inspired in part by Elizabeth Anscombe's paper "Modern Moral Philosophy" (1958), began returning to a more ancient, character-based approach to ethics in an effort to avoid flaws which they regarded as endemic to modern moral philosophy. In the decades that followed, this migration gained considerable momentum, with virtue ethics being regarded by many today as a veritable "third force" (alongside Kantianism and consequentialism) within normative ethics.[12]

It was not until 1980 that a return to virtue began to take hold in the neighboring field of epistemology. That year, Ernest Sosa argued in "The Raft and the Pyramid" that the concept of an intellectual virtue provides a way of dealing with various longstanding debates in mainstream epistemology. Like Aristotle, Sosa did not conceive of intellectual virtues as traits of character; instead, he thought of them as (roughly) reliable or truth-conducive cognitive faculties or abilities like memory, vision, hearing, reason, and introspection.[13]

[10] This shift was not complete, however. For instance, works by Descartes (1968: 38–44), Locke (1996: 172–5, 292–35), and Hume (1997: 102–3, 111–12) contain fairly extensive treatments of some of the more volitional or characterological aspects of the intellectual life, often mentioning various intellectual virtues and vices by name.

[11] As Guy Axtell (1998; 2000) and others have noted, what contemporary virtue epistemologists regard as intellectual character virtues were at the heart of some of the (broadly epistemological) work of American pragmatists like John Dewey in the first half of the twentieth century.

[12] For an instructive account of the relation between virtue ethics and virtue epistemology, see Solomon (2003). For a recent overview of virtue ethics, see Copp and Sobel (2004).

[13] This is not to say that Aristotle's and Sosa's positive accounts of intellectual virtue are very similar; indeed they are not. Again, Aristotle does not treat cognitive faculties like vision or memory as intellectual virtues; and Sosa's conception of intellectual virtue does not include states like *techne*, *phronesis*, or *sophia*. It would, however, be worth exploring how exactly the two groups of qualities are related.

Finally, in 1984, Lorraine Code, receiving some inspiration from virtue ethics and Sosa's view in epistemology, proposed a distinctively *character*-based version of epistemology. Her primary interest was "epistemic responsibility," which she identified as the chief intellectual character virtue—a virtue "from which other virtues radiate" (1987: 44). Distinguishing it from Sosa's faculty-based "virtue reliabilism," Code dubbed her approach "virtue responsibilism" on the grounds that the traits in question are the defining qualities of a responsible thinker or inquirer.[14]

As this quick overview suggests, contemporary virtue epistemology has, since its early days, been comprised of two notably different approaches: a faculty-based or "reliabilist" approach and a character-based or "responsibilist" approach. Each camp has continued to attract its share of converts. John Greco (2000a; 2010) and Alvin Goldman (1992; 2001) have given the notion of an intellectual virtue conceived as a reliable ability or faculty a central role in their accounts of knowledge. Jonathan Kvanvig (1992), James Montmarquet (1993), Linda Zagzebski (1996), Christopher Hookway (2000; 2003), and several others have followed Code in making matters of intellectual character a primary focus. Of special note in the latter domain is Zagzebski's book *Virtues of the Mind* (1996), which provided the first comprehensive and systematic virtue-theoretical approach to epistemology. More than any other work in the field, Zagzebski's book is responsible for putting character-based virtue epistemology on the philosophical map.

While I shall have some occasion to address faculty-based or "reliabilist" varieties of virtue epistemology in the course of the book, and while (as we will see in Chapter 4) the distinction between these and character-based approaches is considerably less sharp than it might initially appear, my primary focus will be "responsibilist" or character-based forms of virtue epistemology—for again I am most interested in the nature and epistemological significance of the relevant excellences of intellectual *character*.[15]

[14] Axtell (1997) helped codify these labels. See that paper and Chapter 4 of this book for extended discussions of the distinction between "virtue reliabilism" and "virtue responsibilism."

[15] Some philosophers today (e.g. Harman 1999 and 2000 and Doris 1998 and 2002) object to the very concept of character or virtue in light of certain experimental data suggesting that human behavior is often influenced more by arbitrary situational factors than by any personal or characterological qualities like virtues or vices. These "situationist" objections to virtue ethics have been met with no shortage of critical replies in recent years. For a sampling of these replies, see Merritt (2000), Sreenivasan (2002), Miller (2003), Kamtekar (2004), Sabini and Silver (2005), Adams (2006), and Snow (2009). While I find the situationist literature fascinating and challenging in various ways, I think the critical response succeeds at showing that it does not present a mortal threat to many reasonably traditional conceptions of virtue. Nonetheless,

1.2.2 *Four varieties of character-based virtue epistemology*

In light of this focus, it will be helpful to take an even closer look at the theoretical terrain of character-based virtue epistemology and to mark some distinctions between the different approaches that have emerged in recent years.[16] (Henceforth, for ease of discussion, I shall use the term "virtue epistemology" to refer

I offer here a very brief outline of my own six-part perspective on the topic and its relevance to the present inquiry. (1) The experimental data in question concern the possession of *moral* virtues. As such, they do not immediately bear on the possession of intellectual virtues, and thus do not immediately threaten standard ways of thinking about intellectual virtues. (2) I make very few claims in the book concerning any *persisting* or *broadly efficacious* aspects of intellectual virtue. Rather, my characterization of the relevant traits focuses mainly on the particular desires, beliefs, and other psychological states that constitute them—states that need not be thought of in the "globalist" terms that situationists find objectionable. (3) I think standard views of the minimal or basic requirements for (moral or intellectual) virtue are more attenuated and situation-specific than situationist critiques of them tend to suggest (see e.g. Doris's "globalist" target on pp. 22–6 in 2002). Consequently, I think they are considerably less threatened by the relevant experimental data than many situationists would have us think. (4) Similarly, I think "full" or "complete" intellectual virtue is not very widely distributed and thus that we should not expect it to make a very strong showing in the relevant experimental contexts. (5) Some situationists may see (4) as an indication that the concept of (at least *full* or *complete*) virtue is useless or irrelevant. My own take on this matter, however, is that many accounts of moral and intellectual virtue are intended as accounts of a particular (moral or intellectual) *ideal*. As such, I think the accounts in question have considerable *regulative* or *action-guiding* power, and thus are not at all useless or irrelevant (see Roberts and Wood 2007 for a prime example). (6) That said, I do not think that an account of, say, ideal epistemic character is the *only* source of information that might be helpful for regulating our intellectual lives. In fact, were situationists to provide empirical data concerning the factors that tend to influence our intellectual (vs. our moral) development and activities, I think this data could also play an important regulative role. It might, for instance, shed significant light on our *present* intellectual situation in a way that would be helpful vis-à-vis our attempts to move beyond this situation and closer to the intellectual ideal. In this way, I am inclined to regard traditional and many situationist portrayals of character and virtue as complementary. This irenic picture does not appear to occur to Doris, who seems to think (2002: 149–52) that one must choose *between* thinking of virtue as a kind of action-guiding ideal, on the one hand, and giving serious attention to what situationist experimental data (allegedly) suggest concerning the rather less than ideal state of human character, on the other. This brief sketch of my response to situationism obviously is no substitute for an elaboration or defense of it; but it is all I have the space for here.

[16] A further motivation for the classification that follows is the remarkable theoretical heterogeneity of the published work in this area. As William Alston (2005) observed, "What is nowadays called 'virtue epistemology' is a sprawling, diverse, even chaotic territory. There is not even a rough commonality as to what counts as an intellectual virtue, much less how it functions in belief formation or how this bears on epistemic status" (153). For more on this point, and for an elaboration of (something very much like) the classification I articulate here, see my (2008).

specifically to character-based approaches and "intellectual virtues" to refer to intellectual *character* virtues.)

One important and salient difference among the various authors working in this area is how they conceive of the relationship between (1) the concept of an intellectual virtue and (2) the problems and questions of traditional epistemology.[17] For some, an appeal to intellectual virtue promises a solution to many of the most difficult and longstanding problems in traditional epistemology. Zagzebski (1996), for instance, argues that giving the concept of intellectual virtue a central role in an account of knowledge yields a satisfactory account of the nature of knowledge, a rebuttal to skepticism, a solution to the Gettier problem, and a way of resolving the debate between internalists and externalists. She sees an appeal to intellectual virtue as having a kind of salvific and transformative effect on traditional epistemology.[18] Others, however, see reflection on matters of intellectual virtue as motivating fundamentally new directions and inquiries in epistemology—directions and inquiries that are largely independent of traditional concerns about the nature, structure, limits, or sources of knowledge.[19] Hookway (2000; 2003), for instance, commends an approach to epistemology that focuses on the domain of *inquiry* rather than on individual beliefs or items of knowledge; and because intellectual character virtues like carefulness and thoroughness, sensitivity to detail, intellectual perseverance, honesty, and adaptability often play a critical role in successful inquiry, he contends that such an approach will be virtue-based. Robert Roberts and Jay Wood (2007) have recently defended an approach to virtue epistemology that focuses on *individual* intellectual virtues and makes little attempt to address or "solve" the problems of traditional epistemology in virtue-theoretic

[17] By "traditional epistemology," I mean (roughly) epistemology in the Cartesian tradition, the central focus of which is the nature, structure, limits, and sources of knowledge. Some of the topics and debates that have been or are central to this tradition include global and local skepticism, the nature of perception, rationalism vs. empiricism, the problem of induction, the analysis of knowledge, foundationalism vs. coherentism, internalism vs. externalism, and the Gettier problem. For an overview and representative sample, see BonJour (2002).

[18] See, for example, pp. 279–81, 291–5, or 329–34. Fairweather (2001), Axtell (2007; 2008; 2010), and Napier (2009) also support giving the concept of intellectual virtue a significant role in an account of knowledge. Axtell, however, does not limit his conception of intellectual virtue to the relevant character traits; instead he endorses a "thinner" conception of intellectual virtue which incorporates both character virtues and faculty virtues.

[19] These two approaches are not mutually exclusive. Indeed, even Zagzebski (1996), who again is the leading proponent of the former approach, sees important connections between intellectual virtue and certain epistemic concepts that have been neglected by traditional epistemologists, for instance, wisdom and understanding. Moreover, her extensive work on the nature and structure of an intellectual virtue fits squarely in this second category.

terms. Their aim is rather to provide something like a "conceptual map" of the domain of excellent intellectual character. Accordingly, they offer chapter-length analyses of several individual virtues, including love of knowledge, intellectual firmness, courage and caution, humility, autonomy, generosity, and practical wisdom.

There are, then, two general approaches to character-based virtue epistemology: "conservative" approaches that appeal to the concept of intellectual virtue as a way of engaging or addressing traditional epistemological problems and questions; and "autonomous" approaches that focus on matters of intellectual virtue in ways that are largely independent of traditional questions, but that are still broadly epistemological in nature.

Each of these main varieties admits of two sub-varieties. Conservative approaches to virtue epistemology can be either strong or weak, depending on how substantial they think the connection is between the concept of intellectual virtue and the problems and questions of traditional epistemology. Zagzebski's approach is a clear instance of what I shall refer to as Strong Conservative VE, since again, she envisions the concept of intellectual virtue playing a *major* and *central* role within traditional epistemology. But a weaker variety of conservative virtue epistemology is also possible. In recent years, for instance, I have argued (and will argue again in subsequent chapters) that the concept of an intellectual virtue cannot form the basis of an adequate analysis of knowledge (2006a; Ch. 3), but that it does merit a kind of *secondary* or *background* role in both reliabilist (2006b; Ch. 4) and evidentialist (2009; Ch. 5) accounts of knowledge. While supporting the idea that there is some theoretical connection between intellectual virtue and traditional epistemology, the suggestion is that this connection is considerably more modest and less extensive than Zagzebski and others have thought. Thus I refer to the view that the concept of intellectual virtue might play a weak or minimal or secondary role in connection with traditional epistemology as Weak Conservative VE.

Autonomous varieties of virtue epistemology also come in stronger and weaker forms. The guiding assumption in this area is that matters of intellectual virtue have epistemological "traction" or significance independent of more traditional epistemological concerns. According to what I shall call Strong Autonomous VE, an autonomous virtue-based approach should *supplant* or *replace* traditional approaches. In this vein, Kvanvig (1992) argues that there is no significant role for the concept of intellectual virtue to play within traditional epistemology, but that this concept is nonetheless central to epistemology proper; consequently, he goes on to claim that the traditional, Cartesian approach to epistemology should be jettisoned in favor of a virtue-based approach. Other proponents of an autonomous virtue epistemology have staked out a less ambitious position, claiming instead that their approaches are a proper *complement* to—and thus can exist peaceably alongside—more traditional approaches to epistemology. Code, for instance, makes clear that her approach is not aimed at replacing traditional epistemology, but rather at shedding light on areas that traditional epistemology has tended to neglect (1987: 63–4; 253). Roberts and Wood adopt a similar line (2007: ch. 1). I shall refer to this less radical perspective on autonomous virtue epistemology as Weak Autonomous VE.

We have seen that virtue epistemology as a whole is comprised of two main approaches: a faculty-based or "reliabilist" approach and a character-based or "responsibilist" approach. The latter, again, is my main concern in the present work. We have seen furthermore that the domain of character-based virtue epistemology itself admits of two varieties—one "conservative" and the other "autonomous"—and that each of these varieties can take either a weaker or stronger form. For a more detailed reiteration of the structure of character-based virtue epistemology, see Table 1.1.[20]

Table 1.1 *Varieties of character-based virtue epistemology*

Conservative VE: the concept of intellectual virtue is useful for addressing one or more problems in traditional epistemology		**Autonomous VE:** the concept of intellectual virtue can form the basis of an approach to epistemology that is independent of traditional epistemology	
Strong Conservative VE: the concept of intellectual virtue merits a central and fundamental role within traditional epistemology	*Weak Conservative VE*: the concept of intellectual virtue merits a secondary or background role within traditional epistemology	*Weak Autonomous VE*: an independent focus on intellectual character and virtues complements traditional epistemology	*Strong Autonomous VE*: an independent focus on intellectual character and virtues should replace traditional epistemology

[20] This is but one possible way of carving up the territory in virtue epistemology. It is inspired mainly by the particular way in which the literature in this area has evolved over the past decade or so. Thus it is aimed primarily at providing an illuminating account of the field in *its present state* (not in a state that it merely might have taken or that it might take some time in the future).

1.3 *An overview of the book*

We are now in a position to consider the central project and claims of the book. In Chapter 2, I extend the present introduction to intellectual character virtues. I do so by undertaking two main tasks. First, I identify six "natural groupings" of these traits based on the role they play in the context of inquiry. Second, I distinguish intellectual character virtues from a range of other intellectual excellences, including intellectual faculties, talents, temperaments, and skills. I argue that while intellectual virtues are often closely related to these other excellences, they nonetheless are distinct from them. This chapter, together with the present one, is aimed at providing an overview of the intellectual virtues for the relatively uninitiated, that is, for readers who presently lack a very firm or robust conception of the traits in question. (Those already well-acquainted with the intellectual virtues and virtue epistemology may wish to skip ahead to Chapter 3).

In Chapter 3, I turn to a discussion of Strong Conservative VE, focusing mainly on Zagzebski's virtue-based account of knowledge. I begin by arguing that an exercise of intellectual character virtues (or anything similar) is not, when added to true belief, sufficient for knowledge. I go on to argue that neither is an exercise of intellectual virtues necessary for knowledge. The immediate conclusion is that the concept of intellectual virtue (where an intellectual virtue is understood as a trait of character) is unlikely to play a central role in a plausible analysis of knowledge. But this in turn entails, or so I argue, that the concept of intellectual virtue is unlikely to play a central role within traditional epistemology at large. I conclude that the prospects of Strong Conservative VE are poor.

In the two chapters that follow, I turn to a defense of Weak Conservative VE, that is, of the thesis that reflection on the intellectual virtues merits a secondary or background role in connection with one or more issues in traditional epistemology. In Chapter 4, I argue that intellectual character virtues satisfy the conditions for reliabilist "knowledge-makers" or justifiers, and that consequently reliabilists of any stripe must give greater attention to matters of intellectual character. I also show how this expansion of the focus of reliabilism generates new theoretical questions and challenges for any reliabilist epistemology.

In Chapter 5, I consider the significance of intellectual virtue for evidentialism, that is, for the view that a belief is epistemically justified at a given time just in case it is supported by the believer's evidence at that time. I begin by identifying cases in which a belief satisfies the evidentialist's central condition for epistemic justification but intuitively is unjustified. I proceed to argue that the solution for evidentialism is to adopt a further condition according to which (within a certain range of cases) justification also requires conducting oneself in a minimally intellectually virtuous way. The conclusion of Chapters 4 and 5 is that while the concept of intellectual virtue may not have a central or transforming role to play within traditional epistemology, neither is it wholly irrelevant. Weak Conservative VE therefore prevails.

The three chapters just described (Chs. 3–5) are the most straightforwardly epistemological chapters in the book and thus are likely to be of special interest to more traditionally minded epistemologists. In Chapter 6, the focus of the book shifts in ways that are, I hope, still likely to engage the interest of traditional epistemologists, but that are also likely to be appealing to many other philosophers, including (but not limited to) moral philosophers. The overarching question in Chapters 6–9 is whether reflection on the intellectual virtues considered more or less in their own right (or apart from the issues of traditional epistemology) can form the basis of an independent, broadly epistemological research program; and, provided that it can, just what such a program might amount to.

In Chapters 6 and 7, I develop an account of the nature and basic structure of an intellectual virtue. Chapter 6 is a defense of what I call a "personal worth conception" of intellectual virtue, according to which the traits in question are intellectual virtues because they contribute to their possessor's "personal intellectual worth," that is, to their possessor's intellectual goodness or badness qua person. According to the account, the primary basis of personal intellectual worth, and thus of intellectual virtue, is a positive psychological orientation toward or "love" of epistemic goods like knowledge and understanding. I elaborate on the content of this orientation and respond to a range of potential objections.

In Chapter 7, I situate this conception of intellectual virtue vis-à-vis several accounts of intellectual and moral virtue in the literature. Here I give special attention to the views of Linda Zagzebski (1996), Rosalind Hursthouse (1999), Julia Driver (2000), Thomas Hurka (2001), and Robert Adams (2006). In addition to identifying several similarities and differences between my account and these others, I also develop a number of substantive criticisms of the latter.

Chapters 8 and 9 examine the nature and structure of two *individual* intellectual virtues: namely, open-mindedness and intellectual courage. These chapters are aimed mainly at specifying the "characteristic psychology" of the virtues in question. In Chapter 8, I begin by considering an initially plausible account of open-mindedness according to which this virtue consists primarily of a disposition to temporarily "set aside" one's viewpoint about an issue in order to give a fair and impartial hearing to an opposing viewpoint. I argue against this view, opting instead for a broader account which allows, first, that open-mindedness can be manifested outside the context of intellectual opposition or conflict, and second, that an exercise of open-mindedness need not involve any kind of rational assessment. I also consider the question of when, or with respect to which ideas or viewpoints, one ought to be open-minded.

In Chapter 9, my focus turns to intellectual courage. Here I defend the view that intellectual courage is a disposition to persist in a doxastic state (e.g. belief) or course of action (e.g. inquiry) aimed at an epistemic good despite the fact that doing so involves an apparent threat to one's well-being. In the course of this defense, I explore a number of issues, including the significance of fear and danger relative to the essential "context" of intellectual courage, the sorts of states and activities in which intellectual courage can be manifested, the possibility of ill-motivated intellectual courage, and when an exercise of intellectual courage is appropriate or virtuous.

Chapter 10 draws together several elements of the preceding chapters by considering their implications for the viability of the four main varieties of character-based virtue epistemology outlined in Chapter 1. The central focus here is Strong Autonomous VE and Weak Autonomous VE (the prospects of the other two varieties will already have been made clear by this point). I argue that the central challenge for Strong Autonomous VE is to make good on the claim that an autonomous, virtue-based approach to epistemology ought to *replace* more traditional approaches to the discipline. I examine the only extant defense of Strong Autonomous VE (Kvanvig 1992) and argue that it falls short. While I reject Strong Autonomous VE, I go on to argue that Weak Autonomous VE has considerable promise, and indeed, that it likely represents the way of the future in character-based virtue epistemology. I also offer an overview, based mainly on the discussion in Chapters 6–9, of the theoretical substance of such an approach. Finally, I explain why an approach of this sort is indeed proper to *epistemology* (broadly construed), rather than to ethics or any other philosophical discipline.

In the Appendix, I consider the relation between intellectual virtues and moral virtues. I begin by delineating three possible views of this relation: (1) what we call "intellectual virtues" just *are* moral virtues; (2) intellectual virtues are a proper subset of moral virtues; and (3) intellectual virtues are fundamentally distinct from moral virtues. I defend a position according to which a trait's being an intellectual virtue depends on its being oriented toward distinctively epistemic goods, while a trait's being a moral virtue depends on its being others-regarding. The result is that there is substantial overlap between the class of intellectual virtues and the class of moral virtues, and that consequently a position somewhere between (2) and (3) is correct.

As this overview makes clear, the book proceeds on two main tracks. On the one hand, it is intended to shed substantial light on the nature and structure of an intellectual virtue (Chs. 6 and 7), the defining character of two individual virtues (Chs. 8 and 9), and the relation between intellectual virtues and other intellectual and moral excellences (Ch. 2 and the Appendix). It is also, however, intended to support the following three meta-epistemological claims: (1) the concept of intellectual virtue does not merit a prominent or central role within traditional epistemology (Ch. 3); (2) it does, however, merit a secondary or background role (Chs. 4 and 5); and (3) apart from any concern with traditional epistemology, philosophical reflection on intellectual virtues can form the basis of a more or less autonomous epistemological research program (Chs. 6–10). My hope is that the book will advance the discussion within virtue epistemology both by providing a lens through which to understand what has gone on in the field over the past couple of decades and by identifying several new and promising lines of inquiry.

Chapter 2

INTELLECTUAL VIRTUES

The aim of the present chapter, like that of the previous one, is largely introductory. Its purpose is to provide an account of intellectual virtues and their role in the cognitive economy for the reader who presently lacks a very firm or informed conception of these things. Given this focus, I shall refrain from getting bogged down in theoretical issues or problems pertaining to the fundamental nature or structure of intellectual virtue. These topics will be taken up in earnest in later chapters. My aim here is rather to approach the subject matter in a relatively preliminary and intuitive way. While I shall, at points, be forced to depart from this course, my hope is to be able to say enough at a reasonably commonsense or theory-neutral level so as to adequately "fix the referent" of the rest of the book.

I begin with a delineation of six "natural groupings" of intellectual virtues based on ways in which these traits are useful for overcoming certain familiar obstacles to successful inquiry. I then go on to distinguish intellectual character virtues from a range of related cognitive excellences: namely, intellectual faculties, talents, temperaments, and skills.

The discussion in this chapter will position us to begin thinking, in the three chapters that follow, about the role that reflection on intellectual virtues should play within traditional epistemology. Given its introductory status, readers already well-acquainted with the intellectual virtues may wish to skip ahead to Chapter 3.

2.1 *Some natural groupings of intellectual virtues*

One natural way of approaching the intellectual virtues from an initial and intuitive standpoint is to identify various categories, types, or groups of intellectual virtues. Accordingly, in the present section, I enumerate six "natural groupings" of intellectual virtues. As the label suggests, the categories in question are not intended as a strict classification or taxonomy; they are neither jointly exhaustive nor mutually exclusive.[1] But this does not prevent them from shedding some worthwhile light on ways in which the intellectual virtues are related to each other and to a certain kind of success in the cognitive life.

The basis of the groupings is the role that intellectual virtues play in the context of *inquiry*, by which I mean an active and intentional search for the truth about some question.[2] The underlying idea is that inquiry makes certain fairly generic demands on us as cognitive agents, and that the possession of different clusters or groups of intellectual virtues equips us to meet or overcome these demands.

Before specifying the groups, it will be helpful to reflect on some general connections between inquiry, knowledge, and intellectual virtue. Note first that a considerable amount of knowledge can be acquired independently of anything like a "search" for truth. This includes knowledge of the appearance of one's immediate surroundings, a great deal of memorial and introspective knowledge (e.g. that I drove to work this morning or that I am experiencing discomfort in my right foot), and even some a priori knowledge (e.g. that two plus three equals five or that the conclusion of modus ponens follows from the premises). Knowledge of this sort is relatively immediate and automatic; it requires little more than the brute or default operation of our basic cognitive faculties.[3]

In other cases, however, knowledge can be much more difficult to come by. This includes knowledge of microscopic or subatomic reality, challenging metaphysical matters, and states of affairs far removed in space or time (e.g. ancient history). Here the acquisition of knowledge does typically require inquiry. As such it makes demands on us as cognitive *agents*—it requires that we think, reason, judge, evaluate, read, interpret, adjudicate, search, or reflect in various ways. But this, of course, is also the domain of personal character, and of *intellectual* character in particular. An intellectually virtuous person is one who thinks, reasons, judges, interprets, evaluates, and so on, in an intellectually appropriate or rational way, while an intellectually vicious person is one who is deficient or defective in this regard. Thus where cognitive success requires

[1] For an attempt at what is apparently intended as a strict taxonomy, see Montmarquet (1993). My own view, which I will not try to defend here, is that the deep interrelatedness of the intellectual virtues makes a strict classification extremely difficult (perhaps impossible).

[2] See Hookway (2000) and (2003) for a discussion of the role of intellectual virtues in the context of inquiry.

[3] This claim is explored and defended at length in Chapter 3.

inquiry, it also typically requires an exercise of one or more intellectual character virtues.[4]

What can be said about the sorts of demands or challenges imposed by successful inquiry? One such demand is fundamentally *motivational*, for inquiry must be initiated or undertaken. Thus an intellectually lazy or unreflective inquirer is unlikely to enjoy much success, since he is unlikely to get the process started in the first place. Accordingly, intellectual virtues like inquisitiveness, reflectiveness, contemplativeness, curiosity, and wonder can be essential to a successful pursuit of the truth. An inquisitive person, for instance, is quick to ask why-questions, which in turn are likely to inspire inquiry. A person with the virtue of curiosity, or whose mental life is characterized by wonder, is quick to notice and be inclined to investigate issues or subject matters of significance. And a reflective or contemplative person is prone to ponder or reflect on her own experience in ways that also are likely to lead naturally to inquiry.

A second fairly standard requirement of inquiry is that of getting and remaining properly *focused*. This might involve having to attend to certain fine-grained features of a physical object, to the semantic subtleties of a text, or to the exact logical structure of an argument. Thus it might require intellectual virtues like attentiveness, sensitivity to detail, careful observation, scrutiny, or perceptiveness. An attentive person, for instance, exhibits a general alertness concerning the object of inquiry. A scrutinizing person adopts an appropriately critical mindset toward her subject matter. And a perceptive or observant inquirer is quick to zero in on salient issues and details.

A third challenge that regularly emerges in the context of inquiry is a function of the fact that inquiry often involves consulting and evaluating a wide variety of sources, some part or parts of which one may already accept or reject. This dynamic gives rise to the temptation to evaluate certain views (those, say, that we are already inclined to accept) according to one (relatively lax) set of criteria or standards and other views according to a different (more demanding) set. And even where no such temptation exists, the appropriate evaluation of a range of different views can be challenging when the views in question are, say, evaluated over a long period of time (thus increasing the likelihood that the standards applied in the evaluation of the views will differ). Accordingly, successful inquiry often requires the virtues of intellectual fairness,

[4] I elaborate on this point in Chapter 4. It would be a mistake, however, to think of intellectual virtues as relevant strictly to the domain of inquiry. For, as Roberts and Wood (2007) convincingly argue, they also bear importantly on the *transmission* of knowledge (e.g. on teaching, reporting, and other intellectual practices).

consistency, and objectivity. And where one has a vested interest in one or more of the views or explanations being evaluated, it can also require virtues like impartiality and open-mindedness.

A fourth and related obstacle to successful inquiry is a function of our capacity for self-deception—of our ability, for instance, to distort or even block out considerations or evidence within our ken or to fail to recognize logical tensions or inconsistencies among our beliefs. Such deception obviously can have a deleterious impact on the process of inquiry. It can lead one to trust unreliable sources, to cease an inquiry prematurely, or to regard certain implausible hypotheses as compelling. To avoid the mire of self-deception, a kind of cognitive integrity is needed. Such integrity bears on how we confront and process new evidence and on how we treat or regard evidence we already possess. It requires that we be aware of the evidence we have and how it bears on the propositions we accept or are considering. Accordingly, it calls for the virtues of self-awareness and self-scrutiny; and it calls for honesty and transparency concerning what this awareness or scrutiny reveals. Finally, avoiding self-deception demands that we do what we can in response to an honest assessment of our cognitive situation, and specifically, that we attempt to bring about an appropriate harmony or agreement among our beliefs and between our beliefs and experiences. This might require abandoning a belief, suspending judgment, or conducting further inquiry. A person motivated to do such things in an effort to bring about the relevant doxastic coherence or harmony embodies the virtue of intellectual integrity.[5]

The remaining two groups of intellectual virtues correspond to challenges in inquiry that are somewhat less common. One such challenge occurs when a person confronts a subject matter that is in itself extremely complex and demanding or that is simply foreign to her usual way of thinking. Here what is needed is an ability to "think outside the box." This can require any of the following virtues: imaginativeness, creativity, intellectual adaptability, flexibility, agility, or open-mindedness. The imaginative or creative person is particularly effective at conceiving of alternate possibilities, hypotheses, or explanations. She can move beyond standard ways of thinking in order to make sense of data or to arrive at solutions to intellectual problems. An intellectually agile or flexible person has a general ability to think quickly and in a range of different ways. She

[5] As this description suggests, I am inclined to think of intellectual integrity (conceived as an intellectual character virtue) as largely parasitic (perhaps as supervening) on several other intellectual virtues. For more on this sort of relation among intellectual virtues, see the chapter on open-mindedness (Ch. 8).

does not easily get stuck in intellectual ruts or routine ways of thinking. And an intellectually adaptable person is especially effective at conforming her mind to new ideas and subject matters.[6]

Finally, there are occasions in the context of inquiry where success requires an unusual amount of exertion or endurance. This can be the result of a wide range of factors: getting to the truth may be dangerous; it may be especially time-consuming; it may require a protracted repetition of a certain mundane technical procedure, etc. In such cases, what is required is a willingness to persist or persevere. Depending on the situation, this willingness might take the form of virtues like intellectual courage, determination, patience, diligence, or tenacity.

We have briefly touched on a variety of ways in which certain clusters of intellectual virtues can be helpful for meeting some of the familiar and generic demands of inquiry (see Table 2.1.). While the connections in question could

Table 2.1. *Inquiry-relevant challenges and corresponding groups of intellectual virtues*

Inquiry-relevant challenge	Initial motivation	Sufficient and proper focusing	Consistency in evaluation
Corresponding intellectual virtues	Inquisitiveness, reflectiveness, contemplativeness, curiosity, wonder	Attentiveness, thoroughness, sensitivity to detail, careful observation, scrutiny, perceptiveness	Intellectual justice, fair-mindedness, consistency, objectivity, impartiality, open-mindedness
	Intellectual "wholeness" or integrity	**Mental flexibility**	**Endurance**
	Intellectual integrity, honesty, humility, transparency, self-awareness, self-scrutiny	Imaginativeness, creativity, intellectual flexibility, open-mindedness, agility, adaptability	Intellectual perseverance, determination, patience, courage, diligence, tenacity

[6] A common element of several of these virtues is a kind of "transcending" of a default cognitive standpoint which, in Chapter 8, I argue is a defining feature of open-mindedness. This illustrates the deep interrelatedness of intellectual virtues and the fact that one and the same virtue can be proper to more than one of relevant groupings (given that open-mindedness also facilitates consistency in evaluation).

be explored in much greater depth (and will be, to some extent, in chapters that follow), this initial account underscores the complex and varied role that intellectual virtues play in the context of an intentional and sustained pursuit of truth.

2.2 *Virtues, faculties, talents, temperaments, and skills*

Having distinguished between various groups of intellectual virtues, I turn in this section to address the relationship between intellectual virtues as a whole and several related varieties of cognitive excellence: in particular, cognitive faculties, talents, temperaments, and skills. For each of the latter, I explain how the traits or abilities in question are distinct from but still importantly related to intellectual virtues.[7] My aim is to continue to clarify, again in a reasonably intuitive and theoretically neutral way, the unique epistemic function and significance of intellectual virtues.

2.2.1 *Faculties*

We may begin with a consideration of cognitive faculties, which include our sensory modalities (vision, hearing, etc.), as well as memory, introspection, and reason. Cognitive faculties differ from intellectual virtues in at least three main ways.[8]

First, faculties are innate; they are part of our natural or native cognitive endowment. We are born with the ability to see, remember, introspect, and make basic logical inferences just as we are born with the ability to eat, breathe, and walk. Intellectual character virtues, by contrast, are cultivated traits. They are settled states of character that come about by way of repeated choice or action. While the "perfection" or refining of a cognitive faculty may, as I explain below, depend on one or more character virtues, cognitive faculties are not themselves character traits, and therefore are not intellectual virtues in our sense.[9]

[7] For a related and sometimes overlapping discussion, see Zagzebski (1996: 102–16), in which intellectual virtues are distinguished from various "natural capacities" and skills.

[8] See Plantinga (1993b) for more on the nature of cognitive faculties. Also, as we saw in the previous chapter, there is a different, broader conception of intellectual virtue according to which cognitive faculties *are* intellectual virtues. While I have no principled objection to this conception, my concern in this book is with the relevant excellences of intellectual *character*.

[9] See Book II of the *Nicomachean Ethics* and Zagzebski (1996: 102) for developments of the view that character virtues are acquired in the indicated way. *Must* they be acquired in this way?

A second major difference between cognitive faculties and intellectual virtues is that the former are impersonal in a way that the latter are not. Intellectual character virtues plausibly bear on their possessor's "personal worth," that is, on their possessor's goodness or badness qua person. To say of someone that she is inquisitive, attentive, fair-minded, or intellectually honest, that she prizes knowledge and understanding above reputation, wealth, or pleasure, that she is open and responsive to rational criticisms of her beliefs, and so forth, is to convey something positive about who she is as a person. It is to suggest that she is, albeit in a certain distinctively intellectual way or capacity, a *good* person or good *qua* person.[10] Excellent cognitive faculties, by contrast, do not have a significant bearing on their possessor's personal worth. One is not a better *person* on account of having perfect vision or a photographic memory. Indeed, a thoroughly rotten person could, it seems, possess cognitive faculties that are, on the whole, extremely well functioning.

A third and related difference between faculties and virtues concerns the role of personal agency in their operation. The operation of cognitive faculties does not typically require an exercise of agency.[11] While, as I get to below, agency can enhance or perfect the performance of a cognitive faculty, the basic or

Or could, say, God create a ready-made virtuous person? I will not attempt to settle this question here, given the introductory nature of this chapter. I will note, however, that while I am open to the possibility that a person's virtues might not *originate* with any exercises of her agency, I think the *maintenance* or ongoing existence of these virtues must be substantially attributable to her agency. That is, the agent (as such) must be part of the explanation of why she presently has the traits in question, even if her agency played no role in their coming to be (because they were imputed to her by God, say).

[10] Zagzebski (1996) makes a similar point, noting that a "critical" difference between virtues and natural capacities concerns "the distinction between the personal and subpersonal," with virtue "being a deep quality of a person, closely identified with her selfhood, whereas natural faculties are only the raw materials for the self" (104). Similarly, Roberts and Wood (2007) remark: "We think of human beings as persons and of the virtues as excellences of persons, traits that make one excellent as a person" (65). For a detailed account of personal worth and its relevance to intellectual virtue, see Chapter 6.

[11] The faculty of reason may seem to be an exception here, since its operation is commonly tied to an exercise of the *will*. Whether reason really does stand in a unique relation to intellectual virtues depends, however, on how exactly we understand the nature of reason. For instance, to the extent that we think of reason as deeply or essentially involved with the will, then the present contrast between virtues and faculties may not apply to reason; however, I suspect that, to the same extent, we will also be disinclined to regard reason as a "cognitive faculty," or at least as a faculty *on par* with our sensory modalities and other faculties. On the other hand, if by "reason" we have in mind merely the rudimentary cognitive ability to, say, grasp basic logical, mathematical, semantic, and similar contents and relations, then while reason may be more on par with the senses and cognitive faculties, it is unlikely to seem like an exception to the present contrast between intellectual virtues and cognitive faculties.

rudimentary functioning of cognitive faculties is more or less automatic (we needn't *try* to have visual or auditory or olfactory sensations). An exercise of intellectual character virtues, by contrast, does characteristically involve agency. We *choose* to listen in a careful and open way to an interlocutor or to persevere in our attempt to understand a particular subject matter.

This is not to deny that the operation of intellectual virtues can be automatic or spontaneous in a way that resembles the default or mechanistic functioning of cognitive faculties (as when an intellectually virtuous person automatically or without thinking listens or reasons in a careful and fair manner). But, even in cases like this, agency is still relevant or involved in a way that it need not be (and often is not) in the untutored or mechanistic functioning of cognitive faculties. At a minimum, agency will have played a role in the person's development or cultivation of the traits in question.[12] But it is also likely to occupy a more occurrent or immediate role. For, in cases of the relevant sort, it is presumably still the person or agent *herself* (rather than some subpersonal psychological mechanism) that listens or reasons or otherwise acts in an intellectually virtuous way. Put another way, the operation of intellectual character virtues does not happen *to* agents in the way that the operation of their cognitive faculties often does.[13]

While fundamentally distinct, intellectual virtues and cognitive faculties are intimately and importantly connected. For instance, intellectual virtues typically (if not always) are manifested in the use or operation of cognitive faculties. Being intellectually vigilant, observant, or sensitive to detail, for example, is often a matter of making excellent use of one's eyesight. Fair-mindedness is a matter of judging or of using reason in a consistent or even-handed manner. And an intellectually honest person is one whose introspective ability is broad in scope and largely unhindered by self-deception. Indeed, while there is no doubt that a person who is, say, blind or deaf can still be intellectually virtuous, the idea of an intellectually virtuous person bereft of any cognitive faculties makes little sense. Therefore, while intellectual virtues are distinct from cognitive faculties, their operation is partially constituted by an employment of them.

[12] Or, at any rate, in their present *existence* or *maintenance*—see note 9 above.

[13] This idea could be further explicated in a couple of different (and potentially related) ways: for example, in terms of the *regulative* or *controlling* (though still non-deliberative) role of agency in the spontaneous exercise of character virtues; or in terms of certain counterfactuals, for instance, in terms of whether the agent could "intervene" and cease the operation of the trait in question. Thanks to Dan Speak for a helpful conversation on these points.

Similarly, optimal performance of cognitive faculties sometimes requires intellectually virtuous agency. Maximal use of one's perceptual abilities, for instance, requires certain elements of training, discipline, and education. And it is reasonable to think that success in these areas at times depends on the extent to which the activity in question has been guided by something like a desire for knowledge. Similarly, certain levels or kinds of self-awareness—for example, an awareness of what one believes or of how present and incoming evidence bears on one's beliefs—might require or be facilitated by virtues like reflectiveness, open-mindedness, or intellectual integrity.[14]

2.2.2 *Talents*

Now let us turn to the relation between intellectual character virtues and what might be referred to as intellectual "talents." Here I am thinking of certain innate intellectual abilities or powers—generally, the sort of thing we tend to identify with *intelligence*. This includes superior capacities for pattern recognition, problem- or puzzle-solving, three-dimensional thinking, mathematical or other abstract forms of thinking, linguistic manipulation and usage, and more. To have an intellectual "talent" in the present sense is to be capable of excelling in one or more of these or other closely related areas.

Intellectual talents are similar to cognitive faculties because they are innate. We tend to speak, for instance, of the intellectually talented as being "gifted," the idea being that their talent or ability is not their own doing, but rather is an endowment of nature. Yet talents are not identical to faculties, for they are not broad belief-forming capacities. Instead they are more plausibly regarded as localized *enhancements* or *excellences* of faculties, and in most cases, enhancements or excellences of reason in particular.[15] Thus intellectual talents as I am conceiving of them are narrower than and in some respect parasitic on cognitive faculties.

Despite the difference between intellectual talents and cognitive faculties, talents differ from intellectual character virtues in essentially the same ways as faculties. For again, talents are largely innate; they are part of our inborn or native cognitive equipment. Intellectual virtues, by contrast, are cultivated; they are the product of repeated choice or action. Intellectual talents, while

[14] For more on the intimate connection between cognitive faculties and intellectual virtues, see Chapter 4 and my (2006b).

[15] The capacity for abstract thought, for instance, is a special power or ability of reason; similarly for the capacity for three-dimensional thinking. Talents involving pattern recognition might involve reason *and* one of the senses (e.g. hearing or vision).

not typically "brute" or subpersonal like some of the faculties discussed above, also can be distinguished from intellectual virtues on the grounds that they fail to contribute to personal worth. Again, while someone's having an IQ of 170 reveals something significant about his overall intellectual acumen, it says little or nothing about his goodness or badness qua person.[16] Finally, the operation of intellectual talents is potentially independent of agency in a way that the operation of character virtues apparently is not. The savant, for instance, might from a very early age simply find herself struck by or cognizant of certain visual or numerical patterns; qua rational agent, she might be entirely passive in the relevant perceptions.[17]

While distinct, intellectual virtues and talents are closely related, and related in a manner that resembles the connection between virtues and faculties. First, intellectual virtues can be manifested in the use or deployment of intellectual talents. An intellectually generous person, for instance, might make use of her superior mathematical ability by offering to tutor some of her struggling classmates. Similarly, an intellectual talent might be enhanced if it is supported or motivated by a certain intellectual character virtue. A person's superior capacity for pattern recognition, for instance, might be maximized if this capacity is accompanied by a desire for truth or by virtues like intellectual carefulness and attentiveness. Thus intellectual virtues can serve to motivate or regulate—and thereby to *enhance* or *perfect*—intellectual talents.[18]

2.2.3 *Temperaments*

While a distinction between intellectual virtues, on the one hand, and intellectual faculties and talents, on the other, may be fairly intuitive, the difference between intellectual virtues and what I shall refer to as intellectual "temperaments" is at least somewhat less apparent. Intellectual temperaments are "natural" psychological dispositions. We might refer to such a disposition by saying of a particular person that he is "naturally intellectually courageous" or

[16] Zagzebski claims that intellectual talents may be "deeply constitutive" of selfhood (1996: 125). This strikes me as plausible; thus I think that intellectual talents can be relevant to (and might partly constitute) their possessor's personal identity in some sense. It does not follow, however, that they make their possessor *good* qua person.

[17] And in contrast with similar "passive" or spontaneous exercises of intellectual virtue, these perceptions or appearances need not be traceable in any way (past or present) to their subject's agency. See note 13 above.

[18] One difference concerning the relation between faculties and virtues, on the one hand, and talents and virtues, on the other, is that the possession or use of talents is in no way essential to the possession or operation of virtues (while virtues typically, and perhaps necessarily, are manifested in the operation of faculties).

"naturally open-minded." Like intellectual virtues, and unlike cognitive faculties and talents, intellectual temperaments are robustly psychological in nature: they are dispositions to manifest certain attitudes, feelings, judgments, and the like. Indeed, as the foregoing examples suggest, temperaments are sufficiently similar to virtues so as to be properly describable in virtue terminology.

The fact that intellectual temperaments are natural does not, however, entail that they are innate, since a person might, say, be "naturally" intellectually courageous or "naturally" open-minded largely on account of having been raised in a certain way or having grown up in a certain type of community. Nevertheless, the fact that intellectual temperaments are natural, even in this relatively broad sense, suggests a notable difference between them and intellectual virtues. For again, intellectual virtues are not "natural"—either in the sense of being innate or in the sense of being a mere product of one's upbringing or communal influences. Certainly a person's upbringing or community can influence whether or the extent to which he possesses an intellectual virtue; but again, virtues are to a significant extent a product of their possessor's repeated choices or actions—choices or actions that are under their possessor's voluntary control.[19]

This is not the case, however, with intellectual temperaments. Indeed, I take it that part of what we mean when we say that a person is "naturally" a certain way (naturally open-minded, say) is that his being this way is, in some deep sense, not his own doing. There is, at any rate, no problem with thinking that a person's intellectual temperaments might be entirely the product of his intellectual nature or upbringing. If, on the other hand, we were to learn of someone that his open-mindedness and intellectual tenacity, say, are *entirely* a matter of the way he was parented or the community in which he was raised—if we learned that the person does not himself figure in any notable way in an explanation of why he has these traits—then I take it that we would not regard him as possessing genuine intellectual character virtues.

A second and related difference between intellectual temperaments and intellectual virtues is that temperaments do not appear to bear in any substantial way on personal worth. Admittedly, they come closer to doing so than either cognitive faculties or talents, and this again is evident in the fact that virtue terminology is sometimes applicable to intellectual temperaments. But this does not support the claim that intellectual temperaments are identical to

[19] Though again, as pointed out in note 9 above, a virtue's being a "product" of its possessor's choices in the relevant sense may not entail that the agent is responsible for bringing the virtue about. Instead the agent may be responsible merely for the maintenance or present existence of the virtue.

intellectual virtues. To illustrate, suppose I try to defend the claim that Jones is a genuinely good person by citing his fair-mindedness, intellectual openness, honesty, and the like. And suppose you respond by pointing out that Jones is just *naturally* that way—that Jones is not himself in any way responsible for his possession of the relevant traits. I take it that this response would, if accurate, undermine my claim that Jones is a genuinely good or better person on account of the relevant qualities.[20]

A third salient difference between the two sets of traits is that intellectual virtues presumably involve the possession of a kind of rational perspective on or understanding of the traits in question, while the possession of intellectual temperaments need not. Intuitively, an intellectually virtuous person has some kind of grasp (albeit perhaps a limited and largely implicit one) of the traits that make her intellectually virtuous that a person who merely possesses the corresponding intellectual temperaments very well may not. She has some sense, for instance, of the value of the ends at which she aims (of knowledge, truth, understanding, etc.) and of how the activity characteristic of her virtues is likely to promote these ends (of how or why behaving in an intellectually courageous or cautious way, for instance, tends to be truth-conducive).[21] But this is not necessarily or even typically the case with intellectual temperaments. Again, to the extent that a trait is simply a deposit or consequence of one's nature or upbringing, one might very well have virtually no grasp or even a grossly mistaken grasp of its goal or "point" or of how the activity associated with this trait is related to its goal.

This way of distinguishing between intellectual virtues and temperaments is related to Aristotle's distinction in the *Nicomachean Ethics* between genuine (moral) virtue and "natural virtue." He says:

> For all men think that each type of character belongs to its possessor in some sense by nature; for from the very moment of birth we are just or fitted for self-control or brave or have the other moral qualities; but yet we seek something else as that which is good in the strict sense—we seek for the presence of such qualities in another way. For both children and brutes have the natural

[20] Again, a much more detailed account of the basis of personal worth is provided in Chapter 6. At present, I am simply trying to draw out and rely on certain intuitive ways of thinking about this notion.

[21] Compare Aristotle's claim in ch. 4 of Book II of the *Nicomachean Ethics* (2000: 28) that performing just or temperate actions "in a just or temperate way" (or as just or temperate person would perform them) requires a certain kind of *knowledge* of these actions. I say more in Chapters 6–7 about the cognitive dimension of intellectual virtues.

dispositions to these qualities, but without reason these are evidently harmful. (2000, 1144^b 1–10, trans. Ross)

Aristotle goes on to identify *phronesis* or "practical wisdom" as the rational component of genuine virtue. His point, then, is that there are certain natural traits that have the appearance of moral virtues, but that are not sufficiently "infused" with or regulated by reason to be such.

Aristotle's distinction resembles the distinction between intellectual temperaments and character virtues. Like Aristotle's natural virtues, intellectual temperaments are—or at least can be—innate. And, as just indicated, an intellectually virtuous person possesses a kind of knowledge of or rational perspective on her virtue that at least resembles practical wisdom and that is unlikely to be had by a person who possesses only the corresponding intellectual temperaments. Finally, intellectual temperaments, like Aristotle's natural virtues, lack a certain normative dimension or value that is characteristic of the virtues they approximate.

2.2.4 *Skills*

Now let us turn to consider the relation between intellectual character virtues and intellectual skills.[22] Intellectual skills, as I am thinking of them, are abilities to perform certain reasonably specific or technical intellectual tasks. One might, for instance, be a skilled orator, teacher, or copy editor; or one might be skilled at designing and executing experiments in the lab, at conducting a certain kind of technical research, or at identifying logical fallacies. Several such skills may in fact be more aptly described as "skill sets," since they may be comprised of one or more subsets of skills (as in the case of teaching or research skills).

Like intellectual virtues, intellectual skills are characteristically cultivated through repetition or practice, that is, through repeated performance of the task associated with the skill in question. While a certain cognitive nature or temperament, say, might naturally dispose or position one to acquire certain skills, the latter typically involve a kind of technique or refined competence that is unlikely to be innate. In this respect, intellectual skills bear a closer resemblance

[22] For extended and illuminating discussions of the distinction between moral virtues and skills, see Wallace (1978: 39–59), Zagzebski (1996: 106–16), Foot (2002: 7–8). Descartes (1968: 35–44) illustrates some of the ways that intellectual virtues and intellectual skills or techniques can be intertwined in the context of inquiry. Battaly (2011) is also a helpful discussion and covers the distinction between skills and both moral and intellectual virtues.

to intellectual virtues than do intellectual faculties, talents, or temperaments, all of which are either innate or otherwise "natural."

But like these other excellences, intellectual skills are fundamentally distinct from intellectual character virtues. First, and most notably, intellectual skills are not personal in the way that intellectual virtues are. While skills may involve a complex psychology, they do not bear significantly on personal worth. To know of someone that she is a particularly skilled or effective researcher, teacher, or orator is not necessarily to know anything about her "goodness or badness" as a person. Intellectual character virtues, on the other hand, do clearly contribute to personal worth. The person who desires truth or understanding for its own sake, and consequently is careful and fair in her assessment of others' views, takes seriously and is appropriately responsive to objections and criticisms of her own beliefs, perseveres in inquiry, and so on, is better qua person as a result.[23]

A second and related point concerns the motivational dimension of the two sets of traits. Skills are fundamentally a kind of competence: essential to their possession is an ability to perform a certain task. And, presumably, the abilities constitutive of the skills in question are compatible with a wide range of underlying motivations. While one might employ various intellectual skills in the context of researching or teaching out of a desire, say, to acquire or convey the truth, such a motive clearly is not essential; one's use of such skills might instead be driven by a desire for professional recognition or a fear of being disliked by one's students. As indicated earlier, however, intellectual character virtues are partly constituted by certain admirable and distinctively intellectual motives.

Imagine, for instance, a person who is disposed to engage in careful and thorough scientific research, but whose ultimate concern lies strictly with professional status or a potential financial payoff. Such a person would not be good or better qua person on account of these traits. While he might be intellectually careful or thorough in some sense, his carefulness and thoroughness would not be genuine intellectual virtues.[24] Again, I am not denying that intellectual skills are often accompanied by something like a love of truth or

[23] This does not mean that this person is "worth more" or possesses a greater fundamental dignity than someone who lacks the relevant virtues. For more on this point, and on the concept of "personal worth," see Chapter 6.

[24] The point here need not be made in terms of personal *worth*. For instance, on Zagzebski's (1996) account of virtue, which makes no appeal to personal worth as such, the lack of a motivational requirement on intellectual skills would also prevent them from qualifying as intellectual virtues.

knowledge; rather, my claim is that, in contrast with intellectual virtues, such a motive is not an essential or defining feature of an intellectual skill. And if this much is true, then intellectual virtues and skills must be distinct.

Once more it is worth looking briefly at a related discussion from Aristotle. In a well-known passage in Book II of the *Nicomachean Ethics*, Aristotle distinguishes between "art" (*techne*) and virtue, claiming that one essential feature of a virtue is that it involves choosing the activity characteristic of the virtue, and choosing it *for its own sake*. According to James Wallace (1978) and Sarah Broadie (1991), Aristotle is thinking of "arts" as skills, in which case he can be read as claiming that while it is not essential to the possession of a skill that one choose the activity characteristic of the skill for its own sake (or at all), this is a requirement for the possession of a virtue.[25]

Aristotle's claim is not identical to the one made above. For not only is his concern moral rather than intellectual virtues, it is also apparently the *activity* associated with these traits rather than their ultimate intentional *object*. Nonetheless, the two points are clearly related. To bring them together, we might say that an intellectually virtuous person necessarily chooses or pursues the object of her virtue (e.g. knowledge or understanding) for its own sake, but that a person with various intellectual skills (skills with the same intentional object) might be motivated substantially or even entirely by other ends.

As with the other cognitive excellences discussed above, intellectual skills nevertheless are importantly related to intellectual virtues. The possession of intellectual virtues often leads to the cultivation or deployment of certain intellectual skills.[26] A person's inquisitiveness about a given technical subject matter might lead her either to develop or to make use of the skills necessary for acquiring an understanding of this subject matter.

Conversely, skills can be refined or enhanced when accompanied by virtuous agency. Compare, for instance, two people with the skills required for conducting technical research in some area, but only one of whom has any desire to reach the truth or to achieve understanding in this area. It is plausible to think that, other things being equal, the skills of the latter person will be greater and more refined than those of the person who lacks the relevant desire—that a desire for truth or understanding, which is characteristic of intellectual virtue, will play an enhancing or perfecting role in connection with these skills. The person who lacks such a desire, by contrast, may be disinclined to use her skills when doing so strikes her as tedious or inconvenient, or she may be prone to

[25] See Zagzebski (1996: 111f) for a discussion of this point.

[26] Here again, see Zagzebski (1996: 115).

use them in a sloppy or careless manner. Thus, as with cognitive faculties and talents, intellectual skills can be refined or perfected by intellectual virtues.

We now have before us at least a general idea of some of the ways in which intellectual virtues differ from other, related cognitive excellences. These differences may be summarized as follows: (1) intellectual faculties, talents, temperaments, and skills fail to bear on personal worth in the way that intellectual virtues do; (2) faculties, talents, and temperaments are "natural," while skills and virtues are cultivated; (3) faculties and talents can operate independent of personal agency in a way that distinguishes them from virtues; (4) temperaments, while similar to virtues on account of being robustly psychological, lack a certain kind of rational grasp or perspective essential to virtues; and (5) skills, while resembling virtues on account of being cultivated, need not involve the kind of admirable intellectual motivation essential to intellectual virtues.

2.3 *Conclusion*

My aim in this chapter has been to provide an initial, reasonably intuitive sketch of intellectual character virtues and their place in the cognitive economy—one that will help "fix the referent" of the rest of the book and position us to begin thinking, in the three chapters that follow, about the role that reflection on intellectual virtues might play within traditional epistemology. In section 2.1, we examined ways in which different groups of intellectual virtues bear on the challenges internal to the process of inquiry. In section 2.2, we considered some similarities and differences between intellectual virtues, on the one hand, and intellectual faculties, talents, temperaments, and skills, on the other. With this initial account of intellectual virtues before us, we can now begin to take a more focused and theoretical approach to our subject matter.

Chapter 3

KNOWLEDGE AND INTELLECTUAL VIRTUE

One major goal of the present work is to identify the role that reflection on intellectual character virtues should play within epistemology. In this chapter, I explore what is perhaps the most interesting and salient possibility along these lines: namely, that the concept of intellectual virtue should occupy a prominent place in an analysis of knowledge, that is, in a specification of a set of purportedly necessary and jointly sufficient conditions for knowledge. The formulation and critique of analyses of knowledge has, of course, been central to the epistemological enterprise for some time. Thus if we are interested in gauging the significance of intellectual virtue to this enterprise, a virtue-based analysis of knowledge is a very natural place to begin.[1]

My immediate target in the chapter will be Linda Zagzebski's (1996) account of knowledge, according to which knowledge is true belief arising from "acts of intellectual virtue" (271). Zagzebski's is by far the most careful and sophisticated virtue-based account of knowledge in the literature.[2] And she goes to considerable lengths to anticipate possible objections to it and to identify a wide range of possible replies and modifications. I argue here, however, that Zagzebski's conditions for knowledge are neither necessary nor sufficient, and that the problems with her view appear to spell trouble for *any* virtue-based account of knowledge. I then go on to explain why this in turn presents a problem for

[1] Such an analysis would also be the epistemological counterpart of the kind of virtue-based analysis of morally right action that has recently gained considerable momentum in ethics. See, for example, Hursthouse (1999).

[2] Recall that we are thinking of intellectual virtues as *character traits*, not as reliable cognitive mechanisms or faculties like vision, memory, introspection, or the like. Thus I am not passing judgment here or elsewhere in the chapter on the theories of knowledge defended by virtue "reliabilists" like Sosa (1991; 2007) and Greco (2000a; 2010). See section 1.2.1 of Chapter 1 for an explanation of this exclusion.

trying to establish any major conceptual connections between intellectual virtue and the subject matter of traditional epistemology, the central focus of which is the nature, structure, sources, and limits of knowledge.[3] I conclude that the prospects of the view identified in Chapter 1 as Strong Conservative VE—the view that the concept of intellectual virtue merits a central and fundamental role in connection with one or more problems in traditional epistemology—are poor.

While this conclusion undermines a certain ambitious view of the prospects of a character-based approach to epistemology, it leaves open at least two other significant possibilities: (1) that the concept of intellectual virtue has a kind of secondary or background relevance to issues in traditional epistemology; and (2) that this concept can form the backbone of an independent or autonomous approach to epistemology (an approach that is distinct from traditional epistemology). In Chapters 4 and 5, I defend a version of (1); and in Chapters 6–10, I defend a version of (2). Therefore, while the thrust of the present chapter is negative, its target is but one way of thinking about the role that reflection on intellectual character virtues might play in epistemology.

3.1 *Zagzebski's account of knowledge*

As we have already noted, Zagzebski (1996) defines knowledge as true belief arising from "acts of intellectual virtue." The concept of an "act of intellectual virtue" is largely technical.[4] According to Zagzebski's formulation, a subject S performs an act of a particular intellectual virtue V just in case S possesses the *motivation* characteristic of V, *does* what a person with V would characteristically do in the situation, and *reaches the truth as a result* (270).[5]

Zagzebski herself is quick to identify one obvious problem with this account of knowledge: namely, that the concept of truth is built into the concept of an act of intellectual virtue, such that it is redundant to describe knowledge as *true*

[3] This is, roughly, epistemology in the Cartesian tradition. Some of the topics and debates that have been or are central to it include global and local skepticism, the nature of perception, rationalism vs. empiricism, the problem of induction, the analysis of knowledge, foundationalism vs. coherentism, internalism vs. externalism, and the Gettier problem. See BonJour (2002) for an overview.

[4] Zagzebski takes some pains to show that the concept has some basis in ordinary thought and language (246–53). However, as I get to below, I think it remains largely artificial. For a relevant discussion, see Roberts and Wood (2007: ch. 1).

[5] All other references to Zagzebski's work, unless otherwise noted, are taken from her (1996).

belief arising from acts of intellectual virtue. Again, to perform an act of intellectual virtue just is to get to the truth or to form a true belief via intellectually virtuous motives and actions. In response, Zagzebski modifies her initial proposal, claiming instead that knowledge amounts to *belief* arising from acts of intellectual virtue (271). But this reformulation clearly does not go far enough, for the concept of an act of intellectual virtue incorporates not just the concept of truth, but also the concept of belief. Once more: to perform an act of intellectual virtue is to form a true *belief* as a result of virtuous motives and actions. It follows that a more accurate rendering of her view is that knowledge is identical to one or more *acts of intellectual virtue*.[6]

This clarification underscores, to my mind, the artificiality of the concept of an "act of intellectual virtue." But this issue need not be settled here, for the substance of Zagzebski's view can be expressed in a considerably less technical way: namely, as the view that *knowledge is* (a) *true belief* (b) *resulting from* (c) *intellectually virtuous motives and actions*.

Intellectually virtuous motives and actions, according to Zagzebski, are motives and actions that an intellectually virtuous person would characteristically possess or perform in the situation in question (248–53). And the idea behind (b)—which is mainly aimed at avoiding the Gettier problem—is that a true belief is knowledge only if this belief is the *result* of or has been *caused* by the believer's virtuous motives and actions; that is, only if the believer's virtuous motives and actions explain *why* she has formed a true belief.[7] We will have occasion later in the chapter to return to the various aspects of Zagzebski's account, but the gist of it should be sufficiently clear. Again, knowledge, for Zagzebski, is a matter of reaching the truth or forming a true belief as a result of intellectually virtuous motives and actions. In somewhat looser terms, knowledge can be thought of as true belief resulting from intellectually virtuous *inquiry*.

Let us briefly consider an example that illustrates what knowledge might amount to on Zagzebski's view. Imagine a medical researcher investigating the genetic foundations of a particular disease. As she conducts her research, she exemplifies the motives characteristic of the virtues of intellectual carefulness, thoroughness, fair-mindedness, and tenacity. She also acts in the manner of one who has these virtues: she examines all the relevant data carefully and in

[6] In very recent work (2008: 127, nt. 20), Zagzebski acknowledges that this is the most accurate formulation of her original view.

[7] Zagzebski employs a range of more or less interchangeable concepts to describe this relation, including "creditable," "attributable," "best explained," "because of," etc. See her (1999: 108) for more on this point.

great detail and refrains from cutting any corners; when she encounters information that conflicts with her expectations, she deals with it in a direct, honest, and unbiased way; in the face of repeated intellectual obstacles, she perseveres in her search for the truth. Over time, this leads to a successful inquiry, as she eventually discovers the sought-after gene. The researcher's belief about the genetic basis of the disease satisfies all of Zagzebski's conditions: the belief is true and it is the product of intellectually virtuous motives and actions.

3.2 *Are intellectual virtues (plus true belief) sufficient for knowledge?*

We may begin assessing Zagzebski's analysis by asking whether it is possible to satisfy its conditions while failing to achieve knowledge. I have argued elsewhere (2006a) that this is indeed a genuine possibility—and for a variety of reasons. Here I shall focus on just one of these reasons.

The most familiar and formidable challenge to any set of purportedly sufficient conditions for knowledge is the Gettier problem (Gettier 1963). Gettier-style cases are aimed at showing, contrary to what was previously the consensus view among epistemologists, that a person can have a "justified true belief" that nevertheless does not amount to knowledge. Suppose, for instance, that near the middle of the day I look at the generally highly reliable clock in my kitchen and find that it reads a quarter past 12. I form the belief that it is a quarter past 12 and this belief is true. Unknown to me, however, the clock unexpectedly malfunctioned exactly twelve hours prior, at 12:15 a.m. While I am justified in believing that it is a quarter past 12, and this belief is true, my belief does not amount to knowledge.

Zagzebski herself has made profitable contributions to the literature on the Gettier problem (1994; 1996). She has shown, for instance, that the distinctive feature of Gettier cases is that they involve a stroke of bad epistemic luck (e.g. the fact that my clock is broken) getting remedied or canceled out by a stroke of good epistemic luck (e.g. the fact that my clock happens at present to read correctly). She has also taken considerable pains to show that her own account of knowledge can handle such cases (1996: 283–99). The solution, she argues, lies with part (b) of her account, which stipulates that a certain causal relation must obtain between the virtuous motives and actions of a knowing agent, on the one hand, and the agent's true belief, on the other (again, it requires that knowers reach the truth *through* or *as a result of* their virtuous motives and actions).[8] According to Zagzebski, what is problematic about Gettier cases is that the subjects in question reach the truth on account of certain (fortuitous) factors *other* than those that justify their beliefs. Again, in the clock case she would say that what explains why I form a true belief is that the time on the stopped clock just happens to coincide with the actual time—*not* any virtuous motives or actions that I may or may not exhibit. In this way, Zagzebski is able to conclude that the belief fails to satisfy her conditions and therefore fails to amount to knowledge.

While I think Zagzebski is right to focus on the relevant causal relation in her attempt to overcome the Gettier problem, I do not think that her own account of knowledge fares much better than many competing views. To see why, it will be helpful to consider a Gettier-style case that is more clearly suited to an assessment of her view. Suppose, then, that person A believes that her careless disposal of cigarette butts is the cause of a wildfire that has begun raging in the hills just behind her house. In a moment of desperation and appalling moral judgment, A decides to plant evidence around her neighbor B's house and yard indicating that B is responsible for the fire. A detective is then dispatched to ascertain the cause of the blaze. He proceeds to conduct an intellectually virtuous investigation of the case. His work is motivated by a desire for truth and other virtuous ends. His actions are also characteristic of intellectual virtue: he handles all of the evidence with great care, thinks through the relevant possibilities, avoids drawing hasty conclusions, consults a wide range of reliable sources, and so on. Nevertheless, A's engineering of the evidence is such that the detective is led to conclude that B is responsible for starting the fire. In the typical case, the detective's belief would be false but justified. In the present case, however, it turns out that unknown to A, B actually did ignite the blaze, and thus that the detective's belief is true.

On the face of it, the detective's belief seems to satisfy Zagzebski's conditions for knowledge, for the belief is true and caused or produced by virtuous inquiry. And yet the detective would not appear to know that B caused the fire.

Zagzebski would likely respond by elaborating on condition (b) of her analysis, which again says that to count as knowledge, a true belief must result from or be caused by virtuous motives and actions.[9] She would likely claim that for this condition to be satisfied, it is not enough that the relevant belief simply be true and be a causal product of virtuous motives and actions; rather, she would

[8] Others have followed suit here. See, for example, Riggs (2002) and the contributions by Sosa and Greco to and DePaul Zagzebski (2003).

[9] This is how she responds to a similar case on pp. 297f.

likely insist that the *truth* of the belief itself be attributable to the relevant motives and actions. Applied to the detective case, the idea would be that while the detective's belief is true and the result of virtuous motives and actions, the fact that the belief *is* true is not attributable to these factors. The detective does not get to the truth on account of his virtuous motives and actions. Rather, the truth of his belief is a matter of luck.

But in what sense exactly does the detective fail to reach the truth "on account of" his virtuous motives and actions? Indeed, there is a way of describing the case in which his getting to the truth clearly *is* attributable to these factors. For we can easily imagine that had the detective *not* exhibited virtuous motives and actions in his investigation, he would have been led to the conclusion that some person other than B was responsible for the fire. In this sense, the fact that he reached the truth is a result of his virtuous efforts. Presumably, and perhaps with good reason, Zagzebski would likely opt for some alternative conception of the relevant causal relation—claiming, effectively, that the truth of the detective's beliefs was not caused by his virtuous efforts in "the right way." But, again, what exactly does "the right way" amount to? Zagzebski does not, to my knowledge, address this question. And, without an answer to it, it remains unclear whether her account really does stand a chance of overcoming the Gettier problem.

One strategy Zagzebski could employ at this point would be to claim that for a true belief to count as knowledge, the truth of this belief must be *non-accidentally* caused by or attributable to the believer's virtuous motives and actions. But the limitation of such a reply should be obvious: it provides an entirely negative and therefore unilluminating explanation of the relevant relation. Indeed, Zagzebski herself says that an appeal to the notion of non-accidentality in the context of addressing the Gettier problem is objectionably uninformative (264). It appears, then, that without considerable further elaboration and explanation, Zagzebski's virtue-based analysis of knowledge does not provide an adequate solution to the Gettier problem.

We have found that it is apparently possible to satisfy Zagzebski's conditions for knowledge while failing, in fact, to acquire knowledge. Nor is it clear, as far as I can tell, how an alternative virtue-based account of knowledge might fare any better in this regard.[10] I turn now to consider whether it is possible to acquire knowledge without satisfying Zagzebski's—or any similar,

[10] While certain authors (e.g. Greco 2003) have gone to greater lengths to spell out the nature of the causal relation at issue, what they have had to say would not, in my judgment, prove helpful to Zagzebski in connection with the specific sort of case noted above.

virtue-based—conditions, that is, whether anything like an exercise of intellectual virtues is *necessary* for knowledge.

3.3 *Are intellectual virtues necessary for knowledge?*

At first glance, it might seem obvious that one can acquire knowledge without satisfying Zagzebski's conditions, for these conditions appear to limit the class of knowers to the class of intellectually virtuous persons. This would mean that an intellectually vicious person, or even a mere virtuous-person-in-training, could not know *anything*—an implausible implication, to be sure. However, while Zagzebski's conditions may be demanding, they are not quite this demanding. For, as Zagzebski herself makes clear (275–6), a person can reach the truth via intellectually virtuous motives and actions (and thus acquire knowledge) without actually possessing the corresponding intellectual virtues, that is, without possessing the settled or entrenched dispositions to exhibit the motives and actions in question. Thus a mere virtuous-person-in-training, or even a generally intellectually vicious person in one of his better intellectual moments, might, say, desire to reach the truth, inquire in a careful and thorough manner, and acquire a true belief as a result.[11]

But this hardly places Zagzebski's account in the clear, for we appear to be capable of knowing many things even absent an unstable or fleeting display of virtuous intellectual motives and actions. Right now, for instance, I apparently know that there is a computer monitor before me, that I do not have a splitting headache, that music is playing in the background, that the room smells of freshly ground coffee, that today is Tuesday, that I have been working for at least an hour this morning, and much more. And none of this putative knowledge appears to have involved an instantiation of any virtuous motives or actions. Thus a range of problematic cases remain for Zagzebski's account (and, apparently, for *any* account of knowledge that demands anything resembling an exercise of intellectual virtues).

Zagzebski is well aware of the challenge that such "low-grade" knowledge, as she calls it, presents for her view. Her discussion of this challenge (277–83)

[11] This opens up her view, however, to a version of the "fleeting processes" objection leveled against some versions of reliabilism. See Greco (2000b) and my (2006a). This aspect of her view also raises the question of whether knowers must be intrinsically motivated by epistemic ends. Zagzebski discusses this issue (in connection with a "nosey neighbor" example) on pp. 314–18, ultimately concluding that this is not a requirement.

suggests at least three possible lines of response. I shall consider each one in turn.

3.3.1 *Low-grade "knowledge" is not genuine knowledge*

The first and most radical response is simply to bite the bullet and maintain that apparent items of low-grade knowledge like those noted above do not in fact amount to knowledge at all. While Zagzebski flirts with this possibility (262–3), she seems, in the final analysis, to be committed to regarding the beliefs in question as knowledge and to demonstrating that her analysis can handle them. This is a good thing, for beliefs of this sort have seemed to epistemologists for centuries to be among the clearest and least controversial instances of knowledge.[12] Indeed, the conviction that such beliefs amount to knowledge represents a standard methodological starting point in epistemology. Consequently, a failure to accommodate such cases is likely to be regarded either as a reductio ad absurdum of the account in question or as grounds for thinking that the account is offering an analysis of an epistemic concept that is fundamentally different from the one that has traditionally occupied epistemologists. For these reasons, I will not pursue this response any further here.[13]

3.3.2 *Mimicking an intellectually virtuous agent*

A second response involves a significant modification to Zagzebski's original formulation. In her discussion of low-grade knowledge, she suggests that a true belief counts as knowledge just in case it is *formed in the way that an intellectually virtuous person might form it under similar circumstances* (279–80). When discussing whether young children can acquire knowledge, she remarks: "As long as they are old enough to imitate the behavior of intellectually virtuous persons in their belief-forming processes, young children (and possibly animals) can have

[12] Zagzebski argues on pp. 273–9 that such beliefs should not be understood as "paradigm instances" of knowledge. I might not disagree inasmuch the notion of a "paradigm instance" of knowledge is suggestive of an instance that approximates the pinnacle or upper evaluative boundary of knowledge. But on this understanding, there is no reason to think that the clearest or least controversial instances of knowledge will also be paradigm instances.

[13] A closely related reply is that Zagzebski is offering an account of a high-grade species of knowledge that is distinct from the comparatively low-grade quarry of traditional epistemology. While I think Zagzebski herself makes clear that this is not her strategy (263), I do not wish to exclude the possibility that this is what her account effectively accomplishes. Nonetheless, even this accomplishment is possible, presumably, only if there is a determinate, reasonably pretheoretical concept of high-grade knowledge of which her analysis can be viewed as offering a plausible account. And it is not at all clear to me that this is the case. See my (2008) for more on this point. Thanks to Heather Battaly for pressing this point.

knowledge based on perception and memory" (280). Understood along these lines, Zagzebski's account might in fact be capable of accommodating the cases of perceptual, memorial, and introspective knowledge noted above. Again, these are cases in which a person apparently fails to instantiate any virtuous motives or actions. But cases of this sort need not present a problem for Zagzebski's view understood in the present way, since it is reasonable to think that when an intellectually virtuous person forms beliefs of the relevant sort, she does so in a strictly automatic or mechanistic way—not exhibiting any virtuous motives or actions. If so, then according to the modified version of Zagzebski's view, the beliefs in question amount to knowledge.

While this response is suggested by some of Zagzebski's remarks, it is doubtful that she really endorses it, for it involves rejecting the idea that virtuous motives and actions are necessary for knowledge. This, in fact, points to a significant problem with the reformulation: namely, that it fails to offer a genuinely *virtue*-based account of the knowledge in question. This is because, in its treatment of low-grade knowledge, the concept of intellectual virtue is not doing any real explanatory work. Again, according to the account, the beliefs in question amount to knowledge because they are formed as an intellectually virtuous person would form them. However, we have seen that when a virtuous person forms these beliefs, she apparently does not do so qua intellectually virtuous person; she does not exercise any virtues of intellectual character. Rather, she forms the beliefs via the brute or mechanistic part of her cognitive nature. This is evident in Zagzebski's own remark to the effect that even animals might be capable of imitating the behavior of virtuous persons in such cases. The upshot is that if this alternative formulation is correct, nothing having to do with virtue per se explains why the beliefs in question amount to knowledge. This in turn suggests that the formulation is not genuinely or sufficiently virtue-based.

3.3.3 *"Low-level" virtuous motives and actions*

A third response to the problem of low-grade knowledge is that while the cases at issue appear not to involve any virtuous intellectual motives or actions, this appearance is mistaken. In particular, it might be argued that certain minimal or "low-level" virtuous motives or actions are in fact present in items of low-grade knowledge. If so, this opens up the possibility that Zagzebski's view can account for such knowledge.

This appears to be Zagzebski's preferred way of handling the problem. She asserts that in cases of simple perceptual knowledge an intellectually virtuous person is characteristically guided by a "presumption of truth," which she describes as an intellectual "attitude," and that it is plausible to think that this motive is also possessed by ordinary cognitive agents under similar conditions (280). To add to this suggestion, we might suppose that ordinary knowers in such cases also possess something like a low-level desire for true belief. It might be said, for instance, that when I form the belief that there is a ceramic mug on the table before me, this process is guided by an *interest* in knowing what is on the table before me together with a basic *willingness* to trust that my senses are not deceiving me. The suggestion, then, is that in cases of low-grade knowledge, the beliefs in question do arise from virtuous motives and actions, and thus that they count as knowledge on Zagzebski's model.

I will not dispute that in a range of the cases in question, certain low-level intellectual motives or actions may be operative, that is, that the relevant beliefs are not always the product of strictly brute or mechanical cognitive processes. I do, however, find it at least somewhat implausible to characterize the motives or actions in question as *virtuous*—to think of them as characteristic of intellectual virtue. As Zagzebski herself suggests, these motives and actions are entirely pedestrian: they are routinely manifested by mediocre cognitive agents and by young children (and possibly, she says, by animals). She also characterizes a failure to manifest such actions and motives as a rather extreme kind of intellectual paranoia (280). Character virtues, on the other hand, are typically thought to pick out a rather high and distinguished level of personal excellence—something that is not exhibited by the average cognitive agent or by young children (and certainly not by animals!). Therefore, to the extent that our concern is whether something resembling an exercise of intellectual virtue is necessary for knowledge, the suggested line of response to the problem of low-grade knowledge appears unpromising.[14]

Another serious problem is that even if certain low-level motives or actions (whether virtuous or not) are operative in these cases, they are unlikely to

[14] A similar point applies to Stephen Napier's (2009) recent defense of a virtue-based account of knowledge. Napier marshals substantial empirical evidence for the claim that epistemic motives are present in cases of what might initially appear to be fairly brute or mechanical perceptual knowledge (see especially ch. 3). While I think Napier makes his point with respect to some of the relevant knowledge, I do not think he pays sufficient attention to the most difficult sorts of cases (that is, to the most brute and mechanical instances of perceptual knowledge). More germane to the present point, however, the motives Napier does identify hardly seem worthy of the status of *virtue* (indeed they are likely instantiated by the cognitive activity of a rather wide range of non-human animals). Nor would these motives appear to play a certain critical *causal* role—an issue I turn to presently.

satisfy Zagzebski's *causal* requirement noted earlier.[15] Suppose, for instance, that I form a true belief to the effect that music is presently playing in the background. And suppose that the formation of this belief involves the sort of low-level intellectual motives or actions described above. To satisfy Zagzebski's conditions for knowledge, these motives and actions must explain *why* I form a true belief, and specifically, why the belief I form is *true*. But surely they do not occupy this explanatory role. While I may, at some level, be a bit curious or display a minimal attentiveness to my surroundings, my belief about the music turns out to be true, not on account of these factors, but because *my hearing is reasonably good*. That is, I form a true belief in this case because of the basic or rudimentary quality of one of my perceptual faculties.[16] A similar point could be made relative to many other instances of perceptual or low-grade knowledge. The truth of my belief that there is a computer monitor before me, or that the aroma of coffee is in the air, for instance, is explainable, not in terms of any intellectual motives, actions, or effort on my part, but rather in terms of the routine operation of one or more of my basic cognitive faculties.[17]

It appears, then, that the foregoing response to the problem of low-grade knowledge is unsuccessful. And, indeed, there is one additional consideration worth noting that reinforces this conclusion. I have been assuming that in the cases in question, certain minimal or low-level intellectual motives or actions are at some level operative. But relative to at least some items of low-grade knowledge, this concession is too generous. For there appear to be cases of

[15] Zagzebski could, of course, abandon this requirement. However, as we saw above, it plays (or is intended to play) an important role in connection with the Gettier problem. It also plays an important role in connection with a further thesis that Zagzebski and many other virtue epistemologists have been interested in defending: namely, that knowledge is "creditable" to the knowing agent (see Zagzebski 1996; Riggs 2002; Greco 2003 and 2010; and Sosa 2007). The idea is that a person deserves credit for a given true belief (and thus acquires knowledge) only if the explanation or best explanation of the truth of this belief lies with an exercise of the person's intellectual virtues.

[16] If the music is loud enough, the low-level motives or actions may be completely irrelevant. Indeed, this may be the kind of case in which it is possible to acquire knowledge about a state of affairs that one wants *not* to know about or attend to. I might, for instance, be attempting (unsuccessfully) to block out or ignore the music. In this case, my motives and actions would (in a sense) be *opposed* to truth. And yet I might still come to know that the music is playing. I shall have more to say about cases like this momentarily.

[17] This is not to deny that there are some beliefs (beyond immediate perceptual beliefs) the truth of which *is* explainable partly or even largely in terms of virtuous intellectual motives and actions. Indeed, I develop this possibility at length in Chapter 4. Nor is it to claim that the truth of *no* more or less immediate perceptual belief can be explained in this way. For, in certain cases, the truth of such a belief might be attributable to a kind of perceptual discrimination or concentration expressive of intellectual virtue.

low-grade knowledge that are unaccompanied by any genuine motives or actions. These are cases in which an agent is entirely *passive* with respect to the belief in question. Suppose, for instance, that as I sit working at my desk late one night, the electricity suddenly shuts off, causing the room immediately to go dark. As a result, I immediately and automatically form a corresponding belief: I am, as it were, *overcome* by knowledge that the lighting in the room has changed. By all appearances, this is a case in which I do not manifest any intellectual motives or actions. I do not, even at a "low" or subconscious level, seek the truth about the state of affairs in question. Nor is it plausible to think I am "trusting my senses" in the relevant, motivational sense.[18] And, of course, cases like this are hardly few and far between: they include knowledge that, for instance, a loud sound has just occurred or that one presently has a severe headache or is feeling nauseous. Again, knowledge of this sort seems not to involve or implicate the knower's agency at all. This provides an additional compelling reason for thinking that virtuous motives and actions are not necessary for knowledge.

3.3.4 *Conclusion*

Our main concern in this section has been whether anything like an exercise of intellectual character virtues is necessary for knowledge. We began by noting that an exercise of actual intellectual virtues—of stable and entrenched dispositions of intellectual character—cannot be necessary for knowledge, since this would limit the scope of knowledge in obviously problematic ways. We then turned our attention to the details of Zagzebski's less demanding virtue-based account, according to which knowledge requires an instantiation of virtuous motives and actions that need not be part of any entrenched psychological disposition or habit. We have found, however, that even this weaker kind of virtue-requirement is too strong. For again some knowledge is acquired independently of any virtuous motives or actions at all. Finally, it is very difficult to imagine what an alternative, more plausible, but still genuinely characterological or virtue-based account of knowledge might look like. Barring such an account, we are well-positioned to conclude that the concept of intellectual virtue cannot anchor a plausible analysis of knowledge. In the remainder of the

[18] It might be wondered whether the belief is the product of a perceptual *habit* the etiology of which does include exercises of intellectual virtue. While this may be the case for *some* perceptual habits (again, see the discussion in Chapter 4), it is not a plausible explanation of the belief in question (and surely is not a plausible account of *all* perceptual habits, for at least some of these are entirely brute or natural).

chapter, I consider the implications of this conclusion for the relevance of intellectual virtue to traditional epistemology at large.

3.4 *Prospects for Strong Conservative VE*

What does the conclusion just reached imply about the role of intellectual character virtues within traditional epistemology? Are there, perhaps, other traditional problems or questions—beyond the analysis of knowledge—an adequate treatment of which would require a central appeal to the concept of intellectual virtue? More specifically, what should we make of the prospects of Strong Conservative VE, which again is the view the concept of intellectual virtue is of *central* and *fundamental* importance to traditional epistemology?

There is good reason to think that if the concept of intellectual virtue does not figure prominently in a plausible analysis of knowledge, then neither is it likely to figure prominently in a response to any other traditional epistemological questions or problems, and thus that Strong Conservative VE is unlikely to succeed. In short, the idea is that traditional debates about the nature, structure, sources, and limits of knowledge revolve around the *necessary* or *defining* features of knowledge, such that if something like an exercise of intellectual virtues is not among these features, then the concept of intellectual virtue is unlikely to figure prominently in any of the relevant debates. This is obviously the case with respect to questions about the fundamental nature of knowledge; but it holds with respect to several other traditional questions as well.

Debates about the limits of knowledge, for instance, have traditionally focused on the problem of skepticism about the external world. Non-skeptical replies to this problem attempt to show that some of our beliefs about the external world do qualify as knowledge, which is a matter of showing that these beliefs satisfy the *necessary* (and sufficient) conditions for knowledge. The concern here is not with any properties or features that the beliefs in question instantiate only sometimes or occasionally. It follows that if something like an exercise of intellectual virtues is not a necessary feature of knowledge, a concern with the relevant traits is unlikely to play a central or fundamental role in overcoming the skeptical challenge.[19]

[19] Hookway (2003) might appear to pose an exception. Hookway argues that reflection on the intellectual virtues and their role in inquiry can help us understand how knowledge is "possible" and that in doing so it can help us address the skeptical challenge. However, what Hookway has in mind by the "skeptical challenge" is apparently something very different

An analogous point holds for the debate among foundationalists, coherentists, and others about the logical structure of epistemic justification. Here again the concern is with the *essential* features of justification (in particular, with whether these features should be conceived along foundationalist, coherentist, or other lines), not with any accidental or incidental features. Therefore, if something like an exercise of intellectual virtue is not required for justification, it is unclear how the concept of intellectual virtue could merit a central role in this debate.

This does not, of course, exhaust the full range of traditional epistemological questions and issues; for instance, it leaves unaddressed questions about the nature of perception, how sensory experience can play a justifying role, whether reason is an autonomous source of knowledge, whether or how inductive inferences are justified, how knowledge is transmitted from one person to another, and so forth. But I submit that it is equally unclear, and in certain cases considerably *less* clear, how the concept of intellectual virtue might figure prominently in a plausible discussion of these other traditional issues. With respect to traditional questions about testimony or the transmission of knowledge from one cognitive agent to another, for instance, the focus again is on the necessary or essential features of knowledge and whether or how testimonial beliefs acquire these features. And with respect to questions about, say, inductive logic, how experience can justify a belief, or whether reason is an autonomous source of epistemic justification, it is difficult to see how the concept of an intellectual virtue could even begin to be relevant.

We have reached the conclusion (1) that Strong Conservative VE is viable only if the concept of intellectual virtue figures properly into a plausible analysis of knowledge, but (2) that any virtue-based analysis of knowledge seems bound to fail. As we will see in the chapter that follows, this does not mean that the concept of intellectual virtue merits no role at all within traditional epistemology (and much less that it merits no role within epistemology broadly conceived). It does, however, put a damper on certain especially hopeful or ambitious versions of virtue epistemology—particularly those that suggest that an appeal to intellectual virtue can somehow "save the day" or have a deeply transformative effect on traditional epistemology.

from the traditional, Cartesian version of skepticism. His discussion, at any rate, does not even begin to address the sorts of worries about vicious circularity, underdetermination, and so on that lie at the very heart of the skeptical challenge in its traditional formulations.

Chapter 4

VIRTUE AND CHARACTER IN RELIABILISM

We have seen that the concept of intellectual virtue is unlikely to play a central or fundamental role in connection with traditional epistemology. It does not follow, however, that this concept is irrelevant to traditional epistemology. For, as I argue in this chapter and the next, the concept of intellectual virtue does merit a secondary or supporting role in this context. In these two chapters, then, I shall be defending what was referred to in Chapter 1 as Weak Conservative VE. This again is the view that there are at least some conceptual connections between intellectual virtue and traditional epistemology, albeit connections that do not motivate an overhaul or transformation of traditional epistemology.

My focus in the present chapter is the relevance of intellectual virtue to a reliabilist account of knowledge; in the chapter that follows, I examine the connection between intellectual virtue and epistemic justification conceived in evidentialist terms. Of course reliabilism and evidentialism are typically thought to offer competing accounts of the nature of epistemic justification. My aim in these chapters, however, is not to side with either of these views, but rather to show that each one has some occasion to appeal to the concept of intellectual virtue.

In Chapter 1, I noted that within the field of virtue epistemology, there exist two rather different conceptions of an intellectual virtue. Virtue "responsibilists" conceive of intellectual virtues as I am conceiving of them throughout the present book: namely, as excellences of intellectual *character*. Virtue "reliabilists," by contrast, cite as paradigm cases of intellectual virtue various cognitive faculties or abilities like memory, vision, hearing, reason, and introspection. For ease of reference, I shall call the former traits intellectual "character virtues" and the latter "faculty virtues." One central aim of this chapter is to show that character virtues satisfy virtue reliabilists' formal requirements for an intellectual virtue, and thus that virtue reliabilists must expand their repertoire of intellectual virtues or "knowledge-makers" to include, not just the faculty virtues, but also character virtues. Indeed, I shall argue that a failure to do so leaves them unable to account for much of the knowledge that we as human beings care about most. Toward the end of the chapter, I explain how this inclusion generates several challenging questions and problems that any fully adequate version of reliabilism must reckon with.

To better understand the thrust of this chapter, it will be helpful to consider a complaint sometimes lodged by responsibilist or character-based virtue epistemologists against their reliabilist or faculty-based counterparts. Zagzebski (1996), for instance, claims that, unlike character-based models, faculty-based accounts of knowledge have a difficult time accounting for "high-grade" or "reflective" knowledge (273–80).[1] The idea, as I understand it, is that a focus on cognitive faculties, whose operation is largely brute or mechanistic, makes it easy to explain why beliefs like "I exist" or "I have hands" or "There is a computer monitor before me" count as knowledge (they are the product of reliable mechanistic cognitive processes), but difficult to explain the status of higher grade knowledge, or knowledge that takes significant effort to acquire: for instance, philosophical, historical, scientific, moral, or religious knowledge. While I think this complaint is onto something, it is not sufficiently clear. In what sense exactly do reliabilist or faculty-based accounts have a hard time accommodating or making sense out of high-grade knowledge? Why think that a reliabilist cannot adequately explain the status of such knowledge? This is what I shall attempt to shed light on here. My aim, again, is to show that absent proper attention to intellectual character virtues, reliabilists are unable to give an account of the sort of reliability at play in much high-grade knowledge, and thereby unable to accommodate or explain its status as knowledge. While my immediate focus will be *virtue* reliabilism, I will make clear why all the major claims I make about virtue reliabilism apply equally to any other variety of reliabilism.[2]

[1] The other side of the token here, as Zagzebski herself acknowledges and discusses in the passage just cited, is that character-based accounts of knowledge have a difficult time accounting for "low-grade" knowledge. This point was developed at length in Chapter 3.

[2] My focus is reliabilist accounts of *knowledge*, but the arguments are meant to apply to reliabilist accounts of justification or warrant as well.

4.1 *The exclusion of character virtues within reliabilist epistemology*

Before turning to argue that virtue reliabilists are wrong to neglect matters of intellectual character, it is important to show that in fact this neglect occurs. We may begin with a discussion of some work by Alvin Goldman, who is one of the originators and most able defenders of reliabilism. While it is not entirely clear that Goldman should or even wishes to be classified as a virtue epistemologist, he sometimes aligns himself with the movement. For example, he identifies "the concept of justified belief with the concept of belief obtained through the exercise of intellectual virtues (excellences)," adding that "the virtues include belief formation based on sight, hearing, memory, reasoning in certain 'approved' ways, and so forth" (1992: 157–8). This suggests that Goldman is thinking of intellectual virtues on the model of cognitive faculties or abilities rather than as character traits. Passages like the following confirm this impression:

> In the moral sphere ordinary language is rich in virtues terminology. By contrast there are few common labels for intellectual virtues, and those that do exist—"perceptiveness," "thoroughness," "insightfulness," and so forth—are of limited value in the present context. I propose to identify the relevant intellectual virtues... with the belief-forming capacities, faculties, or processes that would be accepted as answers to the question "How does *X* know?." In answer to this form of question, it is common to reply, "He saw it," "He heard it," "He remembers it," "He infers it from such-and-such evidence," and so forth. Thus, basing belief on seeing, hearing, memory, and (good) inference are in the collection of what the folk regard as intellectual virtues. (162)

Here Goldman identifies certain intellectual character virtues (e.g. perceptiveness and thoroughness) by name. But he seems to think that these traits—as opposed to cognitive faculties like hearing and memory—are not really intellectual virtues (at least not in the sense that he is concerned with), and thus that a consideration of them is irrelevant to an analysis of knowledge or justification.

John Greco is another chief proponent of reliabilism and of virtue reliabilism in particular. Like Goldman, Greco offers a definition of knowledge that gives a central role to intellectual virtues conceived as reliable "abilities or powers" like perception, memory, and reason. He says that "S has knowledge regarding p if and only if S believes the truth regarding p *because* S believes p out of intellectual virtue" (2002: 311; his italics).

Greco, however, has considerably more to say than Goldman about the distinction between character virtues and faculty virtues. Indeed he explicitly addresses the question of which conception is theoretically preferable. He begins by claiming that epistemologists appeal to virtue concepts in an effort to deal with certain substantive philosophical problems (e.g. problems concerning the nature of knowledge) and that whichever conception of intellectual virtue deals with these problems most effectively is superior (296). He goes on to argue—for reasons that overlap with those offered in Chapter 3—that a character-model of intellectual virtue is unhelpful for giving an account of the nature of knowledge (296–7). He concludes that a character-based or responsibilist conception of intellectual virtue should be rejected on the grounds that it is "too strong" to deal effectively with traditional epistemological problems like the analysis of knowledge (297).[3]

While Greco's conclusion does not, for reasons that will become evident shortly, entail that the concept of an intellectual character virtue is irrelevant to a reliabilist analysis of knowledge, Greco seems to have little use for this concept. For instance, no character virtues appear on any of his various lists of intellectual virtues; rather, when citing examples of intellectual virtue (2000a; 2002), he refers exclusively to cognitive faculties or capacities like vision, memory, reason, and the like. Second, Greco clearly aligns himself with Sosa's general account of intellectual virtue, and he attributes to Sosa the view that intellectual virtues are "cognitive abilities *rather than* character traits" (2002: 295; my emphasis). It seems clear, then, that Greco is committed to denying that character virtues should be regarded as "intellectual virtues" in the sense relevant to a virtue reliabilist account of knowledge.

Ernest Sosa is a third major advocate of virtue reliabilism. He claims (1991: 239–42 and 289–90; and 2007) that a true belief is justified and an instance of knowledge only if it is produced or sustained by an exercise of intellectual virtue.[4] Later on I will suggest that some of Sosa's discussions of intellectual virtue support thinking of character virtues as intellectual virtues in a reliabilist sense;

[3] Greco does not, however, dismiss this conception as altogether irrelevant to epistemology, since he thinks there are likely to be other, less traditional epistemological questions to which it might be relevant (297–8).

[4] As I note below, an additional requirement for what Sosa calls "reflective" or "human" knowledge is that the person in question have an "epistemic perspective" on the known belief, which consists of an additional set of coherent beliefs about the source and reliability of the original belief (see 1991: ch. 11). Our concern here, however, lies with the virtue component of Sosa's analysis. Nor is it very plausible to think that the "reflective" component of Sosa's account of reflective knowledge can be analyzed in terms of an exercise of intellectual character virtues. See my (2008) for an explanation.

but relative to his explicit stance on the matter, there is reason to think that he does not endorse this conception. First, Sosa regularly cites examples of the traits he regards as intellectual virtues, and these examples, like Greco's, include the usual reliabilist faculty virtues and other similar traits, but *not* any intellectual character virtues (1991: chs. 8, 13, and 16). Given Sosa's extensive treatment of the structure and epistemological significance of intellectual virtue, it would be very odd if he thought that character virtues qualified as intellectual virtues and yet never mentioned or elaborated on this point. Second, Sosa regularly uses the terms "virtue" and "faculty" interchangeably (138–9, 234–6, and 273–4). While it is natural to refer to capacities like introspection, memory, and so forth as cognitive "faculties," it is much less natural to refer to character traits like fair-mindedness and intellectual honesty in this way. A related point concerns Sosa's tendency to describe intellectual virtues as "input-output devices" (227) and as "truth-conducive belief-generating mechanisms" (271). While, again, this seems like a fitting description of faculty virtues, it is much less fitting as a description of character virtues. Character virtues do, in some sense, give rise to or "generate" beliefs. But they do so in a way that hardly seems mechanistic. Intellectual virtues, as with moral virtues, tend to involve an exercise of personal *agency*: they involve *deliberating* or *choosing* in a particular way.[5] Thus a belief that emerges from activity characteristic of the intellectual character virtues is unlikely to have been produced in a very mechanical or input-output way. This further suggests that Sosa does not think of character virtues as intellectual virtues in the relevant sense. Finally, Sosa sometimes describes a true belief generated by an exercise of intellectual virtue as mere "animal," "servomechanic," or "metaphorical" knowledge (240, 275). But, for similar reasons, this is likely to be an obvious mischaracterization of a belief arrived at through an exercise of intellectual character virtues. Again, reaching the truth via an exercise of character virtues makes demands on a person qua *agent*. Consequently, the resulting knowledge is very unlikely to amount to "animal" or "servomechanic" knowledge. These considerations strongly suggest that Sosa does not regard the character traits in question as intellectual virtues. And since the concept of an intellectual virtue occupies the leading role in his account of knowledge, he also apparently believes that matters of intellectual character do not have an important role to play in a reliabilist analysis of knowledge.

[5] See Chapter 2 for more on the role of agency in the operation of intellectual character virtues.

4.2 *Character virtues as reliabilist knowledge-makers*

Having shown that virtue reliabilists do not regard intellectual character virtues as intellectual virtues of a sort relevant to a philosophical account of knowledge, my aim in this section is to demonstrate that this is a mistake. I shall argue that intellectual character virtues sometimes satisfy virtue reliabilists' formal conditions for an intellectual virtue. This point, together with the fact that virtue reliabilists generally view knowledge as (roughly) true belief arising from an exercise of intellectual virtue, reveals that intellectual character virtues are indeed relevant to virtue reliabilist accounts of knowledge. I also explain why a similar point holds for any reliabilist account of knowledge (whether virtue-based or not).

Virtue reliabilists are committed to a formal conception of intellectual virtue according to which intellectual virtues are personal qualities that, under certain conditions and with respect to certain propositions, are a reliable means to reaching the truth and avoiding error.[6] This general characterization has been specified in numerous ways, but for the moment, I shall note just one such specification. According to virtue reliabilists (see e.g. Greco 2003), a personal quality is an intellectual virtue only if it plays a *critical* or *salient* role in getting a person to the truth—only if it *best explains* why a person reaches the truth. Thus a personal quality is not an intellectual virtue if it tends to play only a minor or supporting role in reaching the truth.

This characterization reveals that virtue reliabilists do not make a *principled* exclusion of intellectual character virtues from their repertoire of intellectual virtues. There is nothing in their formal definitions of an intellectual virtue that would prevent character virtues from qualifying as intellectual virtues in the relevant sense. Nevertheless, when they go on to develop their accounts of intellectual virtue and its relevance to knowledge, they tend to focus exclusively on cognitive faculties and abilities, giving little or no attention to any character virtues.

Is this neglect of intellectual character virtues warranted? Or do intellectual character virtues sometimes play a critical or salient role in a person's getting to the truth? This depends largely on the subject matter in question. With regard to many matters, reaching the truth is a rather simple and straightforward affair. Reaching the truth about the appearance of one's immediate surroundings, for

[6] See, for example, Sosa (1991: 138, 225, 242, and 284), Goldman (1992: 157–63) and Greco (2002: 287 and 302). For simplicity, I will mostly ignore the end of avoiding error and will focus instead on that of reaching the truth. However, similar points apply to the former end.

instance, typically requires only that one's visual faculty be in good working order. A similar point could be made about several instances of introspective, memorial, and a priori knowledge, for example, that one has a headache, that one drove to work, or that two plus three equals five.[7] It may be that if one were entirely uninterested in the truth about these matters, or desired for some reason to avoid the truth, the proper functioning of one's cognitive faculties would be insufficient for reaching the truth. In most cases of this sort, however, what fundamentally explains or causes one to reach the truth is not an attitude or state of character, but rather the proper functioning of one's basic cognitive endowment. Thus if we limit our attention—as most contemporary epistemologists do—to the sorts of ordinary and mundane truths just noted, it seems that intellectual character virtues do *not* satisfy the virtue reliabilist's conditions for an intellectual virtue.

But, of course, reaching the truth is not always so easy. This is so especially with regard to the domains of knowledge that we as humans tend to value most. Getting to the truth about historical, scientific, moral, philosophical, psychological, or religious matters, for instance, can make significant agency-related demands: it can require the possession of certain intentions, beliefs, and desires. While reaching the truth in these areas does typically require that our cognitive faculties be in good working order, this is not usually what explains or at least what *best* explains our actually getting to the truth. Rather, reaching the truth in these areas is often explained largely or most saliently in terms of an exercise of certain traits of intellectual character: traits like intellectual carefulness, thoroughness, tenacity, adaptability, creativity, circumspection, attentiveness, patience, and honesty.[8]

Consider some examples:

1. A field biologist is trying to explain a change in the migration patterns of a certain endangered bird species. Collecting and analyzing the relevant data is tedious work and requires a special eye for detail. The biologist is committed to discovering the truth and so spends long hours in the field gathering data. He remains focused and determined in the face of various obstacles and distractions (e.g. conflicting evidence, bureaucratic road

[7] This point was explored at length in Chapter 3. The claim argued for below is, as it were, the mirror image of this one, namely, that while some instances or kinds of knowledge clearly do not require an exercise of intellectual character virtues, other most definitely do.

[8] For a related discussion of how the volitional demands of knowledge can vary substantially from one known object or subject matter to another, see Locke's discussion of the "improvement of our knowledge " in BK. IV of *An Essay Concerning Human Understanding* (1996: 292–9).

blocks, inclement weather, boredom, etc.). He picks up on important details in environmental reports and makes keen discriminations regarding the composition and trajectory of several observed flocks. As a result of his determination and careful and insightful methods of inquiry, he discovers why the birds have altered their course.

2. An investigative reporter is researching a story on corporate crime and begins to uncover evidence indicating that some of the perpetrators are executives in the very corporation that owns his newspaper. The reporter believes that he and his readership have a right to know about the crimes, so he persists with the investigation, recognizing that it may cost him his job, and perhaps more. Undaunted even by personal threats, the reporter proceeds with his investigation. After several months of rigorous intellectual labor, he uncovers and exposes the executives' misdeeds.

3. An historian has garnered international recognition and praise for a book in which she defends a certain view of how the religious faith of one of America's "founding fathers" influenced his politics. While researching her next book, the historian runs across some heretofore unexamined personal letters of this figure that blatantly contradict her own account of his theology and its effects on his political thought and behavior. She does not ignore or suppress the letters, but rather examines them fairly and thoroughly. Because she is more interested in believing and writing what is true than she is in receiving the praise of her colleagues and readers, she accepts the implications of this new data for her previously published work, and proceeds to repudiate the relevant parts of it, both privately and in print.

In these scenarios, reaching the truth is not simply or even primarily a matter of having good eyesight, a good memory, or making valid logical inferences. Rather, the individuals in question reach the truth because they exhibit certain attitudes or character traits. These traits seem to account most saliently for or to best explain why the individuals form true beliefs. The biologist, for example, discovers why the relevant bird species has altered its migratory course on account of his patient, focused inquiry and his refined powers of observation and discrimination. The reporter uncovers a corporate scandal because he is intellectually courageous and autonomous. And the historian accepts and acknowledges a major error in her work because of her intellectual openness, honesty, humility, and general love of truth.

We have seen, then, that intellectual character virtues *do* sometimes satisfy the virtue reliabilist's conditions for an intellectual virtue: with regard to certain propositions or situations, intellectual character virtues can play a critical or salient role in getting a person to the truth.[9] These are cases in which reaching the truth requires more than the routine operation of a person's basic cognitive endowment—cases that make significant demands on a person qua *agent*. Moreover, they are often cases in which something very important is at stake, for instance, knowledge of important historical events and realities, the complex operation and structure of the natural world, the just or unjust treatment of a particular person or group of people, etc. It follows that virtue reliabilists' inattention to the domain of intellectual character leaves them unable to adequately account for some of the most important items of knowledge.

It is important to note that while virtue reliabilists have generally avoided discussions of intellectual character in their treatment of intellectual virtue, they have (apparently without realizing it) not done so in their discussions of intellectual *vice*. Given the qualities that reliabilists identify as intellectual virtues, one would expect that when discussing intellectual vices, their concern would be defects like a deteriorating memory, far-sightedness, and hardness of hearing. But this is not what one typically finds. Goldman, for example, cites guesswork, wishful thinking, and ignoring contrary evidence as paradigm intellectual vices (1992: 162). Sosa cites haste and inattentiveness (1991: 229). And Greco cites wishful thinking and superstition (2002: 521). Virtue reliabilists are right, even by their own standards, to identify these qualities as intellectual vices, since they significantly hinder a person's ability to reach the truth. But the qualities in question generally are not a result of defective cognitive faculties or abilities of the sort that tend to interest reliabilists. Rather, they are more accurately described as states or manifestations of vicious intellectual *character*.

This adds to the surprise that virtue reliabilists have not given significant attention to virtues of intellectual character, for these qualities are the virtuous counterparts to the qualities they identify as intellectual vices. It is as though virtue reliabilists have recognized that certain traits of intellectual character tend systematically to *block* access to the truth (and hence are intellectual vices) while failing to acknowledge that others play a salient and systematic role in *reaching* the truth (and hence are intellectual virtues).

Before turning to consider a possible objection to this argument, it is important to note that its scope is not limited to *virtue* reliabilism: it has implications for virtually *any* version of reliabilism. Consider, for example, a version of reliabilism

[9] Robert Roberts and Jay Wood (2004) make a similar connection between intellectual character virtues and Alvin Plantinga's reliabilist or quasi-reliabilist epistemology. This connection is developed in ch. 4 of their (2007).

(á la Goldman 1981) that makes the doxastic processes or methods employed by a cognitive agent (rather than any quality of the agent herself) the source of epistemic justification. According to such views, a belief is justified (roughly) just in case it is produced by a reliable process or method. The activity characteristic of intellectual character virtues also satisfies the conditions for a reliable doxastic process or method. This is because forming beliefs via an exercise of intellectual character virtues involves instantiating certain reliable processes or employing certain reliable methods characteristic of these virtues (for instance, the processes or methods involved with fair or careful or tenacious inquiry). And with respect to certain kinds or cases of knowledge, cognitive performances of this sort are essential to reaching the truth. Therefore, even reliabilists of this other sort must give a significant epistemological role to the intellectual character virtues if they hope to account for the full range of human knowledge.

How might a reliabilist or virtue reliabilist try to get around this conclusion? The latter might attempt to make a principled exclusion of intellectual character virtues in something like the following way.[10] Epistemologists like Sosa and Goldman originally introduced the concept of an intellectual virtue into the epistemological discussion in an effort to explain what distinguishes instances of knowledge from instances of mere true belief. The difference, they argued, has to do with the *source* or *origin* of the beliefs in question. A true belief counts as knowledge only if its source is reliable; and an intellectual virtue is a reliable source of belief. Thus, for virtue reliabilists, the class of intellectual virtues is properly limited to reliable sources of belief. Intellectual character virtues like open-mindedness, intellectual tenacity, and carefulness, however, do not appear to be sources of belief—at least not in the same way that cognitive faculties like introspection and vision are such. Therefore, there are principled grounds for excluding intellectual character virtues from a reliabilist account of knowledge.

But is it right to think that character virtues are not "sources" of belief in the sense relevant to virtue reliabilism? This depends, of course, on what reliabilists have in mind or ought to have in mind by a "source" of belief. On a broad construal, something is a source of a belief just in case it is the *cause* or *salient* cause of a belief. This would seem to be the conception most relevant to any version of reliabilism, since reliabilists often define knowledge as (roughly) true

[10] This objection was presented to me by Stephen Grimm in his comments on an earlier draft of this chapter. For ease of discussion, I will focus on a version of the objection couched in *virtue* reliabilist terms. An analogous point could easily be raised from the standpoint of other forms of reliabilism as well. My reply is applicable to either version of the objection.

belief caused by an intellectual virtue or other reliable mechanism. Goldman, for instance, says: "According to reliabilism, the epistemic status of a belief depends on its *mode of causation*" (1998: sec. 1, par. 7).[11] But on this broad conception of what it is to be a source of belief, intellectual character virtues *are* sources of belief. As explained above, intellectual character virtues are sometimes the (salient) cause of a person's reaching the truth.

For the objection in question to have any force, a narrower conception of a "source" of belief must be assumed. According to one such conception, something is a source of belief just in case it generates beliefs independently of other beliefs or generates them in an immediate or noninferential way. This conception coheres well with many of the traits that virtue reliabilists regard as intellectual virtues, for example, introspection, intuitive reason, and the various sensory faculties. Moreover, it may succeed at excluding intellectual character virtues, since these traits do not typically generate beliefs in the immediate or noninferential way typical of many faculty virtues.[12]

But there are good reasons for thinking that virtue reliabilists do not and should not accept this way of thinking about sources of belief. First, it rules out some of the traits that virtually all reliabilists regard as intellectual virtues. As noted above, reliabilists commonly cite certain "approved ways of reasoning" like inductive and explanatory reasoning as paradigm cases of an intellectual virtue. While these forms of reasoning count as sources of belief in the broad sense noted above, they are not sources of belief in the present, narrower sense. Indeed, they are methods of *inference*, of drawing certain conclusions on the basis of other, preexisting claims or beliefs; they do not generate beliefs in an immediate or noninferential way. Sosa himself draws a distinction along these lines between "generation" faculties and "transmission" faculties, both of which he regards as intellectual virtues. He comments: "There are faculties of two broad sorts: those that lead to beliefs from beliefs already formed, and those that lead to beliefs but not from beliefs. The first of these we call 'transmission' faculties, the second 'generation' faculties"

[11] The notion of causation would also seem to unify or explain several other common ways of stating the reliabilist's central claim: for instance, that knowledge is true belief arrived at "by way of," "through," "as a result of," etc., an exercise of intellectual virtue; or that it is true belief "produced by," "generated by," "with its source in," etc., intellectual virtue.

[12] They may do this on occasion, however, as where a person's character virtues are manifested in, say, a visual observation or "noticing" that would not occur to a nonvirtuous perceiver. Here the traits in question might trigger a certain perceptual belief in (more or less) the relevant immediate way.

(1991: 225).[13] Sosa cites intuitive reason, perception, and introspection as examples of generation faculties; he cites deductive, inductive, and explanatory reasoning as examples of transmission faculties. In practice, then, virtue reliabilists do not limit the class of intellectual virtues to those faculties that generate beliefs in an immediate or noninferential way.

Second, virtue reliabilists are *right* not to employ this narrower conception of a source of belief. For if a virtue reliabilist were to limit the class of intellectual virtues to those cognitive faculties that are sources of belief in this sense, the scope of human knowledge would be limited to *immediate* knowledge, for example, to knowledge of (perhaps the mere appearance of) one's immediate surroundings, direct intuitive or a priori knowledge, introspective knowledge, and the like. Inferential knowledge, the kind of knowledge we acquire from various reliable ways or methods of reasoning, would be impossible. Thus to avoid a form of radical skepticism, virtue reliabilists must reject this narrower conception of what counts as a source of belief.

Is there perhaps a less restrictive understanding of what it is to be a source of belief that would exclude intellectual character virtues while including the full range of reliabilist faculty virtues? This is highly unlikely, for as I turn now to consider, close inspection reveals that character virtues and faculty virtues are in a certain sense inseparable. This is because an exercise of character virtues is sometimes (perhaps always) *manifested* in and partly *constituted* by an operation of faculty virtues.

This is most evident in connection with some of the reliable methods of reasoning just discussed. Note first that these methods are more accurately described as forms of intellectual *activity* than as mere default modes of cognitive functioning. There typically is a more active dimension to inductive or deductive reasoning, for instance, than there is to the routine operation of one's sensory faculties. Given that exercising character virtues also typically involves engaging in a certain kind of intellectual activity, it is not surprising that these forms of reasoning might intersect or overlap with intellectual character virtues. Recall the historian who, out of open-mindedness, intellectual humility, and a genuine commitment to the truth, encounters and accepts data that undermines her acclaimed scholarly work. How exactly should we understand the connection between her acts of reasoning and her exercise of various character virtues? One reply is that her intellectual openness and commitment to the truth enable her to continue investigating (rather than to bury) the

[13] Sosa draws a similar distinction between "fundamental" and "derived" faculties or virtues (1991: 278).

relevant data once she realizes that it threatens her position. While this much is correct, the traits in question might also lead her to *think through* the data in reasonable (rather than sloppy and defensive) ways or to *draw valid conclusions* from it (rather than to distort its implications). The historian's open-mindedness, for instance, might cause her to avoid committing a certain logical fallacy that most others in her situation would commit or to perceive an otherwise easily missed logical connection. Here, a sharp distinction cannot be drawn between the person's reasoning and her exercise of various character virtues. It is not as though she displays open-mindedness and subsequently reasons in the ways in question. Rather, her exercise of open-mindedness is partly constituted by her acts of reasoning.

This relation between intellectual character virtues and standard reliabilist virtues is not limited to methods or acts of reasoning. It can also extend to the functioning of basic cognitive faculties like vision. We noted, for instance, that the field biologist discussed above reaches the truth about a change in migration patterns on account of his intellectual carefulness, concern with detail, and other intellectual character virtues. This might involve the following. As the biologist studies the birds' new winter habitat, he *notices* or *sees* certain subtle but critical topographical details that would normally go unnoticed. His exercise of certain character virtues in this case is partly constituted by the operation of his visual faculty: his inquiring in a careful and attentive way just is (or mostly is) a matter of making certain visual observations.

The tight logical connection between character virtues and faculty virtues is also evident in the fact that when epistemologists offer detailed characterizations of the latter, they have a hard time avoiding talk of the former. Sosa, for instance, in a discussion regarding the fallibility of faculty virtues, notes that the reliability of one's cognitive faculties can be affected by one's intellectual *conduct*. Interestingly, the conduct he proceeds to describe is precisely that of certain intellectual character virtues and vices. He says that "[t]hrough greater *attentiveness* and *circumspection* one can normally improve the quality of one's introspection and thus enhance its accuracy" (1991: 228; my emphasis). He also remarks that the process of forming beliefs through introspection "can of course go wrong in various ways," for example, through an exercise of "haste" or "inattentiveness" (229). Sosa concludes that "a belief's justification derives from the endowments *and conduct* that lie behind it" (232; my emphasis). A second example is Sosa's discussion of "ampliative" or "coherence-seeking" reason, which he describes as a subfaculty of reason proper that incorporates nondeductive methods of reasoning including inductive and explanatory reasoning. While at times Sosa describes this trait as a kind of default cognitive capacity (thereby suggesting parity with other faculty virtues like vision or memory), at other times he describes it in more active and psychologically richer terms. He refers to it, for instance, as "reason as we know it, with its *thirst* for comprehensive coherence" (211), as "an *inner drive* for greater and greater explanatory comprehensiveness" (145), and as "a *rational drive* for coherence" (209). Here coherence-seeking reason seems less like a natural or default cognitive mode than it does a cultivated excellence of intellectual character.

It is clear, then, that the kind of fundamental and categorical distinction between character virtues and faculty virtues central to the objection above is unwarranted. Again, an exercise of character virtues is often manifested in and partly constituted by the operation of certain faculty virtues. Moreover, as the passages from Sosa indicate, the reliability of faculty virtues often implicates one or more character virtues. Therefore, the attempt to make a principled exclusion of character virtues from the reliabilist repertoire of intellectual virtues on the grounds that faculty virtues but not character virtues are "sources" of belief seems bound to fail.

4.3 *Theoretical reverberations*

Thus far I have mainly been concerned with showing (1) that virtue reliabilists tend to neglect matters of intellectual character and (2) that because intellectual character virtues sometimes satisfy virtue reliabilists' formal conditions for an intellectual virtue, this neglect is unjustified. One result of this, we have seen, is that virtue reliabilists (and reliabilists in general) must incorporate intellectual character virtues into their repertoire of intellectual virtues (or alternative justification-conferring qualities). But what exactly is the upshot of this conclusion? What bearing does it have, say, on virtue reliabilism itself or on its place within virtue epistemology? And what, if anything, are its theoretical ramifications? To what extent is it likely to affect the way that virtue reliabilists or reliabilists in general go about constructing or applying their theories?

One implication of the argument, which resembles a claim sometimes made by virtue ethicists, concerns the general scope or orientation of virtue reliabilism.[14] Virtue ethicists (e.g. Stocker 1997: 118–27) often claim that modern ethical theories tend mistakenly to neglect or ignore the human *person* in their accounts of the moral life and that a return to the notion of

[14] As in the previous section, I will initially limit my attention to *virtue* reliabilism; later on I will consider the implications for reliabilism in general.

virtue in moral philosophy offers a way of correcting this problem. A similar point could be made about virtue reliabilism. We have seen that virtue reliabilists tend to characterize knowers in highly mechanistic and impersonal terms. This is evident in their tendency to describe intellectual virtues as "truth-conducive belief-forming mechanism[s]" or as "input-output devices," and to liken knowers to thermometers, thermostats, and the like. This is true even of Greco's "agent reliabilist" approach to epistemology, which stresses the natural cognitive faculties and abilities of knowers over their rational agency (2000a: ch. 7).[15] We have also seen, however, that this limited focus yields an incomplete account of epistemic reliability, for epistemic reliability is sometimes a function, not just of one's basic cognitive functioning, but also of one's intellectual *character*. Therefore one lesson to be drawn is that virtue reliabilists must expand their focus to include the character of epistemic agents or the epistemic agent qua agent.

A related implication concerns the general structure of virtue epistemology. I noted at the outset of this chapter and in Chapter 1 that standard characterizations of virtue epistemology divide the field into two main camps: virtue reliabilism and virtue responsibilism. And the impression one gets from the literature is that the division between the two camps runs deep: virtue reliabilists are said to limit their focus to cognitive faculties and related abilities, while virtue responsibilists limit their attention to matters of intellectual character. We are now in a position to appreciate a fundamental asymmetry in this distinction. The theoretical focus of virtue reliabilism is, as the name suggests, the notion of epistemic *reliability*, while the theoretical focus of virtue responsibilism is that of intellectual *character*. What we have seen, however, is that a concern with reliability must incorporate a concern with intellectual character. Reliability is not purely a matter of having properly functioning cognitive faculties. To put the point another way, we have seen that a strictly faculty-based reliabilist epistemology is unsuccessful—that any plausible reliabilist epistemology must attend to the domain of intellectual character virtues. For again, with respect to certain claims or contexts, such traits are the very basis or seat of reliability. Accordingly, it is a mistake to try to divide the field of virtue epistemology into two more or less symmetrical camps, one concerned with faculty virtues and the other with character virtues. Instead, we shall have to think of reliabilist virtue epistemology (ā la Sosa, Greco, etc.) as incorporating a concern with faculty virtues *and* character virtues, and a responsibilist or

[15] While Greco often speaks of "cognitive character," he seems mainly to have in mind one's native cognitive endowment.

character-based approach (ā la Zagzebski) as concerned strictly with character virtues (though even here, given that character virtues can be manifested in the operation of faculty virtues, the division is not especially deep).

But the argument also has certain theoretical implications for reliabilism. We can begin to see what these are by noting, first, that an important requirement of any fully adequate reliabilist epistemology is to give an account of the reliability of the processes or traits that it regards as contributing to knowledge: it must make clear how or in what sense the traits are reliable or truth-conducive. Sosa and others have shed a great deal of ink developing such an account for faculty virtues. However, as I turn now to argue, character virtues are structurally different from faculty virtues such that existing models of reliability seem inapplicable to character virtues in important ways. The result is that a certain amount of theoretical work remains to be done by reliabilists before they can hope to offer an adequate account of the reliability of character virtues.

Two related differences between faculty virtues and character virtues concern the conditionality or relativity of their reliability. Reliabilists often point out that the reliability of faculty virtues is not unconditional; rather, it is relative to certain kinds of truths or to certain "propositional fields" as well as to certain environmental conditions.[16] I will discuss each of these parameters in turn.

Consider the faculty of hearing. Clearly this faculty is reliable with respect to certain kinds of propositions (e.g. those concerning the sound or spatial location of nearby objects) but not with respect to others (e.g. those concerning the color, shape, or the scent of things). In the case of faculty virtues like hearing, it is reasonably easy to arrive at a plausible specification of the relevant propositional fields. A propositional field can be specified or at least substantially narrowed in such cases simply on the basis of the *content* of the propositions in question: propositions about the color and the shape of things, for example, are epistemically relevant to the faculty of vision, but not to the auditory or olfactory faculties, since the former but not the latter is helpful for reaching the truth about the subject matter in question. The fairly obvious and natural correspondence between particular faculty virtues and particular fields of propositions is also evident in the fact that it makes good sense to speak of "visual propositions," "introspective propositions," "a priori propositions," "memorial propositions," and the like.

[16] See, for example, Sosa (1991: 138, 242, 277, and 287). A subtle distinction can be drawn between the "environment" and the "conditions" relevant to a particular virtue; however, for ease of discussion, I shall treat these as a single parameter.

But character virtues are fundamentally different from faculty virtues in this respect. We noted earlier that at a certain level, it is clear that character virtues are critical for reaching the truth with regard to certain subject matters but not others. For instance, while not essential to reaching the truth about, say, the general appearance of one's immediate surroundings, an exercise of character virtues is essential to the acquisition of much "higher grade" knowledge (e.g. to much scientific, philosophical, or historical knowledge). Notice, however, that the correspondence here between character virtues and propositional fields is extremely general. It fails to tell us anything about the propositional fields relevant to any *particular* character virtues.[17]

The problem is that it is difficult and perhaps impossible to provide this kind of narrower specification for individual character virtues. This is due to certain uniquely "situational" aspects of these traits. We generally cannot tell just by considering the content of a particular proposition, for example, which (if any) character virtue is likely to be helpful for reaching the truth about it. Instead, the applicability of a character virtue to a particular proposition or field of propositions usually depends in a very deep way on highly contingent features of the person or situation in question. The virtues of intellectual caution and carefulness, for instance, might be required in one situation to reach the truth about a proposition which in another situation could be known only via an exercise of intellectual courage and perseverance.[18] In contrast with faculty virtues, the relevance of a character virtue to a particular field of propositions is not given by the content of the propositions themselves. This is reflected in the fact that it makes little sense to speak of "intellectual courage propositions," "fair-mindedness propositions," etc. Again, the kind of subject matter with respect to which intellectual courage or fair-mindedness are likely to be reliable is a deeply contingent and variable matter.

It follows that a number of questions must be addressed if we are to have an adequate grasp of the reliability of character virtues: Is the reliability of character virtues "field-relative" at all? If so, how are these fields determined and what

[17] Further, the correlation between character virtues and the fields just indicated is not exact, since some scientific, philosophical, historical, and related sorts of truths presumably can be believed in a reliable way without an exercise of intellectual virtue (via testimony, say, or in any other case in which no significant demand is made on the person's agency).

[18] Imagine, for instance, that the first person is a very free-thinking individual in a very free-thinking society and the second is a rather timid and unconfident inquirer in a society in which the flow of information is highly regulated and censored. Note as well that this is not an exception to the rule for character virtues, for again, there is a general lack of any initial or principled correspondence between individual character virtues and particular propositional fields.

are they? If not, then what alternative parameter or parameters might be useful for characterizing the reliability of character virtues? Without answers to these and related questions, our grasp of the reliability of character virtues is incomplete in important ways.

A second and related point concerns the kinds of environmental conditions under which intellectual character virtues are reliable. As noted above, reliabilists like Sosa regularly point out that any given faculty virtue will be reliable relative to certain environments but not others. Vision, for instance, is reliable in good lighting and in "normal" environments, but not in complete darkness, a funhouse, or a smoke-filled room. Similarly, hearing is reliable only where there is a not a lot of background noise, where one is not submerged in water, and so on. These examples indicate that the environmental conditions relevant to a particular faculty virtue typically can be specified by reference to the faculty's natural or proper function: a faculty is reliable only with respect to environmental conditions that permit or do not obstruct or interfere with such functioning.

The reliability of character virtues is also relative to certain environmental conditions. Open-mindedness or intellectual courage, for example, can do more cognitive harm than good if exercised in the wrong situation. Yet the environmental conditions relevant to the proper functioning of character virtues would seem to be categorically different from those relevant to faculty virtues. This can be seen in the fact that character virtues often are helpful for reaching the truth in the face of the very sorts of environmental conditions that tend to interfere with the performance of faculty virtues.

We can begin to see how by noting that it does not seem quite right to think of the reliability of character virtues like intellectual perseverance or keen attentiveness as relative to environments with good lighting, little background noise, or few distractions. It is not that these virtues are *unreliable* with respect to such environments; it is just that their exercise is often unnecessary. For these are situations in which persons often can reach the truth just by virtue of the functioning of their cognitive faculties. To know that there is a substantial plot of grass outside my window, for instance, I need not be intellectually perseverant or attentive; I just need decent vision and minimal lighting.

Under what conditions, then, do character virtues tend to be reliable? These traits are especially helpful for reaching the truth where the truth is hard to come by. And often what makes the truth hard to come by are precisely those environmental or situational factors that can undermine or interfere with the reliability of faculty virtues: a gap between appearance and reality, dubious interlocutors, incomplete or misleading evidence, and the like. This shows that when compared with faculty virtues, character virtues are reliable with respect to very different sorts of environmental conditions. In fact, the situational relevance of character virtues often picks up precisely where that of many faculty virtues leaves off. Therefore, if reliabilists are to offer an adequate and illuminating account of the reliability of character virtues, they must attempt to clarify the sorts of environmental conditions under which they are reliable.

A third issue related to the reliability of character virtues concerns the tighter "unity" of these traits when compared with that of faculty virtues. Unlike faculty virtues, character virtues typically are reliable only when possessed in *conjunction* with other character virtues. Open-mindedness, intellectual caution, or intellectual tenacity, for example, are unlikely to be very helpful for reaching the truth if possessed in isolation: open-mindedness typically must be tempered by a kind of mindfulness of and adherence to arguments and evidence, intellectual caution by a firm commitment to discovering the truth, and intellectual tenacity by a willingness to revise a belief or course of inquiry if the evidence finally calls for it. Similarly, the possession of one character virtue apparently can presuppose the possession of others virtues. It would seem, for example, that to be genuinely intellectually fair, one must also be intellectually careful and patient, which in turn seems to require that one be intellectually attentive and determined.[19]

The deep interconnectedness of character virtues generates additional questions that must be addressed if we are to have a proper grasp of the reliability of these traits. For instance, to what extent and in what way are character virtues unified? Does the possession of a single intellectual character virtue entail the possession of all the others? If not, which subsets of character virtues "go together"? And how exactly are these virtues related to each other so that when (but only when) taken together they are reliable? Finally, if the relevant traits are reliable only when possessed in conjunction with other such traits, in what sense are they, when considered individually, really intellectual *virtues* at all? Would it not be more appropriate to think of the relevant *clusters* of traits as intellectual virtues—or perhaps (given a strong unity thesis) only the entire *set* of traits?

A fourth challenge posed by the foregoing argument concerns the application of virtue reliabilism (and reliabilism in general—see below) to particular

[19] This is not to suggest that intellectual virtues are unified in the extremely strong sense that one can possess a single intellectual virtue only if one possesses *all* of the intellectual virtues. Rather, it suggests merely that intellectual virtues may necessarily be possessed in certain clusters or subsets.

beliefs. To explain the justification of a particular belief formed by one or more character virtues, the virtue reliabilist must provide a characterization of these virtues according to which they are clearly reliable. And as we saw above, this characterization must be reasonably specific (for again, if the characterization is too general, the reliability of the traits will appear questionable). When providing this kind of specification of *faculty* virtues, virtue reliabilists appeal to certain logical parameters like the propositional field and environmental conditions relevant to the faculty in question. (Vision, for instance, can be characterized as reliable *with respect to* claims about appearances and when operating at close range in normal well-lit environments.) We have seen, however, that it is far from clear how or whether these parameters apply to the reliability of character virtues. Thus until further light is shed on how best to understand and characterize the reliability of character virtues, virtue reliabilists' ability to explain the justification of particular beliefs produced by such virtues will remain significantly limited.[20]

This problem is compounded by the apparent "unity" of the intellectual virtues. We saw above that, unlike the possession of faculty virtues, the possession of a single character virtue often seems to presuppose that of several others. Because the internal relations among character virtues are often highly complex and far from obvious, the task of providing a precise and accurate description of the character virtue or virtues involved in the production of particular beliefs is likely to prove extremely challenging. To complete this task effectively, we shall need a much better understanding than we presently have of the deep interrelatedness or unity of the character virtues. And again, absent such an understanding, virtue reliabilists will be unable to give a full account of the justification of various beliefs.

Once more it is worth noting that the theoretical questions and problems identified in this section are relevant, not just to virtue reliabilism, but to any version of reliabilism. Like the virtue reliabilist, the method or process reliabilist, say, also must provide an illuminating explanation of the reliability of those methods or processes they regard as capable of conferring epistemic justification. Since, as was pointed out earlier, these include the methods or processes characteristic or expressive of intellectual character virtues, reliabilists of this stripe must also reckon with questions about the logical parameters and

[20] This problem bears an obvious similarity to the "generality problem" for reliabilism. The challenge here, however, is not that of choosing in a non-arbitrary way between a *variety* of applicable characterizations of the relevant faculty or process, but rather that of identifying just a *single* applicable characterization.

unity of these traits. For again, in the absence of a better understanding of these matters, they will be unable to account for the reliability of some of the very methods or processes they deem (or at least should deem) central to justification. And, as noted in connection with virtue reliabilism, this is a problem both in its own right and as it relates to the application of their view to individual beliefs.

4.4 *Conclusion*

We have seen that virtue reliabilists and reliabilists in general must expand their focus to include, not just the more mechanical or faculty-based dimension of human cognition, but also the more active, volitional, or character-based dimension. At a minimum, this includes incorporating intellectual character virtues into their repertoire of intellectual virtues or knowledge-makers. But it also includes reckoning with a range of new theoretical challenges and questions that arise as a result of this expansion. The cost of *not* doing so, we have seen, is that reliabilists are unable to account for the sort of reliability involved with—and thus the very epistemic status of—much of the knowledge that we as humans care about most. This, then, goes a significant way toward vindicating Weak Conservative VE, which again is the view that the concept of intellectual virtue has at least a secondary or peripheral role to play in connection with one or more problems in traditional epistemology.[21]

[21] While not insignificant, the thrust of the chapter does not vindicate Strong Conservative VE. It does not, for instance, require making the concept of an intellectual character virtue per se central to a reliabilist epistemology. For, again, it is consistent with the (plausible) view that a great deal of knowledge can be acquired via reliable means that do not involve anything like an exercise of intellectual character virtues. Instead, the basic point is that intellectual character virtues *along with* faculty virtues can satisfy the reliabilist's formal conditions for an intellectual virtue, and thus can contribute to knowledge understood in reliabilist terms.

Chapter 5

EVIDENTIALISM, VICE, AND VIRTUE

In this chapter we turn to consider another way in which reflection on matters of intellectual character is relevant to traditional epistemology. In the previous chapter, I argued that reliabilists must expand their focus to include a consideration of intellectual character virtues and that doing so leads to new theoretical questions and challenges. In the present chapter, I examine the relevance of intellectual character virtues to an alternative account of epistemic justification. The account in question is evidentialism, which is the view (roughly) that the justificatory status of a belief depends on the extent to which the belief is supported by good evidence.[1]

Evidentialism has been subjected to a barrage of criticisms in recent years, many of which have been aimed at showing that the satisfaction of its central condition is not necessary for justification.[2] I will not be addressing these objections here. Rather, my concern is with the *sufficiency* of the evidentialist's condition. I begin by discussing several cases in which a belief apparently satisfies this condition but fails to instantiate one or more varieties of epistemic justification presumably of interest to evidentialists. I go on to argue that this does not warrant abandoning the thrust of evidentialism. Instead, it calls for supplementing traditional formulations of evidentialism with a certain virtue-based constraint, according to which, in a limited range of cases, justification requires an exercise of *intellectually virtuous agency*. The discussion therefore reinforces the case made in the previous chapter for Weak Conservative VE, which again is the view that the concept of intellectual virtue merits a secondary or background role in connection with one or more problems in traditional epistemology.[3]

[1] Recent defenders of this general approach include Laurence BonJour (1985), Roderick Chisholm (1989), Richard Swinburne (2001), and Earl Conee and Richard Feldman (2004).

[2] See, for example, Plantinga (1993a).

[3] As this brief description suggests, my aim in this chapter is not to defend evidentialism per se (any more than the discussion in the previous chapter was aimed at defending reliabilism).

Before getting started, an important methodological point is in order. There are at least two notably different ways of attempting to argue that the satisfaction of the evidentialist's condition is insufficient for justification. The first is predicated on the idea that there is a single determinate and univocal concept of epistemic justification and that disputes about the nature of justification are disputes about this concept. Here the strategy is to show that a belief can satisfy the evidentialist's condition but fail to instantiate the concept in question. There are, however, serious problems with the idea that there is a single determinate and univocal concept of justification. As William Alston (1993; 2005) has argued, much of the debate in epistemology in recent years suggests that there are in fact several such concepts or several "epistemic desiderata." But if concepts of epistemic justification are manifold, what would it mean to argue that the satisfaction of the evidentialist's condition is not "sufficient" for justification?

We can see an answer to this question by noting that while there may be a rather wide and diverse variety of epistemic desiderata, it is plausible to think that evidentialists are interested in a certain limited subset of them—and perhaps just in a single desideratum. This is, at any rate, what I shall be assuming here. Accordingly, my concern will be limited to what I shall call "evidentialist-relevant" or "e-relevant" varieties of justification, which again are varieties the nature of which at least some evidentialist accounts of justification presumably are intended to capture.[4] My immediate aim, then, is to show that a belief can satisfy the evidentialist's central condition while failing to instantiate one or more e-relevant varieties of justification.

5.1 *Problem cases*

As indicated above, I shall begin with a consideration of cases in which a belief enjoys the required kind of evidential support but does not appear to instantiate any e-relevant variety of justification. Before turning to these cases,

Rather, given the central project of the book, my aim is merely to identify any theoretical "points of contact" between intellectual virtue and traditional epistemology.

[4] I will not attempt to spell out the notion of e-relevant justification in any detail here. However, given the close association between evidentialism and *internalism* (an association discussed in more detail below), e-relevant varieties of justification are likely to be internalist in nature; and paradigmatically externalist varieties of justification (e.g. the kind picked out by crude reliabilism) are likely *not* to count as e-relevant.

however, it will be helpful to specify evidentialism's principal condition more precisely. Evidentialists endorse the following general claim:

> (E) A person S is justified in believing a proposition P at time T if and only if S's evidence at T supports P.

What counts as "evidence" is a matter of some dispute among evidentialists and other epistemologists; however, for our purposes, we can think of evidence as including things like supporting beliefs, sensory experiences, memories, and rational insights.[5] There are also challenging questions surrounding the relevant notion of "support"; but here again we may stipulate that a body of evidence E "supports" a proposition P just in case P is more probable than not given E. As this formulation suggests, evidential support is a matter of degree.[6]

5.1.1 *Cases of defective inquiry*

In the first pair of problem cases, a belief satisfies (E) but only because the believer either fails to inquire at all or inquires in a manner that is clearly defective.

> Case 1. George represents the epitome of intellectual laziness, apathy, and obliviousness. He goes about his daily routine focusing only on the most immediate and practical of concerns: feeding himself, getting to work on time, doing his job in a minimally satisfactory way, paying the bills, etc. He lacks any natural curiosity and is almost entirely tuned out to the news of the day. Unsurprisingly, George has many beliefs he should not and fails to believe many things he should. In the former category is George's belief that exposure to secondhand smoke poses no significant health risks.[7] Given his extremely narrow and practical focus, George is oblivious to all of the well-publicized research indicating the hazards of secondhand smoke. In fact, George has positive evidence in *support* of his belief. He recalls having learned from a reliable source some years ago that a considerable amount of research had been conducted concerning the effects of exposure to secondhand smoke and that this research had failed to establish any correlation between such exposure and any serious health problems. And, as far as George knows, the research on this topic has not changed. (Nor, we may suppose, does he have any reason to think that it might have changed.)

> Case 2. Gerry holds the same belief as George and on roughly the same grounds. Therefore he too has positive evidence for thinking that secondhand smoke is

[5] For more on what might count as evidence, see Conee and Feldman (2004: chs. 4 and 9).

[6] For more on the evidential support relation, see Swinburne (2001: ch. 3).

[7] If necessary, the reader should think of her own example here. As I found when delivering a version of this chapter in Europe, a denial of global climate change is a more compelling example for some than a denial of the threat posed by secondhand smoke!

> not a health hazard. Unlike George, however, Gerry is not oblivious to the news of the day. In fact, he is a reasonably inquisitive person and enjoys checking things for himself. The problem is that his inquiries tend to be insufficiently demanding and discriminating: they are prone to gullibility, carelessness, and hasty generalization.[8] Upon hearing the news reports affirming the danger of secondhand smoke, Gerry decides to look further into the matter. The first item he comes across happens to be a report published by an organization with major financial ties to the tobacco industry. The report is aimed, not at a fair and balanced treatment of the issue, but rather at exposing any apparent weakness or grounds for doubt in the recently publicized research. To any reasonably intellectually demanding and discriminating inquirer, the dubious nature of the report would be evident. But to Gerry it is not. And the result is that Gerry's total evidence (which again includes his initial evidence for thinking that secondhand smoke is benign) supports his belief.[9]

In each of the above cases, a person's belief is well supported by his evidence. As a result, the beliefs seem clearly to satisfy (E). The problem is that the *reason* these beliefs are well supported traces back to certain *defects* on the part of the individuals who hold them. George has good evidence for his belief only on account of his intellectual "tunnel vision." Gerry's belief remains well-supported because of his undemanding and undiscriminating habits of inquiry. In light of these shortcomings, the beliefs of George and Gerry seem clearly to be unjustified. Furthermore, it is plausible to think that the variety of justification in question is e-relevant.[10]

In response to cases of this general sort, Richard Feldman (2005) offers a defense of the sufficiency of (E) the upshot of which is that there is no e-relevant sense of justification according to which the beliefs of George and Gerry are unjustified. According to Feldman, an evidentialist theory of justification is concerned strictly with the relation between a person's evidence and her belief. It makes no difference whether this evidence is the result of (say) uncritical or hasty inquiry or whether the person has the evidence only on account of failing to inquire at all. While these factors may bear on an evaluation of the believer's intellectual *character* or doxastic *methods*, Feldman claims,

[8] We may stipulate that this is something of which Gerry is unaware.

[9] For a similar case, see Kornblith (1983). Greco (2005) raises a related worry for internalist accounts of epistemic justification.

[10] This is evident in the fact that there is something *irresponsible* about the cognitive conduct—and the resulting beliefs—of both George and Gerry. For, as we shall see in more depth below, some evidentialists (e.g. BonJour 1985) draw a close connection between cognitive responsibility and epistemic justification.

they have no bearing on the epistemic status of beliefs that result from such character or methods (2005: 281; cf. Conee and Feldman 2004: 90, 101).

Perhaps there is some epistemic value simply in having a belief that fits one's evidence—regardless of whether this evidence is the result of defective inquiry. Such beliefs might be said to involve a kind of logical coherence or consistency, which indeed is often regarded as an epistemic desideratum.[11] Moreover, as Feldman reasonably asks, what *other* doxastic attitude could plausibly be required of agents like George or Gerry (2005: 282)? Clearly it would be problematic, given their evidence, to suggest that either of them ought to believe that secondhand smoke *is* harmful—or even, for that matter, to suspend judgment on the issue (for again, they have reason to believe that it is *not* harmful). Thus there does appear to be a sense of justification according to which the beliefs of George and Gerry are justified. And there is little reason not to regard this as an e-relevant species of justification.

But this hardly puts (E) in the clear. For the fact that the beliefs of George and Gerry instantiate *some* e-relevant variety of justification guarantees neither (1) that there is not an additional variety of e-relevant justification that these beliefs fail to instantiate, nor (2) that the variety of justification they do instantiate is particularly worthy or significant. Both of these possibilities merit further consideration.

First consider (1). Despite whatever justification the beliefs of George and Gerry may enjoy, there is indeed an additional intuitive and e-relevant sense in which these beliefs are unjustified. For while these beliefs are well supported by the agents' evidence, this evidence clearly is not what it should be. George, for instance, ought to have taken notice of some of the widely publicized research establishing a link between exposure to secondhand smoke and various diseases. Similarly, it ought to have occurred to Gerry to undertake a broader inquiry and pay closer attention to the source of the relevant report. He too should have been aware of the evidence against his belief. Since the beliefs of George and Gerry are based on evidence that ought to be other than it is, there is a straightforward sense in which they ought not believe as they do; that is, there is a straightforward sense in which their beliefs are unjustified. And again, the kind of justification in question seems clearly to be e-relevant.[12]

[11] See, for instance, Swinburne's discussion of "synchronic justification" in (2001: ch. 1). See also Feldman (2005: 277–8).

[12] Trent Dougherty has suggested to me that the concept of justification I am getting at here is strictly a deontological one, that evidentialism is not really a thesis about deontological justification, and that my cases therefore fail to pose a problem for their intended target. But I think there are several problems with this objection. First, while I have employed the language

One way of drawing further attention to this variety of justification is to consider how we might evaluate certain *actions* of George or Gerry that are based on the beliefs in question. Suppose, for instance, that on the basis of his belief that secondhand smoke is benign, George proceeds to smoke on a regular basis in the company of his children. Clearly we would condemn George's behavior, despite the fact that from his own perspective he is doing no harm. And the reason is that he ought not to have this perspective in the first place; he ought not *believe* as he does. For again, evidence against this belief is abundant and readily available to him. He ought to be aware of this evidence and to believe in accordance with it. This strongly suggests that his present belief is, in a genuine and e-relevant sense, unjustified.[13]

Now consider (2). While the beliefs of George and Gerry may instantiate a certain epistemic desideratum, the real significance or worth of this desideratum is questionable. To see why, note that the evidence possessed by George and Gerry is in a certain substantial way *defective* or *contaminated*—and, again, for reasons that trace back to these individuals' own epistemic malfeasance. Had either George or Gerry been even minimally attentive and discriminating in his thinking about the respective subject matter, his perspective concerning

of "ought" in characterizing what goes wrong in the cases, I do not think that the sort of justification that George and Gerry lack is merely the standard deontological variety. This will become clearer when I discuss point (2) below. Second, if evidentialism really should be understood as limiting the scope of epistemic evaluation strictly to the present "fit" between a person's belief and her evidence, with no regard whatsoever for *how* the person acquired this evidence or *why* she possesses the evidence she does, then in fact it looks as though the beliefs of George and Gerry are *justified* from the standpoint of a deontological conception of justification. For, again, if we completely disregard the quality of their inquiry, then given their evidence, they would appear to be perfectly entitled to believe as they do. It must, then, be a mistake to think that the sense in which George and Gerry are *unjustified* is strictly deontological. Third, I see no reason to think of "evidentialism" as necessarily excluding deontological accounts of justification. For instance, suppose someone were to maintain that a belief is justified if and only if it is supported by good evidence, but that the *explanation* for this is that our sole intellectual duty is to believe in accordance with our evidence. Surely this could be regarded as a version of evidentialism (or as picking out an "e-relevant" variety of justification). Indeed, just such a possibility is at least suggested (if not endorsed) in Steup (2001) and (1995).

[13] John Greco offers a similar assessment of some similar cases. He says that where "two persons arrive at the same internal [read: evidential] perspective, but . . . one does so in a way that is epistemically responsible, whereas the other does so on the basis of carelessness, thick-headedness, and stupidity," "[t]he two persons will not be alike in epistemic justification" (2005: 262). His conclusion is that "etiology matters" when assessing the justificatory status of a belief. While Greco's immediate target here is internalism, his criticism applies to the formulation of evidentialism that we are concerned with here.

the truth of the claim in question would have been very different and much more accurate. Things being what they are, however, why think that either George or Gerry does particularly well from an epistemic standpoint to believe on the basis of his evidence? What is especially epistemically good or worthy about believing in accordance with a defective or contaminated evidence base, particularly when the defects in question are attributable to one's own cognitive failure? It would seem not much. My suggestion is not that George or Gerry ought to believe, against his evidence, that environmental smoke is harmful. It is rather that the alternative has relatively little to recommend it.[14]

Cases like that of George and Gerry are analogous to what moral philosophers sometimes refer to as "tragic dilemmas," which are situations in which a person is forced to choose between "sin and sin" or between "the lesser of two evils."[15] Consider the case of Bertie, who, having squandered the semester partying with his friends and playing video games, is presently faced with the dilemma of cheating on one of his final exams (his only hope for passing a course that he needs to graduate on time) or devastating his parents (who have sacrificed a great deal to pay for Bertie's education and have planned a family reunion in honor of Bertie's graduation). On at least one plausible analysis of the situation (assuming, say, that these really are Bertie's only options), Bertie "ought" to cheat on the exam. Indeed we might say that, given the circumstances, this is the only "real" or justifiable option. At the same time, however, this is not to say anything very positive about Bertie's action. While it may be the "lesser of two evils," it is an "evil" nonetheless. Similarly, while George and Gerry in some sense do well to believe in accordance with the evidence they have (in doing so they avoid believing or withholding belief on no basis whatsoever), this does not entail anything very positive about them or their beliefs, for again, each believes in accordance with a defective evidence base, the very defects of which are a result of his own cognitive wrongdoing. The point is that while the beliefs of George and Gerry may instantiate a certain e-relevant concept of justification, this variety of justification is not a very significant epistemic desideratum. Their beliefs are, as it were, the lesser of two epistemic "evils" in the situation. It appears, then, that

[14] This characterization of the problem with the relevant beliefs, which has largely been in terms of epistemic *significance* or *worth* or *value*, underscores the point that the kind of justification I am concerned with (the kind that George and Gerry lack) is not strictly a deontological one. That is, the point is not strictly that these beliefs stand in violation of epistemic duties, but rather that they fail to meet some other normative (but non-deontological) epistemic standard.

[15] See, for instance, Geach (1977) and Hursthouse (1999).

a belief can satisfy (E) while failing to instantiate any *significant* e-relevant concept of justification.[16]

5.1.2 *Cases of defective "doxastic handling" of evidence*

In the cases just discussed, the epistemic status of a belief is undermined on account of some *prior* mistake or defect on the part of the believer, and specifically, on account of whether or how the believer inquired at some point in the *past.* In a second set of cases indicating the insufficiency of (E), the epistemic status of a belief is affected by an *occurrent* mistake or defect on the part of the agent. Specifically, it is affected by the agent's "doxastic handling" of information that threatens to defeat or undermine her justification, that is, by the way in which she treats or regards this information *at the time of belief.* In the first case, the agent ignores or suppresses the potential defeater; in the second case she distorts or misrepresents it.

> Case 3. Like George and Gerry above, Daphne believes that exposure to secondhand smoke poses no serious health risks; she also has some positive evidence in support of this belief. However, she is neither intellectually lazy nor undiscriminating. Upon hearing about the relevant research, she does some looking into the matter and nearly all the information she comes across indicates that in fact environmental smoke *is* hazardous. Daphne's problem is that she is a hypochondriac raised by two chain-smoking parents. Owing to extreme anxiety about her health, she cannot accept any of the relevant evidence; indeed, she quickly and conveniently (though genuinely) forgets about or suppresses it. The result is that, from her perspective, her evidence continues to support her belief.[17]

> Case 4. Doris also believes with some positive evidence that secondhand smoke is benign. Upon hearing news reports to the contrary, she too engages in reasonably careful and discriminating inquiry on the matter and in doing so

[16] Greco (2005) makes a similar observation on this score. The upshot of his discussion is that while the beliefs of George and Gerry might be "justified" in some very weak sense, the relevant conception of justification is objectionably abstract, uninteresting, and unimportant. In reference to this conception, he remarks that "'time-slice' evaluations that abstract away from the formation of beliefs, their relation to the world, and the character of believers will not be very important." And he offers the following comparison with moral evaluation: "Neither do we care about whether some action A is right relative to S's own moral norms, in abstraction from questions about how S did A, or why S did A, or whether S's norms are themselves any good" (267).

[17] We may stipulate that she has no recollection of having encountered the counterevidence or having suppressed it. Thus, from her standpoint, the totality of her evidence clearly supports her belief.

encounters a host of data that threaten to refute her belief. Like Daphne, Doris is unable to accept this data. But in Doris's case, this is due to her own extremely strong attachment to smoking. Being able to smoke whenever and wherever she wants is one of few sources of comfort in her otherwise lonely and difficult life. Unlike Doris, Daphne's cognitive constitution is such that she cannot simply "forget" or suppress the relevant evidence. Instead she *distorts* or *misrepresents* certain critical aspects of it. The result is that, from her standpoint, the case for thinking that environmental smoke is hazardous is weak, and her belief remains well supported.[18]

There can be little doubt that there is an e-relevant sense in which the beliefs of Daphne and Doris are unjustified. Daphne is suppressing evidence of which she has recently been made aware and that casts major doubt on her belief. Doris, though not exactly suppressing or ignoring such evidence, is distorting or misrepresenting key elements of it. Nevertheless, the beliefs of Daphne and Doris are well supported from their respective standpoints.

While evidentialists are unlikely to deny that the beliefs of Daphne and Doris are unjustified, they may attempt to argue that these beliefs fail to satisfy (E) and hence do not present a problem for their position. Specifically, an evidentialist might argue that what matters for justification is not whether it *seems* to a person that her belief is well supported by her evidence, but rather whether her belief really *is* well supported. This objection draws attention to a certain ambiguity in (E). It indicates the need to distinguish between the following two more precise formulations of the central evidentialist principle:

(E2) S is justified in believing P at T if and only if S's evidence at T *appears to S* to support P.

(E3) S is justified in believing P at T if and only if S's evidence at T *in fact* supports P.

The suggestion is that an evidentialist might respond to the cases of Daphne and Doris by claiming that evidentialism should be understood along the lines of (E3) rather than (E2), and that once it is, these cases cease to pose a problem for evidentialism.

(E3) does apparently provide the evidentialist with a way around the Daphne and Doris cases.[19] For both Daphne and Doris are in some sense "in possession

[18] Again we can stipulate that Doris is unaware of having distorted or misrepresented the relevant data and thus that as far as she can tell, her belief is well supported by her evidence.

[19] Note, however, that (E3) is still susceptible to the George and Gerry cases discussed earlier; for their beliefs, while intuitively unjustified, are in fact well supported by their evidence.

of" evidence that in fact tells decisively against their beliefs.[20] The problem, in Daphne's case, is that she is ignoring or suppressing this evidence; Doris, on the other hand, is distorting or misrepresenting it. But given that the evidence in question is in their possession, and that it *actually* tells against their beliefs, (E3) rules (plausibly) that these beliefs are unjustified.

But (E3) is problematic on other grounds. Consider beliefs that involve what might be referred to as "deeply hidden" evidential relations, which are relations that obtain between a person's evidence base and one of her beliefs, but that are extremely difficult to discern, even from the standpoint of an entirely normal and well-functioning cognitive agent. Along these lines, Richard Swinburne (2001) discusses a case in which a detective is in possession of a great deal of evidence regarding a certain murder. It follows from the detective's evidence "by a complicated line of argument" that a particular suspect is guilty. However, "the detective is overwhelmed by the sheer quantity of evidence and so has not seen the relevance of this piece of evidence" (154).[21] Assuming, then, that there are indeed instances of "deeply hidden" evidential relations, (E3) entails that if a person's evidence in such a case seems clearly to support a certain claim P, but on the basis of a "deeply hidden" entailment relation in fact supports a different claim Q, this person is justified in believing Q. But this is extremely implausible, for the person in question is entirely unaware of the fact that her evidence actually supports Q.[22]

To see how an evidentialist might try to amend (E3) in light of this problem, note that most evidentialists also embrace *internalism* about epistemic justification. According to one standard version of internalism,[23] a person is justified in believing a given claim only if he has "direct and unproblematic access" to any factors that justify this belief. If supplemented with an internalist condition, (E3) becomes:

[20] On the assumption that the relevant evidence is *not* actually in their possession, matters are even worse for (E3). For in that case the beliefs in question *are* well supported by the relevant evidence and so turn out (implausibly) to be justified.

[21] Conee and Feldman (2001: 73) discuss a similar sort of case; as does BonJour (1998: 128).

[22] Perhaps the belief is justified in a certain robustly *externalist* sense. But such justification presumably is not e-relevant and therefore need not concern us here.

[23] See, for instance, BonJour (1992). "Mentalism" is an alternative version of internalism according to which justifying factors are necessarily "internal" in the sense of being "internal to the person's mental life" or "in the person's mind" (Conee and Feldman 2004: 55). However, as I explain in note 24 below, an appeal to a mentalist version of internalism would be of no help in dealing with the case in question.

> (E4) S is justified in believing P at T if and only if S's evidence at T *in fact* supports P *and* S has direct and unproblematic access to this fact at T.

(E4) allows the evidentialist to deal with one problematic aspect of the case just noted, since it entails (plausibly) that the person in question is not justified in believing Q (the proposition supported by the hidden evidential relation).[24] But a serious problem remains. For not only is it implausible to think that this person is justified in believing Q, it is extremely *plausible* to think that she is *justified* in believing P (the proposition supported by "all appearances"). But if (E4) is correct, this person is *not* justified in believing P, for her evidence *in fact* supports Q.

One way around this difficulty would be to narrow the scope of the internalist element of (E4) by claiming that justification is a function of the actual relation between a person's belief and *those aspects of the person's evidence to which she has direct and unproblematic access*. This would yield the following principle:

> (E5) S is justified in believing P at T if and only if *the aspects of S's evidence to which S has direct and unproblematic access at T* in fact support P.[25]

(E5) can handle both aspects of the case under consideration. It rules (plausibly) that the subject is not justified in believing Q because, while Q is supported by the totality of this person's evidence, it is not supported by that part of her evidence to which she has direct and unproblematic access (i.e. the "unhidden" part). It also rules (plausibly) that the person *is* justified in believing P, for the part of this person's evidence to which she has direct and unproblematic access does in fact support P.

But while (E5) is an improvement over (E4) in one respect, it is vulnerable in a way that (E4) is not. For unlike (E4), (E5) generates the *wrong* result in the very cases that led us to distinguish variations of (E) in the first place: namely, the Daphne and Doris cases. The details of these cases can easily be refined so that

[24] By contrast, if (E3) were supplemented with a *mentalist* internalist condition, it would still entail that the person in question is justified in believing Q, for the support relation between the person's evidence and her belief that Q presumably would be internal in the relevant sense. Thus an appeal to a mentalist version of internalism does not provide a way around the objection.

[25] "Aspects" should be understood to include *items* of evidence themselves (e.g. experiences, other beliefs, etc.) or any evidential *relations* between these items and the believed proposition. Thus there is no need to stipulate further that S must have access to the fact that the aspects of S's evidence to which S has access in fact support P, for as it stands (E5) can handle the sort of case that led to the adoption of an access-clause in (E4).

Daphne and Doris lack the kind of access required by (E5) to the relevant counterevidence, with the implausible result that their beliefs satisfy (E5) and thus are justified. We might imagine, for instance, that Doris is so attached to smoking at will that if she were to curtail her habit in any way (which she would feel compelled to do if she were honest with herself about the relevant evidence), her psyche would begin to unravel. Thus it would take extreme measures (hypnosis or therapy, say) to get her to confront this evidence. On this rendering of the case, Doris presumably lacks anything like "direct and unproblematic" access to that part of her evidence that she is distorting. Therefore, since the evidence to which Doris does have the required kind of access in fact supports her belief, (E5) rules (implausibly) that her belief is justified.[26]

There is in fact a notable irony in such cases that further tells against the plausibility of (E5). It consists in the fact that the more defective the individuals in question are, the more likely they are to be justified according to (E5). For instance, the more Daphne suppresses or ignores the relevant counterevidence, the more problematic and less direct her access to this evidence becomes, and thus the more likely it is that her belief will count as justified according to (E5). This is problematic, of course, because it is precisely Daphne's self-deception that intuitively undermines the justification of her belief.

We began this section by considering how two additional cases pose a problem for the sufficiency of (E). This led to a distinction between (E2) and (E3). According to the former, justification requires mere "apparent support" between one's belief and one's evidence, while according to the latter, it requires "actual support." Problems with (E3) led to a consideration of two related principles, (E4) and (E5), both of which we also found susceptible to serious objections. My concern in the remainder of the chapter is with (E2). I argue that (E2) can be modified in a way that preserves the thrust of evidentialism and avoids the problems that plague these other formulations.

5.2 *Modifying evidentialism*

We have examined two sets of cases in which a belief satisfies (E2) but fails to instantiate any interesting variety of e-relevant justification. Thus (E2) clearly

[26] A similar story could be told about Daphne. It might, for instance, take the same sort of extreme measures to get Daphne to "recall" the evidence she is suppressing. Therefore, she too can be viewed as lacking the kind of access to this evidence that is required by (E5) and thus as being justified in believing as she does.

stands in need of modification. To see what form this modification might take, it will be helpful to look again at the various cognitive defects manifested in the cases in question. Doing so will provide an indication of what further, positive requirement should be added to (E2).

The defects in question include the following: intellectual laziness, inattentiveness, lack of intellectual discrimination, gullibility, carelessness, disregard for the truth, ignoring and distorting counterevidence, self-deception, and more. One striking feature of this list is that it consists entirely of intellectual *vices*, that is, of bad or defective traits of intellectual character. It is on account of an exercise of such traits that the individuals in Cases 1–4 above lack justification for their beliefs. One strategy for amending (E2), then, would be to make the antidote to intellectual vice a necessary condition for justification.[27] This antidote consists, of course, in various intellectual *virtues* like carefulness and thoroughness in inquiry, inquisitiveness, attentiveness, fair-mindedness, open-mindedness, intellectual honesty, and intellectual integrity. Thus it might be thought that (E2) should be supplemented with an additional condition that makes an exercise of intellectual virtue a necessary condition for justification. This would yield (something like) the following principle:

> (E6) S is justified in believing P at T if and only if S's evidence at T *appears to S* to support P *and* S exercises virtues of intellectual character in the formation of this belief.

There is, however, at least one immediate and formidable problem with (E6). As we examined at length in Chapter 3, justified or known beliefs sometimes arise from the brute or default functioning of a person's basic cognitive machinery or endowment (*not* from an exercise of any intellectual character virtues). Recall the case in which, while working late one night in my well-lit study, the electricity suddenly and unexpectedly shuts off, immediately causing the room to go dark. In response, I automatically and without thinking form a belief to the effect that the room has grown dark. Intuitively, my belief is justified. It is also justified according to (E2), since my belief is (and appears to me to be) well supported by my visual experience. However, it is *not* justified according to (E6), for there is little reason to think that I have exercised any virtues of intellectual

[27] Another strategy would be to incorporate a purely negative condition according to which justification requires *not* exercising any vices of intellectual character. One problem with this condition is that it sheds no light on what, positively, is required for justification beyond the satisfaction of (E5). Moreover, as I explain in note 29 below, it seems possible for a belief to be justified from an e-relevant standpoint even though the person who holds the belief displays intellectual vices at the time the belief is formed.

character in the formation of this belief.[28] Cases like this show that an exercise of intellectual virtue is not a necessary condition for justification.[29]

We have found, then, that a belief can be unjustified on account of the believer's exhibiting vicious agency, but that it is implausible to make virtuous agency a necessary condition for justification. If so, how can (E2) be modified—beyond the addition of a purely negative and unilluminating amendment to the effect that justification requires an *absence* of vicious agency—so that it precludes the relevant manifestations of intellectual vice? The apparent solution is to modify (E2) so that it makes something like an exercise of intellectual virtue necessary for justification, but only in cases like the ones discussed earlier (not in cases of passive or brute justification). This can be done by supplementing (E2) with a virtue-based *proviso* or *constraint.*

To get an idea of what exactly this constraint might look like, we must examine more closely the difference between Cases 1–4 above, on the one hand, and cases of brute or passive justification, on the other. As already suggested, the principal difference between the two concerns the role of personal agency in the formation of the relevant belief. In the former set of cases, the agency of the believer is involved; in the latter kind of case, it is not. Recall, for instance, the case of Gerry. His agency bears immediately on the content of his evidence: his evidence is what it is largely because he has inquired in an undiscriminating and careless way. He then forms his belief on the basis of this evidence. Personal agency is also involved in the formation of the beliefs of Daphne and Doris. Here it bears most immediately, not on the content of their evidence, but rather on how they handle or regard this evidence. Doris, for instance, distorts or misrepresents critical

28 It need not be the case that my agency is completely idle. For as Linda Zagzebski (1999) has shown (and as we saw in Chapter 3), any plausible virtue-based account of justification or knowledge must posit a rather strong connection between virtuous agency and the relevant justified or known belief, such that a belief counts as justified, say, only if an exercise of intellectual virtue (or something like it) is the *best explanation* of the relevant belief. Accordingly, in the present case, even if my agency were operative at some level, surely it would not be the best explanation of why I form the relevant belief; rather, the best explanation would be the brute or routine functioning of my visual faculty.

29 A variation on the case just noted shows that a person's agency might in fact work *against* the formation of a belief that nonetheless amounts to knowledge. Being under an imminent writing deadline, for instance, I might try to *deny* that the lights have gone out—I might, to an extent, be *incredulous*. Here I would be attempting to resist the truth and so would be displaying a kind of intellectual *vice*. Nevertheless, there can be little doubt that I would be unable to resist the force of my own (brute) cognitive nature and would come to believe (and indeed to know) that the lights have gone out.

elements of her evidence. She then forms her belief on the basis of the resulting perspective.[30]

Thus, in Cases 1–4, personal agency makes a salient contribution to what we might call the "evidential situation" of the person in question, meaning that it largely determines either the *content* of the person's evidence or how the person *handles* or *regards* this evidence. By contrast, in cases of brute or passive justification, the believer's agency does not contribute to his evidential situation. In the case of passive justification discussed above, for instance, I acquire and confront the relevant evidence concerning the lighting in the room simply as a result of the brute or natural functioning of my vision. My evidential situation does not implicate or involve my agency in any significant way.

We are finally in a position to see how (E2) ought to be amended:

> (E*) S is justified in believing P at T if and only if S's evidence at T appears to S to support P, *provided that* if S's agency makes a salient contribution to S's evidential situation with respect to P, S functions, qua agent and relative to that contribution, in a manner consistent with intellectual virtue.

Several elements of (E*) require further comment. First, note that the virtue requirement in (E*) does not have universal application: it applies only to cases in which a person's evidential situation involves or implicates her agency in the relevant sense. Thus (E*) does not stipulate an additional necessary or defining condition for knowledge. Instead it is lays down a constraint regarding when or under what conditions a belief's being supported by good evidence generates justification. The idea is that while justification is essentially a matter of having good epistemic reasons in support of a belief, there are cases in which having such reasons generates justification only if the reasons are had against the "backdrop," so to speak, of virtuous cognitive functioning.[31] Second, the "qua agent" qualification in the final clause of (E*) serves to underscore the fact that while an agent's brute cognitive machinery might be in good working order, and thus that the agent might be "functioning" well or virtuously at one level, justification (in the relevant cases) requires virtuous *agency*. Third, (E*) does not require that a believer actually *be* intellectually virtuous. It does not require, for instance, that the virtuous conduct in question flow from a fixed or settled

[30] A similar story could be told regarding the beliefs of George and Doris. George's agency is involved in the formation of his belief to the extent that it explains his intellectual laziness and obliviousness. And Daphne's is involved to the extent that it is the cause of her ignoring or suppressing the relevant counterevidence.

[31] For a related and suggestive discussion, see Locke's treatment of "degrees of assent" in ch. 24 of BK. IV *An Essay Concerning Human Understanding* (1996: 306).

disposition on the part of the believer. Fourth, (E*) does not demand that a believer exhibit the very "height" of intellectual virtue or that her intellectual conduct be *maximally* intellectually virtuous. It requires merely that she function in a manner *consistent* with intellectual virtue (alternatively, that she refrain from functioning in a way that a virtuous person characteristically would *not*).

Two final observations concerning (E*) are also in order. First, (E*) generates the correct result in connection with Cases 1–4 above. None of the subjects in these cases turn out to be justified according to (E*), for in each case, while the person's agency does make a salient contribution to his or her evidential situation, the person fails to function in a manner consistent with intellectual virtue. Moreover, (E*) explains why, in cases of brute or passive justification, a person can be justified without engaging in any virtuous intellectual activity. For, again, these are cases in which the subject's agency does not bear on his or her evidential situation. Second, a commitment to (E*) does not require the repudiation of internalism, at least on a standard way of understanding this doctrine. Internalism is typically said to require that the factors which *justify* a belief be "internal" in the relevant sense. While there are problems with regarding as "internal" the factor of whether a belief is the product of virtuous agency, (E*) is consistent with this tenet, for as indicated above, it does not treat virtuous agency as a *basis* of justification, that is, as a "justifying factor." Rather, on (E*), the concept of virtuous agency plays a mere background or constraining role vis-à-vis the actual basis of justification, which again is the possession of adequate *evidence*.

5.3 *BonJour's evidentialism*

Before concluding, I want to consider how something like (E*) has in fact been gestured at—though not elaborated on—in some recent evidentialist literature. Laurence BonJour is a prominent defender of an evidentialist-type account of epistemic justification. According to BonJour (1998: 1), justification depends on the possession of good epistemic reasons, or reasons for thinking that the belief in question is true. For present purposes, this may be read as the claim that justification depends on the possession of good evidence.[32]

[32] Some evidentialists (e.g. Conee and Feldman 2004) seem to equate the notions of good evidence and good epistemic reasons. Given a broad enough understanding of evidence, this strikes me as a plausible identification.

In some of his early work (1985), BonJour draws an explicit and apparently strong connection between the notion of good epistemic reasons and that of epistemic *responsibility*. He says that epistemic responsibility is the "core notion" of epistemic justification conceived in terms of such reasons (8). In more recent work, however, BonJour describes the relation between justification and epistemic responsibility in weaker terms. He maintains that while justification and responsible epistemic conduct often go hand-in-hand, they do not always do so, and thus that justification should not be *defined* or *analyzed* in terms of epistemic responsibility or related concepts.[33] Nevertheless, in a more recent book on a priori justification (1998), BonJour suggests that the concepts of epistemic responsibility or intellectual virtue might yet have some role to play in connection with an analysis of justification.[34]

According to BonJour's initial proposal (106–10), a person is a priori justified in believing a given claim just in case he has "rational insight" into the necessity of this claim. Without getting into the details of the account, it should be noted, first, that rational insight as BonJour understands it is a source of good epistemic reasons: it is capable of providing believers with good or cogent grounds in support of the truth of necessary propositions. Thus BonJour's position on a priori justification conforms to his broader position on justification noted above, and can reasonably be regarded as evidentialist in nature. Second, while the above represents BonJour's initial formulation of his view, he goes on in a discussion regarding the fallibility of a priori justification to claim that, strictly speaking, a priori justification requires mere *apparent* rational insight; that is, he rejects the idea that a priori justification is a *guarantee* of truth. This qualification enables BonJour to account for a variety of putative cases of a priori justification in which the beliefs in question later turn out to be false (110–15).

As this brief sketch suggests, BonJour seems clearly to favor a version of evidentialism along the lines of (E2) rather than (E3) above, that is, a version according to which justification is a function of whether, from the believer's standpoint, her belief is well supported by the evidence. BonJour is aware, however, that a quasi-subjective account of justification like (E2) is open to certain objections to which a more objective account along the lines of (E3) is not. One such objection is what he refers to as the argument from "dogmatism

[33] See, for instance, BonJour and Sosa (2003: 175–7). BonJour cites cases of "epistemic poverty" as one reason for not identifying justification and epistemic responsibility.

[34] Unless otherwise indicated, references below are to his (1998).

and bias" (133–7). The worry here is roughly that an account of justification that requires mere *apparent* support between a person's evidence and her beliefs will (implausibly) sanction beliefs that enjoy such support only on account of bias or dogmatism on the part of the believer (cases in which, were the person in question not thinking in a biased or dogmatic way, her belief would not appear to her to be supported by her evidence). Such cases bear a clear resemblance to the Daphne and Doris cases discussed above. Again, these are cases in which a belief appears to be well supported but only because the person in question is suppressing or distorting a potential defeater.

In response to this objection, BonJour makes the critical point that on his view, only rational insights that have been arrived at on the basis of "reasonably careful reflection" have any epistemic significance (113).[35] Such reflection, he maintains, is inconsistent with dogmatism and bias; elsewhere he indicates that it is inconsistent with other intellectual vices like carelessness, inattention, and intellectual sloppiness (112, 116). Thus, on BonJour's view, if a given claim appears to be well supported by one's evidence, but this appearance is a product of one's vicious or irresponsible cognitive activity, then one is not justified in believing the relevant claim. BonJour characterizes the requirement in question as a "background condition" on a priori justification (137).

This condition bears a close similarity to the constraint incorporated into (E*). First, it requires a certain level of virtuous or responsible conduct (e.g. "careful reflection" on one's beliefs) (136). Second, BonJour apparently does not regard the virtuous or responsible activity in question as a *defining* element of a priori justification. On his view, the sole positive basis of such justification is the possession of good epistemic reasons acquired via pure thought or reason; and he makes clear that the relevant kind of cognitive activity does not itself enter into such reasons (137).[36] Rather, BonJour's view is apparently that to generate justification, the possession of such reasons must occur within a certain context or against a certain backdrop, namely, one in which the believer functions in an intellectually virtuous way. Thus for reasons that reflect some of the points discussed earlier, BonJour apparently thinks that a suitable version of evidentialism must include something like a virtue constraint.

[35] BonJour hints at but does not develop a similar requirement for empirical justification in (1985: 42).

[36] If it were to enter, then the reasons and the resulting justification would no longer be purely a priori, for the activity in question is knowable only introspectively or by some other empirical means.

There are, however, at least two notable ways in which the virtue constraint included in (E*) may differ from the one that BonJour has in mind. First, BonJour's constraint appears to be concerned merely with the "doxastic handling" of evidence, that is, with how an agent is presently treating or regarding his grounds for his belief.[37] It is not clear that he intends for the constraint to apply to the process or inquiry that generated these grounds. Second, the intended scope of BonJour's background condition may differ from that of (E*). BonJour discusses the condition only in connection with a priori justification; and he seems to think that it is applicable to *every* instance of such justification. But this way of thinking about the scope of the condition may be, at once, too narrow and too broad. First, we have witnessed the need for a virtue constraint relative to certain cases of empirical justification. Thus its proper scope is not limited to cases of a priori justification. Second, there is at least some reason to think that there are cases of a priori justification to which the constraint does not apply. These are cases in which a priori justification is relevantly brute or mechanistic, that is, cases in which the believer's agency fails to make a salient contribution to his evidential situation. It seems, for instance, that someone might come to "see" and believe that the conclusion of modus ponens or disjunctive syllogism follows from its premises, or that two plus three equals five, without his agency's making a "salient contribution" to his evidential situation with respect to these claims. The rational perception or intuition in question might be a function of the relatively brute or mechanistic operation of the person's rational capacity. If so, then the scope of BonJour's suggested constraint is also too broad.

5.4 *Conclusion*

We have seen that a plausible account of any significant e-relevant variety of epistemic justification must incorporate a proviso or constraint that, when applicable, requires cognitive agents to function in a manner characteristic of intellectual virtue. We have also seen that such a constraint has been gestured at (though never fully developed) in some of the evidentialist literature. This provides further support for the idea that the concept of intellectual virtue

[37] This is suggested, for instance, by his various characterizations of the way in which dogmatism or bias (which the virtue-requirement is intended to rule out) might be involved with a belief. See, for instance, pp. 112–14, 127, and 136–7.

does merit some kind of role within the landscape of traditional epistemology—that while it does not merit pride of place, neither can it be ignored.[38] In other words, while Strong Conservative VE may fail, Weak Conservative VE is viable indeed.

[38] The discussion also underscores other potential lines of inquiry in the same general vein. For instance, it would be worth considering, from the other direction as it were, just how close the connection is between the notion of believing with good evidence and intellectually virtuous belief formation. Is it reasonable to think that intellectually virtuous agents *always* form beliefs on the basis of good grounds or evidence? Or can believing in the absence of such grounds ever be consistent with or even expressive of intellectual virtue? Moreover, insofar as these are genuine (non-tautological) questions, they presuppose, contrary to certain prima facie plausible ways of thinking about intellectual virtue, that intellectual virtue is not itself to be *defined* in evidentialist terms (that is, as a matter, say, of "following the evidence" in one's inquiries and beliefs). But is this a plausible assumption?

Chapter 6

A PERSONAL WORTH CONCEPTION OF INTELLECTUAL VIRTUE

In the preceding three chapters, we examined ways in which the concept of intellectual virtue might figure (or fail to figure) into the theoretical terrain of traditional epistemology. At this point, the focus of the book shifts to matters of intellectual virtue considered in relative isolation from traditional epistemology. Our concern in this and the remaining chapters is with the intellectual virtues and their role in the intellectual life *as such*—not with how reflection on these traits might help us better understand or "solve" one or more traditional epistemological problems or puzzles. Nonetheless, the discussion in these chapters is likely to be of some interest even to traditionally minded epistemologists, for the concepts of truth, knowledge, rationality, belief, inquiry, and the like remain central throughout.

In this chapter, and to some extent in Chapter 7, I offer an initial sketch and defense of a particular *theory* of intellectual virtue, that is, an account of the basic nature and structure of an intellectual virtue. In Chapters 8 and 9, my attention turns to two *individual* virtues: namely, open-mindedness and intellectual courage. In these chapters, I address the relevant traits, not as intellectual virtues per se, but rather as the specific traits they are. That is, I focus on features of these traits that differentiate them from other intellectual virtues. An important and overriding concern of Chapters 6–9 is the viability of "autonomous" character-based virtue epistemology, which is the view that reflection on the intellectual virtues can form the basis of an epistemological research program that is largely independent of (even if not irrelevant to) traditional epistemology. The bearing of these chapters on the plausibility and probable shape of an autonomous virtue epistemology will be taken up in Chapter 10.

My plan in the present chapter is to defend the view that intellectual virtues can be understood as "personal intellectual excellences," or as traits that contribute to their possessor's "personal intellectual worth." Unsurprisingly, one major aim of the chapter is to clarify these central concepts. A second aim is to defend this account against a range of possible questions and objections, which in turn will lead to some further clarifications and refinements. In the chapter that follows, I proceed to situate this "personal worth" account of intellectual virtue with respect to—and offer at least a minimal assessment of—several other accounts of intellectual and moral virtue in the literature.[1]

6.1 *Preliminaries*

Before getting to the account, three preliminary points are in order. First, recall that we are thinking of intellectual virtues as *character* traits, not as natural or innate cognitive faculties like memory, reason, vision, introspection, or the like. The character traits in question include inquisitiveness, attentiveness, carefulness and thoroughness in inquiry, open-mindedness, fair-mindedness, and intellectual rigor, honesty, and courage. These are (roughly) the character traits of an excellent thinker or inquirer. My primary aim in this chapter, again, is to identify what *makes* the traits in question intellectual virtues.[2]

Second, I endorse pluralism concerning kinds or concepts of intellectual virtue. That is, I believe there is more than one way in which a character trait can qualify as an intellectual virtue, or more than one substantive and univocal criterion for the possession of an intellectual virtue. This is a plausible thesis given that a "virtue" is simply an excellence and that there is presumably more than one way in which the traits in question can be intellectually excellent.[3] Accordingly, my aim here is to identify a single plausible conception of

[1] It should go without saying that an entire book easily could be devoted to an account of the fundamental nature and structure of an intellectual virtue. Thus the account developed here is intended merely as an initial proposal and defense—one that will need to be further explored and defended elsewhere.

[2] As indicated in Chapter 1, some philosophers today (e.g. Doris 1998 and 2002 and Harman 1999 and 2000) are suspicious of the very idea of personal character. Their misgivings are based on certain experimental data suggesting that human behavior is largely governed by situational factors rather than by virtues or other personal traits. While I find this literature fascinating and think it does need to be taken seriously by virtue theorists, I do not think it poses any major difficulties for the account of intellectual virtue put forth here. For a very brief sketch of why, see note 15 of Chapter 1. And for some recent critical discussions of situationism's central claims and arguments, see Merritt (2000), Sreenivasan (2002), Miller (2003), Kamtekar (2004), Sabini and Silver (2005), Adams (2006), and Snow (2009).

[3] Surprisingly, this point appears not to be very widely recognized within the virtue ethics or virtue epistemology literature, for in both fields it is not at all uncommon for an author to

intellectual virtue. A third and related issue concerns how the present (or for that matter *any*) account of the nature of an intellectual virtue should be assessed. On what grounds should such an account be thought to succeed or fail? This question is especially pressing in light of the commitment to pluralism just noted, for this commitment raises questions about which sorts of considerations should be allowed to count *against* a given theory of virtue.[4] While I cannot provide an exhaustive answer to this question here, I propose the following two theoretical desiderata. First, any plausible account of the nature of an intellectual virtue must pick out a distinct and univocal intellectual *excellence* (rather than, say, a mere part or aspect of such an excellence or a discrete and univocal trait that is not necessarily an excellence or intellectually excellent). Second, it must fit with or accommodate a substantial range of the traits that we intuitively regard as intellectual character virtues. That is, it must be plausible, given the account in question, to regard a substantial range of these traits as excellences of the relevant sort. This is necessary, of course, because the task at hand just is to account for the nature of a familiar set of traits: again, traits like fair-mindedness, intellectual courage, intellectual honesty, carefulness and thoroughness in inquiry, reflectiveness, intellectual rigor, and so forth. I say that an acceptable theory must account for a "substantial" rather than, say, the *complete* range of traits we intuitively regard as intellectual virtues because it may be (1) that some of these traits are plausibly regarded as intellectual virtues in one sense or according to one plausible theory of virtue but not according to another, or (2) that the theory in question is explanatorily strong enough in other respects to justify giving up a limited number of intuitive judgments about the status of certain traits. As the latter point suggests, I endorse a "reflective equilibrium" approach to constructing a theory of intellectual virtue. While these are not the only criteria relevant to assessing an account of the nature of an intellectual virtue, they are central and important, and I shall have more to say about them below.

assume that if his account of moral or intellectual virtue is correct, then any substantially different account must be mistaken.

[4] Specifically, it opens up the possibility that if one is defending a particular theory of intellectual virtue and someone objects to this theory on the grounds that it fails to make sense of a certain range of cases or intuitions, one might simply respond by claiming that the cases or intuitions in question are relevant only to some *other* theory of intellectual virtue (i.e. one aimed at capturing the essential features of some *other* kind or concept of intellectual virtue), and thus that one need not be concerned about them. Where a principled justification can be given for this sort of move, it may be entirely appropriate (indeed I shall employ it below); but otherwise it is bound to seem ad hoc.

6.2 *Personal worth and intellectual virtue*

How, then, might we begin to think about the conceptual basis of intellectual virtue? Or about what ultimately makes traits like fair-mindedness, open-mindedness, intellectual carefulness and thoroughness, inquisitiveness, attentiveness, intellectual courage, tenacity, and honesty intellectual virtues? I shall defend a response to this question that gives a central role to the notion of "personal worth," that is, to the notion of being a "good person" or of being good qua person. While no such account has been developed in any detail in the literature, virtue epistemologists have occasionally alluded to a connection between intellectual virtue and vice, on the one hand, and personal worth, on the other. Robert Roberts and Jay Wood (2007), for instance, say: "We think of human beings as persons and of virtues [intellectual virtues included] as excellences of persons, traits that make one excellent as a person" (65). Similarly, Susan Haack (2000) remarks that "to my ear at least, 'he is a good man but intellectually dishonest,' if not quite an oxymoron, really does need an 'otherwise'" (15). And Casey Swank (2000), in a discussion of epistemic *vice*, says:

> Unreasonable persons, persons of bad epistemic character, are also just plain bad. Epistemic vices are not freestanding. They are, rather, natural and unsurprising facets or consequences of more basic and general defects in one's personal character. How might we account for this coincidence? The obvious suggestion is that the badness of epistemic vices *consists in* their being offshoots or manifestations of underlying *personal vices*... It is from the point of view of *personal excellence*, rather than that of truth (or the like), that it is better to be reasonable than unreasonable. (202; my emphasis)

Swank's point is equally applicable to intellectual *virtues*. That is, it is equally plausible to think of intellectual virtues as "offshoots or manifestations" of personal *excellences*; or that the traits in question are virtues, not (merely) from the standpoint of truth or reliability, but (also) from the standpoint of personal worth or excellence.

But how, more precisely, might we understand the connection between intellectual virtue and personal worth? Let us take the following principle as our starting point:

> (PWC) A character trait T is an intellectual virtue just in case T contributes to its possessor's personal intellectual worth.

The central term in (PWC) is that of "personal intellectual worth." While this label may be foreign, the kind of value it picks out is familiar and intuitive—or so I hope to show.

6.2.1 *Personal intellectual worth*

To get a handle on the notion of personal intellectual worth, it will be helpful first to say a bit more about the notion of personal worth *simpliciter*. The concept of a "good person" or of someone's being good or bad qua person is deeply embedded in ordinary normative discourse and thinking. We often express our praise or admiration for other people by saying things like "So-and-so is a remarkably good person" or "So-and-so is a better person than I." Equally familiar are judgments aimed at marking a contrast between a person's worth or excellence qua person and his worth or excellence in some other respect. This includes remarks of the following general form: "While so-and-so may be a terrific X (athlete, musician, artist, legislator, attorney, etc.), he sure seems like a rotten *person*." It also includes judgments of a reverse sort, according to which someone is considered good or admirable qua person but weak or defective in one of the other respects just noted. Few would deny, for instance, that Mother Teresa, while a profoundly good person, might have been hopeless on the tennis court, with a paintbrush, or in the kitchen. At first glance, then, the notion of personal worth picks out a distinctive and familiar kind of excellence—one that may or may not be accompanied by various other kinds of excellence sometimes manifested by persons.

But this initial description suggests that personal worth, while perhaps familiar and intuitive, is an inherently *moral* notion: that to be a good person, or to be good qua person, is to be morally good in some respect. It remains, however, that the domain of personal worth per se is not exhausted by that of personal moral worth. Personal worth or excellence also has an intellectual dimension.[5] The best way to come at this dimension is by way of some observations about our practices of intellectual admiration.

We admire people from an intellectual standpoint, or with respect to intellectual values or criteria, for a wide range of reasons. Sometimes we admire them for their excellent cognitive faculties or abilities. I might, for instance, admire a person's photographic memory or 20/20 vision. Or I might admire a person's

[5] Perhaps it has other dimensions as well, for example, aesthetic and spiritual dimensions. What these other dimensions might involve should be evident by the end of the chapter. For more on the relation between the intellectual and moral dimensions of virtue, see the Appendix.

capacity for highly formal or abstract thought, rigorous and complex mathematical computation, or multi-dimensional mental representation. But these forms of evaluation are largely impersonal or non-personal in nature: they have no obvious or immediate bearing on their subjects' personal worth.[6] Indeed, someone might possess perfect vision, a photographic memory, and an extraordinarily high IQ, while still being a deeply flawed or vicious person.

But intellectual admiration is not always like this. Consider someone with a deep and abiding desire for knowledge and understanding, someone who prizes these as among life's greatest goods, and who, as a result of this desire, is regularly willing to give a fair and honest hearing to "the other side," to persevere in his search for the truth, to entertain counterevidence to his beliefs in an open and patient way, to refrain from caricaturing or distorting positions he rejects, and so on. Such a person surely is admirable, and admirable in a way that is relevant to his excellence or worth qua person. Intuitively, he is a better person on account of the qualities just noted. At the same time, however, he is not necessarily a *morally* better person; rather he is better in a way that is at once personal *and* intellectual.[7]

This suggests the existence of an independent sphere of value that lies between the sort of value instantiated by the person with exceptional vision and a high IQ, on the one hand, and the value instantiated by the moral exemplars noted above, on the other. Again, like the former, the value in question is distinctively *intellectual* or *cognitive*, for it pertains to or concerns distinctively cognitive ends like truth, knowledge, evidence, rationality, and understanding. But, like the latter, it is also relevant to personal worth. It is, we might say, personal worth *as it relates to* cognitive ends or values like the ones just mentioned. My suggestion is that the notion of intellectual virtue can be understood relative to *this* domain of value. According to (PWC), intellectual virtues just are character traits that make their possessor good or excellent in the relevant intellectual-cum-personal way. They are "personal intellectual excellences."

[6] Of course, they are forms of "personal" evaluation in the sense that they involve or are about persons. However, they are not evaluations of persons qua persons. Rather, as the language just employed suggests, it may be more accurate to characterize them merely as evaluations of certain capacities *of* persons (eyesight, memory, etc.).

[7] Perhaps he is a better person in a very broad sense of "moral." However, moral goodness thus conceived would not, I take it, *exclude* the relevant sort of intellectual goodness; rather, the latter would be a *type* of moral goodness. For more on the relationship between "moral" and "intellectual" in this context, see the Appendix.

I take it that this way of thinking about the nature of an intellectual virtue has substantial intuitive plausibility. Indeed, as the above characterization indicates, the very qualities that most clearly illustrate the sort of value in question are precisely those qualities that we tend to associate with intellectual virtue: for example, a love of knowledge, intellectual honesty, open-mindedness, intellectual perseverance, and fair-mindedness. This suggests at least an initial correspondence between a personal worth account of intellectual virtue and standard ways of thinking about the relevant traits.

Let us, then, take for granted that the notion of "personal intellectual worth" picks out an independent and intuitive dimension of value. That is, let us assume that *there is a reasonably familiar and intuitive way of being good or excellent qua person that is distinctively intellectual—or a way of being intellectually good or excellent that is also personal.* Let us also assume an initial correspondence between this dimension of value and the traits we intuitively regard as intellectual virtues.

These assumptions notwithstanding, given how central the notion of personal intellectual worth is to the present account of intellectual virtue, we must attempt to say more about it. What, for instance, is the *basis* of personal intellectual worth? Why exactly do we think of a person with the sort of psychology described above as an intellectually good or excellent person? And once these things are made clear, does a conception of intellectual virtue rooted in the notion of personal intellectual worth still provide a plausible account of the traits we tend to regard as intellectual virtues?

These are important questions; and I shall get to them momentarily. Before doing so, however, I want to head off several potential objections and misunderstandings of the very idea of personal worth as I am conceiving of it.

6.2.2 *Clarifications*

First, while I cannot develop the distinction in any detail here, I maintain that there is an important and fundamental difference between personal worth in the sense noted above and a kind of inherent value or dignity that we tend to ascribe to all persons and in equal measure. The latter refers to a kind of value that all persons have just on account of being persons. It is the sort of value in virtue of which we tend to think of all persons being in some sense "equal" or as possessing certain basic rights. Personal worth, on the other hand, refers to a further, distinct way in which persons can (but need not) be good or excellent. Again, the alternative value is a sort of guaranteed or baseline value, while personal worth is a kind of value that beings with an inherent dignity or worth may or may not instantiate. I see no reason to deny that both types of value can plausibly be called "personal worth." However, I think they are clearly distinct. This is evident in the fact that it is widely agreed (1) that there is a sense in which all human beings are normatively "equal" or possess a common value or dignity, but also (2) that some persons are "better persons" than others. Both of these claims are plausible, and the kinds of value they pick out seem clearly to correspond to the two kinds just noted. While much more could be said about this distinction, the point I wish to emphasize now is that by appealing to the notion of personal worth in the relevant way, I am not suggesting that some people are "worth more" or "more valuable" than others in the sense just indicated.[8]

Second, I repudiate the obviously problematic idea that persons are *categorically* good or bad. The notion of personal worth does not in any way suggest (let alone entail) that some persons are entirely (even mostly) good or bad qua persons. Rather, this notion is consistent with the very plausible idea that we are all of us amalgams of good and bad: that we are good people to some extent or in some respects and not so good in others.[9]

Third, the notion of personal worth should not be confused with a kind of "niceness" or social propriety that is sometimes associated with "being a good person." A person who follows all the rules, does what he is told, avoids causing offense, and so forth, may very well *fail* to be a good person in my sense. Rather, to say of someone that he is a morally or intellectually good person, that he is morally or intellectually good qua person, is to say something significant and clearly positive about him—indeed, about his very *identity* or about who he *is* as a person. And surely there are ways of being "nice" or "upright" that fall well below this standard.

Fourth, I also intend a distinction between personal worth and what might be called "human worth," that is, a person's goodness or badness qua *human being* or member of the human species. While much of what I say about personal worth may also be true of human worth, and while my account of intellectual virtue may turn out to be very similar to one based on the notion of human worth, I intentionally employ the term "person" rather than "human being." This is partly because I think that if there were any non-human persons

[8] For a relevant discussion, see Adams (1999: 115–20).

[9] Thus I distance myself from the sort of exaggerated virtue-ascriptions that (rightly) concern some "situationists" (see e.g. Doris 2002: 92–7 and 114–17). I do not, however, think that the imperfect and often fragmentary nature of personal character requires that we cease using terms like "good person" or "bad person" (though perhaps we would do well to use them more carefully and qualifiedly). Still less do I think this fact poses any problem for the very concept of personal worth as I am thinking of it here.

(e.g. aliens, angels, or the like) my account of personal intellectual worth would likely to be applicable to them as well.[10] But it is also because I think the most promising account of these concepts simply will not have occasion to appeal to any specific features of human nature or to the human species as such. This is all to the good, for the challenges facing a "nature-based" or naturalist account of virtue are manifold and well known. We will examine some of these challenges in Chapter 7 when I contrast a personal worth account of intellectual virtue with an explicitly naturalistic one.[11]

6.2.3 *The basis of personal worth* simpliciter

We have seen that there is at least some initial plausibility to the idea that intellectual virtues are "personal intellectual excellences," that is, that they are traits that contribute to their possessor's "personal intellectual worth," or that make their possessor an intellectually good or better person. We have also noted, however, that more needs to be said about the basis of this value.

Once again I think the best way to proceed is by first reflecting on the concept of personal worth *simpliciter*. A person can be better or worse qua person, but on account of what? What, in general, makes a person good or better qua person? One plausible response is that personal worth is primarily a function of one's "pro-attitudes," of what one loves, desires, or identifies with, and also of what one "hates," is repelled by, repudiates, and so on. Specifically, it is a function of the extent to which one is, in a psychological sense, *positively* oriented to what is good, right, or appropriate and *negatively* oriented what is bad, evil, or wrong.

Something like this idea has recently gained currency within virtue ethics. In *Virtue, Vice, and Value* (2001), Thomas Hurka defends the view (roughly) that a moral virtue is a particular instance of "loving" one or more "baseline" goods like pleasure or achievement, where "loving" a good is a matter of being positively oriented toward it in one's desires, actions, or feelings. Similarly, in *A Theory of Virtue* (2006), Robert Adams argues that moral virtue is matter of "persisting excellence in being *for* the good," which might involve "loving it,

[10] God, conceived as a supernatural person, might be an exception. Here a close analog of the *Euthyphro* dilemma looms. I cannot stop here to address this issue; but for a pertinent discussion, see Zagzebski (2004).

[11] A further reason to maintain a distinction between a naturalistic and a personal worth account of intellectual virtue is suggested by Adams's distinction (1999: ch. 1) between well-being and excellence. Naturalistic accounts of virtue typically are centered on the notion of human well-being or flourishing; my personal worth account, by contrast, is better understood as excellence-based.

liking it, respecting it, wanting it, wishing for it, appreciating it, thinking highly of it, speaking in favor of it," and the like (16). We will look carefully at these accounts of moral virtue in Chapter 7. At present, I merely register the fact that they draw a strong conceptual connection between virtue, on the one hand, and what a person is positively and negatively oriented toward, on the other.

A corresponding account of the basis of "personal worth" may be summarized thus:

> (BPW) A subject S is good or better qua person to the extent that S is positively oriented toward or "loves" what is good and is negatively oriented toward or "hates" what is bad.[12]

A complete assessment of (BPW) would require an explanation and clarification of its various elements that I do not have the space for here. I take it, however, that even in the absence of such elaboration, the principle has considerable intuitive appeal.

There is, for instance, considerable plausibility in the idea that one's goodness or badness qua person must consist in *some* kind of relation between oneself, on the one hand, and other kinds or sources of value or disvalue, on the other.[13] One possibility along these lines is that the relation in question is principally a *causal* one, for instance, that personal worth should be understood in terms of the quality of the outcomes or consequences of one's actions or motives. But this is problematic. For whether we actually succeed, say, in bringing about the good consequences or states of affairs at which we aim is often very largely a matter of luck. It often depends on the cooperation of other rational agents and on a congenial environment: factors that are often substantially, if not entirely, beyond our control. But surely it is mistaken to think that an individual's goodness or badness qua person might depend on whether she is lucky enough to have the cooperation of other agents or her environment. Rather, where the concern is personal worth, what seems relevant are certain "internal" or psychological factors, for example, what the person aims at,

[12] This at least resembles certain claims endorsed by Adams and Hurka. Adams says: "I believe the claim that x is excellent implies not only that it is good to value x, but also that this goodness of valuing x is grounded in the excellence of x and independent of ulterior values that may be served by the valuing. In other words, the claim that x is good implies that it is... *intrinsically* good to value x" (1999: 22). See Hurka (2001) for a similar view. The obvious difference between these authors' claims and (BPW) is that (BPW) makes explicit and central reference to the concept of *personal worth*.

[13] This fits, for instance, with the familiar and plausible view that good or virtuous persons are those that can identify and are appropriately responsive to the morally salient features of their surroundings (see e.g. McDowell 1979).

desires, or strives to achieve: that is, what she "loves" in some intuitive and familiar sense of the term.[14]

While (BPW) enjoys considerable plausibility, we must attempt to say a bit more about the precise character of the orientation to which it appeals. I shall briefly elaborate on three aspects of this orientation. First, in the clearest and most paradigmatic instances of personal worth, the relevant "love" and "hate" are *desiderative* in nature. Personal worth is paradigmatically a matter of "loving" what is good in the sense of wanting or desiring that it obtain and of "hating" what is bad in the sense of despising the bad or desiring that it not obtain. Later in the chapter we will consider whether the orientation in question might take other forms. For now it will suffice to note that personal worth standardly or paradigmatically supervenes on a certain desiderative psychological structure.

A second and related point concerns the strength of the orientation mentioned in (BPW). It might be claimed, for instance, that if a person has only a very mild or weak preference for the good, then this orientation may not have any bearing on his personal worth. This seems to me to be correct. One way of accommodating this point would be to say that the orientation in question must be strong or intense enough that it actually *motivates* its possessor to choose or act on behalf of the good. Therefore, if I have a desire (say) to see justice prevail in my community, but this desire is so weak that it fails to compel me even to lift a finger in support of any just causes, then (plausibly) this desire will not have a positive bearing on my personal worth.

But in fact this requirement is too strong. For there are various ways in which even desires that do contribute to personal worth might fail to be motivating—as where, for instance, there is some countervailing value at stake or where one is prevented by external forces from acting on the relevant desire.[15] Perhaps such cases could be handled by maintaining, alternatively, that a desire for the good contributes to personal worth only if, *other things being equal* or *considered in its own right*, this desire is motivating. But this formulation does not go far

[14] Obviously there is a (limited) similarity between this way of thinking about personal worth and Kant's well-known claim (1993: 7–8) that "moral worth" is a function of a good will, which in turn "has its full value in itself," that is, whose value is not in any way dependent on its effects or consequences. For a development of the idea that virtue possession is immune to the relevant kinds of luck, see Greco (1995), my (2007), and section 7.2.1 of Chapter 7. It is also worth noting that the present exclusion of luck is not intended to exclude *all* forms of luck. It does not, for instance, exclude the kind of "constitutive" luck discussed by Thomas Nagel (1979), Bernard Williams (1981), and many others.

[15] For instance, where the pursuit of a particular good G_1 is incompatible with that of a second and superior good G_2, my desire for G_1 might contribute to my personal worth even if, on account of my pursuit of G_2, I never actually pursue G_1.

enough. For even the sort of very mild preference for the good or weak opposition to the bad noted above might be motivating in this sense. My desire to see justice prevail, for instance, might be such that if I had nothing else to do, no other interests or desires, and nothing holding me back, it would compel me to act in support of a just cause, but also that barring the satisfaction of any one of these conditions, it would, on account of its inherent weakness, fail to motivate any action on my part. This desire would be motivating in the relevant sense; it would not, however, appear to make any contribution to my personal worth.[16] I will not attempt to resolve this issue here. Instead, I will simply conclude that the orientation appealed to in (BPW) should be understood as being *reasonably* strong or intense, so that, when considered in its own right, it will likely (though not necessarily) prove motivating.

A third point concerns the sorts of *reasons* that might underlie or support this orientation. It would appear that a person's being positively oriented toward a good end or negatively oriented toward a bad end will contribute to her personal worth only if she is concerned with the relevant ends *as such* or *for their own sake.*[17] If, by contrast, this person is positively oriented toward a good end merely because this end happens to be causally related to some *other* end that is bad or even evaluatively neutral, then the fact that she is oriented in this way presumably will not make her a good or better person at all (it may in fact make her a *worse* person). Similarly, if a person is negatively oriented toward a certain bad or evil end, but only because of its connection with some other end of questionable value (the person hates poverty, say, because of the potential tax burden it places on him), then this orientation will not enhance her personal worth. Thus (BPW) should be read as requiring that the person in question be positively oriented toward the good and negatively oriented toward the bad *as such* or *for their own sake.*[18]

[16] Indeed, it might even have a *negative* bearing on my personal worth, given its obvious failure to "match" or correspond to the worth of its object. Hurka invokes a "proportionality principle" to explain such judgments. See his (2001: 83f).

[17] More precisely, this requirement holds only where the good in question is *intrinsically* (vs. merely instrumentally) valuable. If M is a (mere) means to a certain good G and I desire M as such or for its own sake, then presumably my desiring M will not contribute to my personal worth. This should not be taken to suggest, however, that a desire for instrumental goods cannot contribute to personal worth. For if I desire M *as a means to* G or because M *tends to produce* G, then presumably my desiring M *will* (or at least might) contribute to my personal worth. See Hurka (2001: 17–18) for a development of a similar point. This way of thinking about personal worth and virtue also bears some resemblance to Richard Brandt's (1992: 270–6, 289, 306f).

[18] A further issue that I will not address in any detail here is whether the ends in question must *in fact* be good or bad—or, alternatively, whether it is possible for a person to be *mistaken*

Before turning to consider the basis of personal *intellectual* worth, one additional question needs to be addressed. It might be wondered at this point whether some further explanation or account of (BPW) is available, that is, whether more might said about just why it is that one is a better person to the extent that one is positively oriented toward the good and negatively oriented toward the bad. Interpreted in one way, this question strikes me as confused. If the question is asking for some further *basis* on account of which "loving" the good, say, contributes to personal worth, then I think that no answer can or should be given. For intuitively the contribution that loving the good makes to personal worth is a brute fact. Being a good person just is a matter of caring about or being motivated by that which is good and of being unmoved by or despising that which is bad.

Nonetheless, the following remark may go some way toward answering the question. To be positively oriented toward something in the relevant way is to *identify* with it.[19] And, paradigmatically at least, it is to do so with both "heart and mind," or will and intellect: it is to *judge* that the thing in question is good or worth loving, and to *desire* it, be *moved* by it, or *choose* it. If, then, we think of persons as constituted primarily by both an intellect and a will, it should come as no surprise that one's goodness qua person would depend on the value of what one identifies with or "loves."[20] This is, at any rate, one way of trying to shed some additional light on (BPW).[21]

6.2.4 *The basis of personal* intellectual *worth*

Suppose, then, that we accept something like (BPW) as a generally accurate account of the basis of personal worth *simpliciter*. Given that our immediate

about their normative status (without a change in personal worth). Strictly speaking, I think such mistakes are possible. However, I think (1) that they are likely to be few and far between; and (2) that the person in question must still have *good reason to believe* that the end or ends in question have the normative status she takes them to have. Thus it would perhaps be more precise to say that personal worth is a matter of loving what one has good reason to think is good and hating what one has good reason to think is bad.

[19] For a related and intriguing discussion, see Nozick (1981: 524–8).

[20] A similar point could be made about the relevant negative orientation. See my (2010) for a relevant discussion. Also, as the present point suggests, I am thinking of the relevant positive orientation or "love" as having a *cognitive* dimension. Though I will not elaborate on this dimension here, I do touch on it briefly in my (2007) and in section 7.2.1 of Chapter 7. See my "The Cognitive Demands of Intellectual Virtue" (manuscript) for a more in depth discussion.

[21] A correlative of account of what it is to be *bad* or *evil* qua person is readily available in terms of "loving" what is evil and "hating" what is good. Here again, see Hurka (2001) and Adams (2006) for relevant discussions.

concern here is personal *intellectual* worth, the next task is to try to narrow the scope of (BPW) accordingly. One obvious way of doing so is as follows:

> (BIW) A subject S is intellectually good or better qua person to the extent that S is positively oriented toward or "loves" what is intellectually good and is negatively oriented toward or "hates" what is intellectually bad.

According to (BIW), personal intellectual worth is a function of how a person is oriented toward certain distinctively intellectual values and disvalues. The precise character of this orientation should be understood along the lines sketched in the previous section. That is, it should be regarded as being paradigmatically desiderative in nature, meeting the relevant threshold of strength or intensity, and involving a concern with intellectual values or disvalues *as such* or considered in their own right.

What about the intellectual values and disvalues themselves? What do these include? A great deal could be said in response to this question, much of which would take us well beyond the scope of this chapter.[22] For now, it will suffice to think of the relevant goods or values in terms of what Linda Zagzebski (1996) has called "cognitive contact with reality," a notion that is intended to encompass a range of familiar cognitive states like true belief, knowledge, and understanding, and to think of the relevant "bads" or disvalues as including states like false belief, ignorance, lack of understanding, and irrationality.[23]

(BIW) fits well with our initial characterization of personal intellectual worth. Recall that we initially identified as a clear case of an "intellectually good person" someone who possesses "a deep and abiding desire for knowledge and understanding, someone who prizes these as among life's greatest goods, and who, as a result of this desire, is regularly willing to give a fair and honest hearing to 'the other side,' to persevere in his search for the truth, to entertain counterevidence to his beliefs in an open and patient way, to refrain from

[22] It would take us, in fact, to the burgeoning subfield of epistemology that explores the nature and scope of *epistemic value*. See Pritchard (2007), Haddock, Millar, and Pritchard (2009), and Pritchard, Millar, and Haddock (2010) for up-to-date discussions. This is perhaps the main point at which my concerns in this book intersect directly with discussions in this neighboring area. And, as the present point suggests, aspects of my account of intellectual virtue depend on the status of claims proper to this other domain.

[23] There is something recognizably Platonic, about the general picture here. While Plato does not discuss intellectual character virtues as such, in 475b–476b of the *Republic* (1997), he describes the philosopher or virtuous "lover of wisdom" as one who "turns gladly to learning and is insatiable for it," "love[s] the sight of truth," and is able to "see and embrace the nature of the beautiful itself." Thus on his view there is apparently an intrinsically *epistemic* dimension to personal worth or virtue.

caricaturing or distorting positions he rejects, and so on." This characterization makes explicit reference to the kind of orientation mentioned in (BIW). And it is plausible to think that the other motives or activities it mentions (for instance, an openness to counterevidence and an unwillingness to caricature competing views) contribute to personal worth only if they are the result of such an orientation. Again, if a person expresses an openness toward and refuses to caricature or misrepresent competing views, but does so only out of a desire to be liked by the people who hold these views, then his openness or fairness presumably will not contribute to his personal intellectual worth: he will not be an intellectually better *person* on account of this activity. It is, then, plausible to think of the basis of personal intellectual worth along the lines of (BIW).

6.2.5 *The account summarized*

We are now in a position to draw together the various parts of the preceding discussion of personal intellectual worth and related notions with my initial proposal about the nature of an intellectual virtue. According to (PWC), an intellectual virtue is a character trait that contributes to its possessor's personal intellectual worth. We have seen that the notion of "personal intellectual worth" corresponds to an intuitive and reasonably familiar dimension of value that is at once personal *and* intellectual. And we have seen that it is plausible to conceive of the basis of such value in terms of a certain psychological orientation toward various intellectual values and disvalues. For ease of discussion, and because I think it has a certain intuitive priority, I shall henceforth focus on the *positive* dimension of this orientation, that is, on the relevant "love" of epistemic goods. My proposal, then, is that *an intellectual virtue is a character trait that contributes to its possessor's personal intellectual worth on account of its involving a positive psychological orientation toward epistemic goods.*

6.2.6 *The broad structure of an intellectual virtue*

The discussion thus far has been aimed at providing a plausible account of what all intellectual virtues have in common that make them intellectual virtues. It does not, however, shed any light on how the various individual traits that qualify as intellectual virtues might be distinguished from each other, that is, it offers no way of *individuating* intellectual virtues. Thus, to provide an idea of how intellectual virtues conceived as "personal excellences" might be individuated, and to further clarify the model of intellectual virtue I am defending, it will be helpful to say something about how I am thinking of the general or broad structure of an intellectual virtue.

I maintain that intellectual virtues have an *integrated, two-tier psychological structure*. At a basic or fundamental level, all intellectual virtues involve, as we have seen, a positive orientation toward epistemic goods. This orientation is the principal psychological basis of personal intellectual worth and thus of intellectual virtues as I am conceiving of them. However, each intellectual virtue also has its own *characteristic psychology*. That is, each virtue involves certain attitudes, feelings, motives, beliefs, actions, and other psychological qualities that make it the virtue it is and on the basis of which it can be distinguished from other intellectual virtues. As I argue in Chapter 8, for instance, the characteristic psychology of open-mindedness is a kind of "cognitive transcending" of a familiar or default cognitive standpoint. An open-minded person, that is, is one who is able and willing to detach or depart from such a standpoint in order to give serious consideration to some alternative or competing standpoint. It is this disposition, and the various psychological qualities that comprise and go along with it, that distinguishes an open-minded person from one who is, say, fair-minded or intellectually honest. Finally, on the present model, the characteristic psychology of each individual virtue is "rooted in" or "flows from" the more fundamental positive orientation toward epistemic goods. Thus an open-minded person "transcends" various epistemic standpoints on *account* of her deeper concern with epistemic goods. She is, say, motivated to acquire understanding, sees the relevant cognitive activity as integral to achieving understanding, and so also has a secondary or derivative motivation to engage in this activity.[24]

This way of thinking about the basic structure of an intellectual virtue is not entirely original. Zagzebski (1996), for instance, summarizes her own view as follows:

> We have seen that all intellectual virtues arise out of the motivation for knowledge and include an internal aim to operate cognitively in a way that is believed to be knowledge conducive, a way that is unique to each virtue. So the aim of open-mindedness is to be receptive to new ideas and arguments even when they

[24] Here too the need for a certain cognitive requirement on intellectual virtue (also alluded to in note 20 above) is apparent, since part of what it is for the characteristic psychology of a virtue to be "grounded" in a desire for truth, say, is apparently for the person in question to *believe* that the activity expressive of this psychology is likely to be helpful for reaching the truth. As I explain in more detail in section 7.2.1 of Chapter 7, this suggests further that while intellectual virtue in a personal worth sense may not require actual reliability, it does require a certain "reliability belief" to the effect that the activity characteristic of the virtue in question is a reliable means to truth or other epistemic ends. Here again, see my (2007) and my "The Cognitive Demands of Intellectual Virtue" (manuscript) for more on this requirement.

> conflict with one's own in order to ultimately get knowledge. The aim of intellectual thoroughness is to exhaustively investigate the evidence pertaining to a particular belief or a set of questions in order to ultimately get knowledge. The aim of intellectual courage is to defend one's belief or a line of inquiry when one has good reason to be confident that it is on the right track, and to fearlessly answer objections from others in order to ultimately get knowledge. (269)

In the chapter that follows, we will examine some notable differences between Zagzebski's view of the structure of an intellectual virtue and my own. However, as this passage suggests, I largely agree with her general account of this structure and believe that it yields a promising way of individuating intellectual virtues.

6.3 *Assessing the account*

How plausible is the foregoing account of intellectual virtue? We have seen that it has considerable intuitive appeal—that there is apparently a dimension of value that is at once personal and intellectual, that it is plausible to think of the basis of such value in terms of something like a desire for truth or knowledge, that the traits we tend to regard as intellectual virtues often involve such a desire, and so forth. What more can be said either for or against the account?

One natural place to begin is with how the account fares relative to the two theoretical desiderata identified at the beginning of the chapter. There I noted that a plausible account of the nature of an intellectual virtue must (1) pick out a distinct and determinate intellectual *excellence* (rather than, say, a mere part or aspect of such an excellence or a discrete and determinate trait that is not necessarily an excellence or intellectually excellent) and (2) accommodate or cover at least a substantial range of the traits we tend to regard as intellectual virtues. It should be clear at this point that the account fares very well in connection with both of these criteria. First, surely it picks out a genuine intellectual excellence. It is entirely reasonable, that is, to regard as "intellectual excellences" character traits that contribute to their possessor's personal intellectual worth, or that make their possessor an intellectually good or better person. Second, we have seen that the account covers a wide range of putative virtues. It is extremely plausible, for instance, to think of traits like inquisitiveness, attentiveness, intellectual courage, honesty, fairness, and openness as contributing to the personal worth of their possessor, and to think of them as doing so on account of something like a desire for truth.

In the remainder of the chapter, I consider a series of individual traits that might appear to pose a problem for the present account of intellectual virtue. We will see that some of the traits pose no difficulty at all, but that others require a broadening of some of our initial ways of thinking about intellectual virtue and related concepts. The discussion will bring into sharper focus what can and cannot be expected of the present account and how the account stands relative to certain theoretical alternatives.

6.3.1 *Intellectual carefulness and thoroughness*

One general worry about the model is that it is too demanding. This worry can be illustrated in connection with traits like intellectual carefulness and thoroughness.[25] I have argued that these traits are intellectual virtues in a personal worth sense only if they are motivated by something like a desire for truth. It might be argued, however, that no such desire is necessary.

Consider, for instance, a bench scientist who does extremely careful and thorough research over the course of his career, but whose work is motivated primarily by a desire to win a Nobel Prize and all the professional accolades that come therewith (*not* by scientific curiosity, a concern for advancing human knowledge, or the like). It might be said that as long as a tendency to engage in careful and thorough intellectual activity under the appropriate conditions is a sufficiently settled and integrated part of the scientist's character, it will make sense to think of him as genuinely intellectually careful and thorough, and further, of his carefulness and thoroughness as genuine intellectual virtues.

I have no objection to the idea that the scientist might be genuinely careful and thorough in inquiry; and indeed, that his carefulness and thoroughness might be "intellectual virtues" in some reasonably familiar and legitimate sense. Here I must reemphasize my acceptance of pluralism about kinds or concepts of intellectual virtue. As indicated above, I think a single trait of character can be intellectually excellent and thus an "intellectual virtue" in more than one way. Indeed, I argue in Chapter 7 that a character trait's being epistemically reliable or truth-conducive is both necessary and sufficient for its counting as an intellectual virtue according to a certain viable "externalist" model of intellectual virtue. It may, then, be reasonable to regard the scientist's carefulness and thoroughness as intellectual virtues in this sense.

[25] These and related traits are relatively formal in the sense that they do not have an obvious immediate motivational component. Similar traits include intellectual courage, perseverance, self-control, and patience. See Roberts (1984) and Adams (2006) for more on virtues of this general sort.

That said, I think we have already seen that with respect to a *personal worth* account of intellectual virtue, the scientist's character traits cannot be considered intellectual virtues. Again, if the scientist is habitually careful and thorough in his research, but *strictly* out of a desire for intellectual approval and status, then presumably he is not really an intellectually good or better *person* on account of these qualities. He has some intellectual or cognitive "excellences," to be sure, but these are not personal excellences in our sense—they do not contribute to his worth or excellence qua person. Indeed, if the motives in question were the dominant ones in the scientist's life as a whole, we might reasonably think of him as rather defective qua person.[26]

Finally, note that traits like intellectual carefulness and thoroughness certainly *can* qualify as intellectual virtues on the present model. Imagine, for instance, what form these traits are likely to take in the psychology or character of a broadly or maximally good cognitive agent. In what way or sense would this person be intellectually careful or thorough? It is plausible to think that she would be such *out of* something like a firm and resolute desire for truth or knowledge, that her high regard and desire for the epistemic good would be what motivates or compels her to think and inquire in careful and thorough ways. This is, of course, precisely the characterization of the virtues in question indicated by the present model.

6.3.2 *Creativity and originality*

I have argued that (1) the sort of motivational state on which personal intellectual worth supervenes is paradigmatically desiderative in nature and that (2) the intentional object of this state can be understood in terms of cognitive ends like truth, knowledge, and understanding. In the present section, and in sections 6.3.3 and 6.3.4, I examine a range of traits that will force us to broaden our conception of one or more of these dimensions of personal intellectual worth—and thus of our conception of intellectual virtue as well.[27]

Creativity and originality are often identified as intellectual virtues (see e.g. Zagzebski 1996: 123–5 and 182–3). It is far from clear, however, that these traits necessarily—even typically—aim at truth or similar cognitive ends. The creative artist's ability to "think outside the box," say, or an academic's propensity for

[26] I commend these judgments on *intuitive* grounds. Thus I intend not to be relying on the very account of personal worth at issue.

[27] As this suggests, the objections that follow are aimed at my account of personal intellectual worth as developed up to this point in the chapter. They do not immediately threaten the claim that intellectual virtues can be understood as traits that contribute to personal intellectual worth—that is, they do not threaten a personal worth conception of intellectual virtue per se.

arriving at original theories or arguments, need not be motivated by a desire to understand or to grasp things as they are. Nor is it obvious that creativity or originality, even in cases of this sort, would necessarily make no contribution to their possessor's personal intellectual worth. This suggests, contra (2) above, that personal intellectual worth does not necessarily involve a positive orientation toward epistemic goods like truth, knowledge, and understanding.

We can begin to address this worry by first identifying and setting aside three types of creativity and originality that are not immediately relevant. First, creativity and originality sometimes take the form of cognitive *skills* or *talents* rather than traits of intellectual character. Thus conceived, creativity and originality, while potentially epistemically and otherwise interesting, have little bearing on their possessor's intellectual goodness or badness qua *person*, and thus are not relevant in the present context.[28] Second, creativity and originality sometimes aim at certain distinctively *aesthetic* ends. A photographer, for instance, might make creative or original use of light or light exposure in order to showcase certain striking or beautiful features of her subject. While characterological "versions" of creativity and originality that flow from a positive orientation toward beauty or other distinctively aesthetic ends may have a favorable bearing on their possessor's personal worth in some sense, they presumably do not have a bearing on their possessor's personal *intellectual* worth. For, as we have seen, it is reasonable to think that a character trait can make a positive contribution to personal intellectual worth only if this trait aims at distinctively *intellectual* or *epistemic* (rather than merely aesthetic or other kinds of) ends.[29] Third, creativity and originality sometimes aim at *themselves*. A poet, for instance, might employ a novel literary device or style simply because it represents a departure from the work of his predecessors (that is, simply because it is creative or original). Here again it is doubtful that the orientation in question would make a positive contribution to the personal intellectual worth of its possessor. This is partly because it is unclear whether creativity and originality per se—or creativity and originality considered in their own right—are genuine *goods*, and thus whether a positive orientation toward them has any relevance at all to personal worth (intellectual or otherwise). But even if they are thus valuable, it remains highly questionable

[28] See Chapter 2 for an explanation of some fundamental differences between intellectual virtues conceived as personal excellences, on the one hand, and intellectual skills and talents, on the other.

[29] The traits in question may have a bearing on their possessor's personal *aesthetic* worth. For more on the relation between different domains of value and corresponding groups of virtues, see the Appendix.

whether the motivation to be creative for creativity's sake or original for originality's sake might make a positive contribution to personal *intellectual* worth, that is, whether it might make its possessor an intellectually (versus, say, an aesthetically) good or better person.

We should, then, attempt to focus our attention on creativity and originality understood in other ways. Again, the question is whether there are *characterological* instances of these traits that aim at distinctively intellectual or epistemic goods that nonetheless are *distinct* from truth or related cognitive ends. When the question is framed in this way, however, it is far from clear whether an affirmative answer is appropriate. That is, it is far from obvious which epistemic or intellectual goods a characterological instance of originality or creativity might aim at *other* than knowledge, truth, understanding, or the like. Of course, an answer to this question may depend on what exactly counts as an "epistemic" or "intellectual" good. But this is an extremely difficult issue, and one that I cannot take up within the limits of this chapter. Therefore, instead of pursuing the matter further here, I will simply conclude that *if* there are any epistemic or intellectual values of the relevant sort, and *if* a "love" of or positive psychological orientation toward these values would seem to contribute to their possessor's personal intellectual worth, then we must expand or elaborate on our conception of the basis of such worth so as to accommodate them.

Finally, here too it is important to note that creativity and originality clearly are capable of making a positive contribution to personal intellectual worth (and thus of counting as intellectual virtues on the present model). Consider again what these traits might amount to in the psychology of an ideal cognitive agent. Presumably such a person would be motivated (in appropriate contexts) to think or reason in original and creative ways, and to do so "out of" something like a desire for knowledge and understanding. This person might see creative and original ways of thinking as an important means to the achievement of his epistemic goals. In this way, his creativity and originality might be an expression of his deeper commitment to epistemic goods, and thus might make him an intellectually good or better person in the relevant sense.

6.3.3 *Intellectual conscientiousness*

Let us turn now to consider a rather different intellectual trait: namely, intellectual or epistemic *conscientiousness*. By contrast with the discussion of creativity and originality above, an examination of epistemic conscientiousness will require a definite elaboration or "thickening" of our initial way of thinking about the basis of personal intellectual worth and thus of intellectual virtue.

Roberts and Wood (2007) offer the following apt description of this virtue:

> We have intellectual duties—to examine some of our beliefs, to question our motives in arguing for one position or another, to collect evidence for our beliefs, to deepen our understanding of important things when we have opportunity, and so forth. We are not in all circumstances obligated to act on all of these duties; but obligations do arise in contexts, and it is part of practical wisdom as it applies to the intellectual life to discern our duties as they become applicable...
>
> At our best, we are motivated "directly" by the intellectual goods, and by other goods connected with them, to do what it takes to acquire, maintain, communicate, and apply the intellectual goods...Sometimes, however, this more direct, and more directly virtuous, kind of motivation fails us. In a circumstance where the transparent love of knowledge would, ideally, impel us to check the data one more time, we just don't feel like checking the data one more time. Or we just don't feel like adding that extra scruple about our argument that we know is needed, or reading one more book before we finalize a paper to send off to a journal. Perhaps we're impatient, or tired, or beginning to get bored with a project. At this point, where the mature, spontaneous attraction to the intellectual goods fails or partially fails us, we may still be virtuously motivated to do what we ought to do, if we have a sense of intellectual duty—a sense of "ought" about intellectual actions. Intellectual conscientiousness is the susceptibility to be motivated by the consideration that behaving well epistemically is *required* of us, is what we *ought* to do, is our *duty*. (78–9)

I see no reason to doubt that the sort of motivational structure described by Roberts and Wood might contribute to its possessor's personal intellectual worth.[30] And yet, the motivating factor in this case is decidedly *not* a desire. Nor is the relevant epistemic end or goal that of truth or knowledge; rather, it is epistemic *duty* or *obligation*.

Intellectual conscientiousness illustrates the need to broaden our conception of both of the main elements of (BPW) and thus of the potential psychological basis of intellectual virtue. It indicates, first, that the positive orientation central to personal intellectual worth is not necessarily desiderative in nature. It shows that it can also take a purely *volitional* form. Again, one can be an intellectually good or better person—and thus intellectually virtuous—on account of having a kind of *respect* for the epistemic good. Second, epistemic

[30] There may be a limit to how *much* this trait can contribute to personal intellectual worth given that, as Roberts and Wood themselves suggest, it apparently involves a kind of "second-best" motivation.

conscientiousness illustrates the point that the goods a "love" of which contribute to personal intellectual worth are not limited to instances of "cognitive contact with reality." It shows that these goods can include one's intellectual or epistemic duties or obligations. Again, a person can be intellectually virtuous in the relevant sense on account of being appropriately sensitive or responsive to these duties or obligations.[31]

Given the present concern with intellectual duties, it is also worth briefly considering the closely related notion of intellectual *rights*. Presumably such rights exist. We have a "right to know" various things about, for instance, our own health or about the actions of our government. Might such rights, then, be a further value a desire or respect for which contributes to personal intellectual worth and thus to intellectual virtue? This seems to me a genuine possibility. Consider, for instance, a war correspondent who consistently puts himself in harm's way in order to provide an accurate account of the latest battle, and who does so out of a conviction that his readers have a "right to know" about the events in question. Similarly, imagine a newspaper editor who agrees, out of a similar motivation, to run a story which is bound to offend the paper's publisher and thus to jeopardize her own employment. I see no reason, in either of these cases, to deny that the person's respect for others' intellectual rights might contribute to his or her personal intellectual worth. Accordingly, we must also include intellectual rights among the sorts of things a "love" of which can contribute to intellectual virtue understood in terms of personal intellectual worth.[32]

6.3.4 *Intellectual generosity*

My earlier characterization of intellectual virtue might also leave the impression that intellectual virtues are fundamentally *egoistic*, that is, that an intellectually virtuous person is necessarily concerned with reaching the truth, acquiring knowledge, and so on, for *himself*. However, as some of the examples just discussed suggest, this too is an overly narrow way of thinking about the basis of intellectual virtue. The case of intellectual generosity illustrates this point nicely.[33]

[31] For a useful discussion of conscientiousness as it relates to moral virtue, see Wallace (1978: ch. 4). Much of what Wallace says there can be applied to intellectual virtue and intellectual conscientiousness.

[32] This is not to say that the rights or duties in question are *irrelevant* to epistemic goods like truth or knowledge. Indeed, they are, after all, *epistemic* rights and duties, or rights and duties pertaining to the goods in question.

[33] See Roberts and Wood (2007: ch. 11) for an illuminating discussion of this trait.

An intellectually generous person is (roughly) one who gives freely of her epistemic capacities or resources in order to benefit the epistemic situation of another. Thus intellectual generosity, like other forms of generosity, is inherently *others*-regarding; it is non-egoistic. Moreover, intellectual generosity is less likely to aim at respecting others' intellectual *rights* than it is at furthering their acquisition of particular epistemic *goods* or at their epistemic or cognitive well-being as a whole. It is entirely reasonable to think, for instance, that a teacher or dissertation supervisor who spends considerable time and effort to help improve her students' paper-writing skills, or who regularly serves as a sounding board for their incipient intellectual contributions, might be an intellectually better person or intellectually better qua person on account of this. Her orientation would not, at any rate, be an exclusively moral one. For again, her concern is distinctively epistemic or intellectual in nature: she is concerned with promoting her students' share in the epistemic goods. Accordingly, it is important that we not conceive of intellectual virtues as necessarily directed at their possessor's own epistemic well-being. They can also be directed at the epistemic flourishing of others.[34]

6.3.5 *Conclusion*

The discussion in section 6.3 has been aimed at elaborating on and underscoring the plausibility of the model of intellectual virtue developed in section 6.2. We have seen, first, that the psychological orientation that I argued is central to personal intellectual worth and thus to intellectual virtue, while typically desiderative, can also be volitional in character. Second, we have seen that this orientation need not aim at one's own acquisition of truth, knowledge, or similar epistemic goods. It can also aim at ends like intellectual duties, intellectual rights, or others' epistemic well-being. The resulting characterization of the psychological basis of intellectual virtue is not intended to be exhaustive or complete.[35] But it does, I hope, provide a reasonably rich and plausible initial account of what makes something an intellectual character virtue.

[34] See Kawall (2002) and the Appendix for more on the others-regarding dimension of intellectual virtues.

[35] For instance, I consider it an open question whether there might be other epistemic ends a "love" of which contributes to personal intellectual worth and thus to intellectual virtue. Some candidates that I have not considered here include certainty, rational coherence, "seeing for oneself" or acquaintance, and intellectual friendship.

Chapter 7

THE PERSONAL WORTH CONCEPTION AND ITS RIVALS

In the previous chapter, I sketched what I called a "personal worth conception" of intellectual virtue, according to which an intellectual virtue is a trait that contributes to its possessor's "personal intellectual worth," or that makes its possessor an intellectually good or better person. In the present chapter, I want to situate this account relative to a number of other treatments of intellectual and moral virtue in the literature. My reason for giving an extended hearing to accounts of *moral* virtue is twofold: first, accounts of the nature and structure of intellectual virtue are relatively few and far between;[1] and second, several extant accounts of moral virtue are such that a structurally isomorphic account of intellectual virtue can easily be extrapolated from them.

I begin with a discussion of two accounts of moral virtue that bear a strong resemblance to my own account of intellectual virtue: namely, those of Thomas Hurka (2001) and Robert Adams (2006). I then proceed to contrast my account with three others: namely, Julia Driver's (2001) consequentialist account of intellectual virtue, Rosalind Hursthouse's (1999) naturalistic account of moral virtue, and Linda Zagzebski's (1996) motivational account of intellectual virtue. My aim, however, is not merely to situate my own account relative to these others. I also hope to show that a personal worth account has certain comparative *advantages*. Thus I also develop several objections to these other accounts—objections to which a personal worth conception is immune. In this regard, the present chapter also amounts to an extended (albeit mostly negative) defense of the personal worth account sketched in Chapter 6.

[1] Two accounts to which I will not give an extended hearing here are Montmarquet (2000) and Wright (2009). While worthwhile discussions, the accounts of intellectual virtue they offer are either not as comprehensive as or insufficiently distinct from the accounts considered below.

7.1 *Similar conceptions*

7.1.1 *Hurka's "recursive" conception*

In *Virtue, Vice, and Value* (2001), Hurka develops an account of moral virtue that can be interpreted as incorporating an account of intellectual virtue. The account begins with the stipulation of a set of baseline intrinsic goods, which include things like pleasure, achievement, and knowledge. It then identifies a moral virtue with an instance of "loving" one or more of these goods for their own sake (11–23).[2]

On Hurka's view, to "love" something is to be "positively oriented" toward it "in one's desires, actions, or feelings." This orientation admits of three main forms: "One can love *x* by desiring or wishing for it when it does not obtain, by actively pursuing it to make it obtain, or by taking pleasure in it when it does obtain" (13). As this suggests, a virtue, for Hurka, amounts to an occurrent desire, action, or feeling that is positively oriented toward one or more intrinsic goods like pleasure, achievement, or knowledge. Desiring another person's pleasure, for instance, is a virtue, as is an active pursuit of a worthy achievement, or an experience of pleasure at having mastered a body of knowledge.

Also central to Hurka's account is the idea that moral virtues are *intrinsically* valuable. This may seem odd given that, on his view, virtues are in some sense parasitic on *other* values (namely, the baseline values at which they are aimed). However, Hurka argues that it is intrinsically good to "love" (for its own sake) that which itself is intrinsically good (13–17). This permits him to draw the conclusion that virtues are intrinsically valuable. It also gives his account a "recursive" character, for he proceeds to claim that it is a moral virtue to "love" the "loving" of an intrinsic good, to "love" the "loving" of the "loving" of an intrinsic good, and so on (20–1).

While Hurka gives no indication that he takes his account of moral virtue to incorporate an account of intellectual virtue, his inclusion of knowledge among the set of relevant baseline intrinsic goods suggests a rationale for doing so. In short, Hurka might say that an intellectual virtue is an instance of "loving" knowledge or related epistemic goods, where this includes desiring, pursuing, or enjoying the goods in question.

[2] I am omitting certain details of Hurka's account, including the role it gives to "hating" baseline evils. These details are not essential to the present discussion.

An account of this sort bears an obvious similarity to the personal worth conception of intellectual virtue sketched in the previous chapter, for the latter says that the basis of personal worth is something like a "love" of epistemic goods or values (including knowledge). Yet there are also some important differences between a personal worth account and the Hurka-inspired one just noted. One difference is that the latter makes no appeal to the notion of a good or excellent *person*. At times, Hurka suggests that virtues improve the *lives* of their possessors, but this is not equivalent to my claim about persons; nor, at any rate, is it part of the conceptual basis of Hurka's account.

This leads to a second and subtler difference, a consideration of which will underscore a requirement on any plausible account of intellectual virtue. On my account, the concept of personal intellectual worth plays an important *constraining* role. To see the importance of such a role, note that not just any desire for truth, nor just any trait rooted in such a desire, is intellectually virtuous or excellent. For a desire for truth might go unharnessed or unchecked in various ways, such that it gives rise to certain intellectual *defects*. It might, for instance, lead to a kind of intellectual fanaticism that overrides other people's intellectual rights or well-being; or it might lead to a kind of vicious dogmatism or narrow-mindedness.[3] The upshot is that an account of intellectual virtue that gives a central role to a desire for or "love" of truth must lay down some constraints as to what sorts of variations on such a state can contribute to intellectual virtue.

On my own account, this is done via an appeal to the concept of personal worth. For again, I maintain that if a person's positive orientation toward truth or related ends fails to contribute to her personal intellectual worth, then it fails to make her intellectual virtuous. But what, if anything, plays a similar role on Hurka's account? While Hurka does not, to my knowledge, address this question, it is plausible to think that he might respond by appealing once more to the notion of intrinsic value. He might say, for instance, that an instance of "loving" the truth is an intellectual virtue only if it is intrinsically valuable; and since fanatical or dogmatic varieties of loving the truth, say, intuitively are *not* intrinsically valuable, they fail to count as intellectual virtues. This illustrates how the notion of intrinsic value might, on Hurka's view, occupy the kind of constraining role which on my view is occupied by the notion of personal

[3] See Montmarquet (1993) or (2000) for a development of this point. Of course, a desire for truth might go awry in other ways as well, for instance, morally. Our present concern, however, is with the dimensions of intellectual virtue.

intellectual worth. It also underscores a further fundamental difference between the two accounts.

A third difference lies with Hurka's rejection of the venerable thesis that virtues are *character* traits, or (reasonably) stable dispositions to act, feel, think, and so forth in various ways. For Hurka, virtues are not character traits. Rather, they are *occurrent* psychological states or episodes; more specifically, they are discrete *instances* of "loving" intrinsic goods. As indicated in several of the previous chapters, I prefer the traditional view that virtues are character traits, and therefore differ with Hurka on this point.

In the remainder of this section, I want to say something about the plausibility of my personal worth account of intellectual virtue as compared with the Hurka-inspired account just sketched. The main point I wish to focus on is the idea that virtues are occurrent psychological states rather than stable dispositions or character traits. Hurka's argument for this claim (42–4) is not easy to pin down. However, it apparently begins with the idea that a stable disposition to instantiate the desires, actions, or feelings of a given virtue V is required for the possession of V only if this disposition contributes substantially to the overall *value* of V. In other words, the virtue of open-mindedness, say, necessarily involves a stable disposition to instantiate the desires, actions, or feelings characteristic of open-mindedness only if the overall value of open-mindedness substantially depends on its being a disposition of the sort in question. Second, Hurka suggests that for one of the relevant dispositions D to make a substantial contribution to the overall value of the corresponding virtue V, D must make a substantial contribution to the value of the individual *desires, actions*, or *feelings* to which D gives rise. Thus his view is apparently that a stable disposition to engage in open-minded thinking is essential to the possession of the virtue of open-mindedness only if the possession of such a disposition substantially contributes to the overall value of open-mindedness; and that it makes a contribution of this sort only if the thinking to which it gives rise is substantially more valuable on account of its having arisen in this way. Put in even simpler terms, the idea is that a stable disposition to engage in open-minded thinking is essential to the possession of open-mindedness only if open-minded thinking is more valuable on account of having its source in a stable disposition. Third, Hurka maintains that dispositions of the relevant sort systematically fail to contribute to the value of the corresponding desires, actions, and feelings. He concludes that virtues are not essentially stable dispositions.

In support of the third premise of his argument, Hurka invites the reader to consider two moral agents A and B, both of whom perform an act of kindness. Person A's act arises from a stable disposition, while person B's does not. In response Hurka asks: "Apart from the values in any associated actions and in his disposition itself, is A's action morally preferable? I see no reason to believe this... A's kind action may be accompanied by more valuable actions at other times in his life and by a more valuable disposition now, but I do not see that it is any better in itself" (43). For present purposes, I shall grant this point and the corresponding premise of Hurka's argument.

The problem with this argument, as I see it, lies with its first and second premises. Consider, first, the idea that a stable disposition to exhibit various virtue-relevant qualities is essential to the possession of the corresponding virtue only if such a disposition makes a substantial contribution to the overall value of the virtue in question. Why should this be the case? Why not think that to be genuinely courageous, say, one must have a stable disposition to engage in courageous actions, even if courage on the whole is not itself better or more valuable on account of involving such a disposition? Hurka's reasoning seems to be that because a virtue is, by definition, a *good* or *excellent* state, any essential feature of a virtue must also be good or excellent. This is evident from the following remark: "The concept of a virtue is essentially that of a kind of desirable state. If what is most desirable in the relevant area required stable dispositions, it would make sense to define virtue in terms of dispositions. But if this is not so, virtue should mainly be found in occurrent attitudes" (44). But why should we accept the main premise here? Why think that just because a virtue is an excellence, anything that figures into its identity conditions must also be excellent?[4] A virtue is, after all, a certain *kind* of excellence. And I see no reason to doubt that part of what makes a virtue the kind of excellence it is might itself be something that is not excellent.[5]

The second premise of Hurka's initial argument is also questionable. Again, this premise says that a disposition to manifest virtue-relevant actions, feelings, and desires is essential to the possession of the corresponding virtue only if this disposition adds substantially to the value of the individual actions, feelings, and desires to which it gives rise. The underlying idea here seems to be that the value of a virtue lies primarily with the value of the individual actions, feelings,

[4] I am treating, fairly I think, Hurka's usage of "desirable" as interchangeable with "good" or "excellent."

[5] Compare, for instance, cognitive *skills* and *faculties*, both of which are cognitive excellences of a certain sort. Here, one of the main things that differentiates the two sorts of excellences is something non-normative: namely, that skills are acquired and faculties are innate. Similarly, even Hurka would agree that for a given quality to be a virtue, it must be a property of a *person*. But again, the fact that something is a property of a person is not itself an excellence—after all, intellectual *vices* are properties of persons as well.

and desires that are characteristic of it (and, more specifically, with the value of these things considered apart from whatever sort of disposition may have generated them). But this is an implausible assumption.

To see why, note that on one venerable and intuitively plausible way of thinking about virtues, to know that someone possesses a virtue is to know something about the person *himself*. It is to know something about who this person is—about the kind of person he is. It is also to know something *positive* about this person: for instance, that he is a good person or that, qua person or human being, he is good or excellent in a certain respect.[6] The problem with Hurka's second premise lies with the fact that an agent can manifest virtue-relevant actions, feelings, desires, and the like, while still failing to be a good or excellent agent, person, or human being. A generally rotten person can, on a good day or in a fleeting moment of moral or intellectual inspiration, take pleasure in what is good or perform a virtue-relevant action. While the fact that such feelings or actions do not arise from a stable disposition to manifest such things may not (à la Hurka's third premise) affect our judgment of these feelings or actions themselves, surely it will and ought to affect our judgment of the *agent*.[7] Thus the value of a virtue is not primarily derivative from the value of the actions, feelings, and desires that are characteristic of it. Virtues have a kind or dimension of value that is not guaranteed or implied by a positive evaluation of these other elements of virtue.

Finally, it is important to be clear about how radical Hurka's position is. For Hurka, a virtue is *identical* to an occurrent desire, action, feeling, or the like. There is nothing more to the "possession" of a virtue than the instantiation of the relevant psychological state or episode. It matters not from whence (or whom) this state or episode has arisen.[8] To many, the claim that a virtue can

[6] I am not intending to appeal to the content of my own theory of virtue here. Rather, I take it that the point in question is independently plausible. One can accept that virtues reveal something positive about their possessor qua person or human being without maintaining (as I do) that this is an *essential* or *defining* feature of a virtue.

[7] This is not to say that we will judge the agent *un*favorably, but rather that our positive assessment of this person's actions or feelings will not carry over to our assessment of the person *herself*. Note, further, that a good person can occasionally perform an action (e.g. tell a lie) or experience a feeling (e.g. envy) characteristic of *vice* without these occurrences warranting a negative assessment of the person herself. This suggests the further point that moral vices cannot be identified with the occurrence of the relevant (characteristically vicious) psychological states or episodes.

[8] Indeed, as indicated by the scare quotes in the previous sentence, there is something odd, given Hurka's account, about the idea of "possessing" a virtue. We do not "possess" actions, episodes of pleasure, or the like. We do, however, "possess" dispositions.

be an experience of pleasure or that a virtue can *be* an action is bound to sound like a category mistake. To be sure, if we accept Hurka's claim that virtue just is a matter of "loving" intrinsic goods, and if we think of "loving" in strictly episodic terms, this conclusion follows naturally. Barring such theoretical commitments, however, it would seem far more plausible to reject either of the forementioned claims about the nature of a virtue than it would to embrace the idea that a virtue just *is* an action, feeling, or other occurrent psychological state.

7.1.2 *Adams and "excellence in being for the good"*

Robert Adams (2006) has recently defended a theory of moral virtue similar to Hurka's that can also be interpreted as incorporating an account of intellectual virtue. The conceptual starting point of his theory is what he refers to as "capital *V* Virtue" or virtue "in a sense in which it normally has no plural and does not take an indefinite article." It is the "holistic property of having a good moral character" (32). I shall refer to this as "holistic" or "comprehensive" virtue. On Adams's view, holistic virtue is a matter of "persisting excellence in being for the good."

There are three parts to this definition. The first and most central is the idea that holistic virtue involves a certain positive psychological orientation toward the good. It is fundamentally a matter of being *for* the good, which can involve "loving it, liking it, respecting it, wanting it, wishing for it, appreciating it, thinking highly of it, speaking in favor of it," and the like (16). The second critical part of the definition is based on Adams's observation that being for the good is no guarantee of virtue. For "[o]ne can seek goods selfishly, only for oneself; or unjustly, only for one's friends, without regard for the rights of strangers; or intemperately, losing track of one's own most central aims and values; or in ways that cheapen human life, preferring goods that are easy or obvious and neglecting others that are more deeply meaningful." Accordingly, Adams says that holistic or comprehensive virtue is a matter of *excellence* in being for the good: it is a way of being for the good that is "worth prizing for its own sake" or "worthy to be honored, loved, admired, or (in the extreme case) worshiped, for its own sake" (24). Third, Adams maintains that momentary, fleeting, merely occurrent excellence in being for the good is not sufficient for holistic virtue. Thus, contra Hurka, Adams regards holistic virtue as a stable and persisting state of personal character.

But what, on Adams's view, is required for the possession of *individual* virtues? One might expect Adams to say that individual virtues are particular instances of or variations on "persisting excellence in being for the good." But this is not the position he takes. Adams allows that a trait can be a virtue even if it does not involve being for the good at all.[9] In support of this claim, he appeals to "structural virtues" like courage and self-control, contending that a person can be courageous and self-controlled—and that her courage and self-control can be *virtues*—even if they are aimed at or employed in the service of *evil* ends (think, for example, of a courageous or self-controlled villain or terrorist). With regard to such cases, Adams says that while the person in question possesses a genuine virtue, she lacks holistic or "capital *V* Virtue" (32–5).

On what basis, then, does Adams allow that traits of the relevant sort are virtues? He claims that they are virtues because they are capable of *figuring into* holistic or comprehensive virtue (35). Here I take Adams to mean that traits like courage and self-control can, as it were, "perfect" or facilitate a person's positive orientation toward or "being for" the good. A generous and compassionate person who is also courageous, for instance, will be more effectively or excellently "for the good" than one who is generous, compassionate, and cowardly. Thus, for Adams, traits like courage, self-control, and patience are virtues, not on account of involving any good or admirable motivation, but rather because of the role they are capable of playing within holistic or "capital *V* Virtue."

Given that states like truth and knowledge should be understood as partly constitutive of "the good," it is not difficult to see how a conception of intellectual virtue might be extrapolated from Adams's account of moral virtue. It might be said, for instance, that "holistic" or "comprehensive" intellectual virtue is a matter of persisting excellence in being for the intellectual or epistemic good.[10] And it might be maintained that a character trait is an individual intellectual virtue just in case it can facilitate "being for" the intellectual good.

Such an account would, in many ways, be very similar to my own. The notion of "being for the intellectual good," for instance, is roughly equivalent to the sort of positive orientation toward epistemic goods that I have argued is the basis of personal intellectual worth and thus of intellectual virtue. Similarly, the Adams-inspired account of intellectual virtue might give a role to the concept of "excellence" similar to the role that the concept of personal intellectual worth occupies on my account. The former concept could, for instance, do the kind of constraining work discussed above. Specifically, the account might

[9] His discussion of this and related points comes in chapters 2 and 10.

[10] Adams makes some remarks along these lines on p. 20.

stipulate that a fanatical or unbridled passion for truth is uncharacteristic of genuine intellectual virtue on the grounds that it is less than excellent, that it does not warrant being "honored, loved, admired" for its own sake. A final similarity is that both accounts portray intellectual virtues as stable dispositions or character traits.

These similarities notwithstanding, there are also some important dissimilarities between the Adams-inspired account and a personal worth account. First, as just indicated, Adams makes no immediate appeal to the notion of personal worth.[11] He says that the kind of excellence with which he is concerned—the kind essential to comprehensive virtue—is non-instrumental or (at least broadly) intrinsic (24–5). Beyond this, however, he does not, to my knowledge, do much to elaborate on the general character of such excellence. Second, and more importantly, Adams and I disagree about whether an individual trait can be a virtue if it fails to involve a "love" of or "being for" the good. As already noted, Adams thinks this is a genuine possibility.[12] On my account, however, an intellectual virtue just is a trait that contributes to personal intellectual worth on account of its involving something like a "love" or positive orientation toward the epistemic good.

I shall pursue the latter difference in a little more detail, for it seems to me that Adams's position, whether applied to intellectual or moral virtue, is not sufficiently motivated. While I shall focus mainly on moral virtue, it should be obvious how a closely analogous line of argument could be developed in connection with intellectual virtue.

As indicated in the discussion of Hurka above, it is plausible to think that if a person possesses a genuine moral character virtue, then he will *himself* be morally virtuous at least to some extent. Let us, then, consider Adams's claim that the courage of a villain, say, is a genuine moral virtue. Does it make sense to think that such a person would himself be morally virtuous on account of his courage? I think this is doubtful. For the moment, however, let us assume this is possible. A further, less straightforward question is whether it makes sense to think that the villain might be morally virtuous on account of a function that

[11] At times this appears deliberate. On p. 26, for instance, Adams registers a concern about identifying moral virtue with "being a good person." His concern, however, is apparently with a kind of exclusivism which I explicitly repudiate in Chapter 6. Elsewhere, however, Adams seems to endorse a connection between moral virtue and personal worth. He remarks: "Courage will not make one virtuous, or *a morally good person*, unless . . . " (34; my italics); and "it seems to me that even if [competitiveness] is typically beneficial to society, it is not a virtue, not the sort of trait that *makes one a morally good person*" (56; my italics).

[12] See also Roberts (1984) for a defense of this possibility.

his courage is capable of playing under conditions very different from those in which he finds himself. Put another way, the question is whether a person with a particular virtue might *himself* be morally virtuous on account of a function this virtue is capable of playing in some *other* possible world or in the psychology of some *other* agent (namely, in a world in which the agent in question is for the good or in the psychology of some other agent who is for the good). Suppose, for instance, that we were to ask of a particular courageous villain: Why is he virtuous? Why do we have some admiration for this otherwise dubious character? I take it that it would not be very plausible to respond by saying, "We admire this character because he has a trait which, if put in the service of the good, *would* enhance a person's overall orientation toward the good." Rather, to the extent that it is plausible to regard the courageous villain as virtuous or admirable at all, this is so, I would suggest, on account of the way in which courage is manifested in *him* or in *his* actions, attitudes, and the like (again, not on account of how it would be manifested, or the role it would play, within a psychological orientation that the villain himself lacks).[13]

Adams's conception of virtue cannot make proper sense of these plausible judgments. For again, on his view, courage is a virtue because it is capable of facilitating or enhancing a positive orientation toward or "being for" the good. Thus, the courageous villain has a virtue, or is virtuous, on Adams's view, because of the role his courage is capable of playing in a rather different—and indeed contrary—orientation toward the good.

Another apparent problem with Adams's claim that a character trait can count as a genuine moral virtue in the absence of an underlying good motivation is rooted in the plausible idea that if a trait of character T is a genuine moral virtue, then T is a quality that a maximally *wicked* agent need not possess.[14] This is, it seems, a very minimal and intuitively plausible requirement. Its corollary is that if T is a genuine moral virtue, then it is at least *possible* that a maximally wicked agent will fail to possess T. The problem is that a maximally wicked

[13] To the extent that such a person would be virtuous (and I will not attempt to rule out this possibility), this may seem to pose a problem for my own account of virtue (since the person is not positively oriented toward the good). My response is that while a courageous villain may have an excellence or virtue of sorts (even a virtue in a more or less "internalist" sense), he is not virtuous in a *personal worth* sense. The latter point becomes evident when we take seriously the character and moral status of his criminal motives and actions. I elaborate on this point in Chapter 9.

[14] Perhaps the stronger claim that if T is a genuine moral virtue, then T is a quality which a maximally wicked agent *cannot* possess is plausible as well. If so, then the conclusion of the present claim is even easier to substantiate.

agent apparently *would* possess traits like courage, patience, self-control, carefulness, and the like. Surely a diabolical character with these traits would be even more diabolical or wicked than one who is impatient, cowardly, lacking in self-control, and so forth. It follows, contra Adams, that courage, patience, self-control, and the like, when possessed in the absence of an underlying good motivation, are not genuine moral virtues.[15]

One additional and closely related argument merits consideration. Again, Adams thinks that a character trait T is a moral virtue if T is capable of facilitating or enhancing a positive orientation toward or "being for" the good.[16] Assuming, as Adams appears to, that moral *vice* is paradigmatically a matter of *opposing* or of being *against* the good (36–44), it seems, by parity of reasoning, that he should also endorse the following principle: a character trait T is a moral vice if T is capable of facilitating or enhancing a negative orientation toward or "being against" the good. But surely an agent with wicked or diabolical intentions would be well-served in his opposition to the good by traits like courage, self-control, carefulness, and patience. Therefore, Adams's view apparently generates the implausible result that the traits in question are also moral *vices*, and indeed, that they are no less vices than they are virtues.

By way of conclusion, it seems that Adams would do well to make it a requirement for the possession of an individual virtue—not merely for the possession of holistic or comprehensive virtue—that the person in question actually be "for the good." While this would require denying that courageous villains and the like are virtuous, we have seen that in fact there is much to be said in favor of this implication. Furthermore, note that this would not require one to hold that the ill-motivated characters in question are less than *courageous* (or careful or patient or self-controlled, etc.). Instead, it would entail merely that courage, carefulness, patience, and related traits are not always genuine virtues, that is, that there can be virtuous and non-virtuous "versions" or instances of these traits.[17]

[15] I recognize that a defender of Adams's account of virtue is unlikely to feel the force of the initial premise of this objection. She might, that is, deny that there is anything problematic in the suggestion that a maximally wicked agent might (and perhaps *must*) possess certain genuine moral virtues. My suggestion, however, is that there is something substantially prima facie counterintuitive about this denial.

[16] This is a sufficient, but not a necessary, condition, given Adams's view of "motivational" (vs. "structural") virtues noted above.

[17] For more on this point, see the account of intellectual courage developed in Chapter 9.

7.2 *Dissimilar conceptions*

7.2.1 *Driver's consequentialist account*

In *Uneasy Virtue* (2001), Julia Driver defends a consequentialist account of moral virtue from which she proceeds, there and in other work, to derive an isomorphic account of intellectual virtue.[18] She identifies the basis of intellectual virtue as follows: "A character trait is an intellectual virtue iff it systematically (reliably) produces true belief." By "systematically" she means that the trait tends to produce more true beliefs than not within the world or context in which it is possessed (2000: 126; cf. 2001: 82). As this brief description suggests, Driver's account is "consequentialist" because it says that a trait's status as an intellectual virtue depends strictly on its epistemic consequences or outputs.

There are some major and fairly obvious differences between Driver's account of intellectual virtue and my own personal worth account. First, not only does her account make no appeal to the notion of personal worth, it also (unlike the accounts of Hurka and Adams) makes no essential appeal to anything like a desire for truth or knowledge. Indeed, for Driver, any psychological or "internal" property is relevant to intellectual virtue only insofar as it contributes to its possessor's epistemic reliability. Thus while something like a desire for truth might be among the most reliable ways of reaching the truth for creatures like us in worlds like ours, nothing about the intrinsic or intentional character of this desire makes it relevant to intellectual virtue. Again, what matters in this regard is strictly the *causal* relation between the relevant desire and the goal of true belief.

A second and related difference is that epistemic reliability is not an essential feature of intellectual virtue on my account. As indicated briefly in Chapter 6, this is due primarily to the fact that reliability is largely a matter of luck. Whether a person is successful at reaching the truth often depends, not just on her own motivation or "best efforts," but also on factors that are largely, if not entirely, outside of her control—for example, the relative epistemic friendliness or hostility of her environment, the cooperation of other epistemic agents, and so on. The basis of personal worth, however, is not susceptible to luck of this sort.[19]

[18] While the accounts are structurally parallel, she maintains a significant distinction between moral and intellectual virtue. See her (2000) and (2003).

[19] This is consistent, however, with its being susceptible to other kinds of luck—for instance, "constitutive" luck as discussed by Nagel (1979), Williams (1981), and many others.

To see why, imagine a victim of an epistemically malevolent Cartesian demon. This person has a genuine and abiding desire for knowledge and understanding about important subject matters. He is intellectually careful, fair, honest, and thorough in his inquiries. He listens well to others. He is sensitive to and responds appropriately to counterevidence. And his disposition to function in these ways is appropriately rooted in his desire for truth. Nevertheless, owing to the manipulations of the demon, he is plagued by a systematic gap between appearance and reality, such that, despite his excellent motivation, best efforts, and the like, and despite what seems to him and everyone else to be his extraordinary cognitive success, he is in fact extremely cognitively unsuccessful. Relatively few of the beliefs that emerge from his inquires are true. While there may, as I will get to momentarily, be a sense of "intellectual virtue" in which the person fails to count as intellectually virtuous, surely his epistemic predicament does not count against his personal intellectual worth. Surely he is not an intellectually worse person on account of his failure to reach the truth—a failure which again is entirely beyond his control and ken. Indeed, given that he has no way of knowing about the systematic gap between appearance and reality, it seems clear that he is an intellectually *good* person, despite his lack of epistemic success.[20]

As these remarks may suggest, I do not regard Driver's account of intellectual virtue as being in competition with my own. Rather, I think we are attempting to shed light on two distinct concepts of intellectual virtue or two different ways in which a trait might qualify as an intellectual virtue. I am prepared to grant, for instance, that epistemic reliability of the sort that interests Driver is both necessary and sufficient for a certain kind or type of intellectual virtue.[21] For surely such reliability is an intellectual *excellence*; and given that a virtue is essentially an excellence, there is little reason to deny that Driver has identified a certain type of intellectual virtue.

At the same time, however, reliability is neither necessary nor sufficient for an intellectual virtue understood on a personal worth model. That it is not necessary is evident from cases like the one just considered. But neither is it sufficient. To see why, consider once again a person who persistently acts in ways that we consider to be intellectually virtuous, but whose motivation for doing so is rooted entirely in a desire for money, fame, or some other

[20] For more on this and related issues, see Greco (1995) and my (2007).

[21] This is (roughly) how authors like John Greco (2000a; 2010) and Ernest Sosa (2007) think about intellectual virtues. Consequently, they tend to count reliable cognitive *faculties* like vision, memory, and introspection as intellectual virtues.

questionable end. This person might have intellectual character traits that are reliable in the world in question, but he would not, insofar as he is motivated strictly by money, fame, or the like, be an intellectually good or better person in the relevant sense.[22]

The apparent upshot of these considerations is again that Driver's account of intellectual virtue and my own account are aimed at shedding light on two fundamentally different ways of being intellectually virtuous. In Driver's terms, hers is a purely "externalist" account of intellectual virtue, while mine is a purely "internalist" account.

It is not clear, however, that Driver would be content with this irenic analysis. For she apparently has a principled opposition to "internalism" about intellectual virtue, that is, to any view according to which a trait's status as an intellectual virtue "is determined by factors internal to agency, such as a person's motives or intentions" (2001: 68). Driver's "main qualm" with an internalist account of intellectual virtue is that it "dispenses with any connection between the agent and the world. The agent's behavior need have no actual implications for what occurs in the world . . . " (80). To illustrate her worry, she considers the following scenario:

> Suppose that, unbeknownst to us, imaginativeness is conducive more to false belief than to true belief. The imaginative person may aim at truth, but not achieve it (maybe she is distracted by too many possibilities, for example). If it were discovered that such were the case, then I doubt that we would continue to call the trait an intellectual virtue, even though it does involve aiming at the truth. There has to be some real connection to the world, or what is true. (2000: 129)

These remarks are aimed, apparently, at showing that *any* viable account of intellectual virtue must involve some kind of reliability requirement.

I have two main responses to Driver's objection. First, concerning the general idea that an intellectual virtue must have some notable causal connection with truth in the world in which it is possessed, I think the plausibility of this claim depends on how we are thinking about the notion of intellectual virtue to begin with. Again, we have seen (here and in Chapter 6) that there are good reasons for thinking that if a given trait contributes to personal intellectual worth, then it is an intellectual virtue in a legitimate and robust sense. But where intellectual virtue is understood in such terms, the necessity of a connection with the world or with truth is much less clear. For, as we have seen, these

[22] See Chapter 6 for a further development of this point.

things can come apart in such a way that the personal worth of the agent in question is not threatened or undermined. Thus, insofar as we are thinking of intellectual virtues as personal excellences, it is a mistake to think that intellectual virtues *must* have a "connection with the world."

On the other hand, it is important not to overstate the potential gap between intellectual virtue thus conceived and the goal of truth. Worlds in which the psychological qualities constitutive of personal worth tend not to be systematically helpful for reaching the truth are likely to be few and far between (as evidenced by the far-fetched Cartesian demon scenario above). Put another way, it is reasonable to think that the psychological requirements of a plausible personal worth account of intellectual virtue will be such that a person who satisfies these requirements will, under normal circumstances or in worlds like ours, be considerably more likely to form true beliefs as a result.[23] For intuitively, if a person's desire for true belief, say, is especially weak or easily overwhelmed by other desires, then this desire will not contribute much to his personal intellectual worth. Thus it is plausible to think that for a desire of the sort in question to make a contribution to its possessor's personal intellectual worth, it must be reasonably robust, and indeed, robust enough that, given normal circumstances, it is likely to play a notable role in establishing a connection with the "real world."[24]

Second, let us further consider the sort of scenario Driver describes in which a trait that we presently think of as an intellectual virtue is discovered to be unreliable. Driver points out, rightly I think, that upon making this discovery, we would no longer continue to regard the trait or traits in question as intellectual virtues. And again, it is on this basis that she concludes that the possession of an intellectual virtue requires "some real connection to the world." But this conclusion does not follow.

While I cannot stop to develop the point in any detail here, I have argued elsewhere (2007) that the kind of positive orientation toward or "love" of epistemic goods that I am claiming is essential to personal intellectual worth has a certain *cognitive* element or dimension. Specifically, I claim that to possess an intellectual virtue (conceived as a personal excellence), one must (at some level) have a *reasonable belief* to the effect that the activity characteristic of this virtue is a reliable way of achieving one's epistemic goals. This requirement is

[23] For an analogous point regarding moral virtue, see Adams (2006: 48–60).

[24] It does not follow that said reliability is a virtue-*making* feature; for again, even this type of epistemic success is susceptible to luck in a way that personal worth is not. Here again, see Adams (2006: 48–60) for a parallel discussion.

needed in order to secure a kind of practical *rationality* that intuitively is essential to personal intellectual worth.[25] If correct, this requirement provides a way around Driver's objection. For if we were to discover that certain traits we thought were reliable in fact are not, then we could no longer reasonably believe that the activity characteristic of these traits is a reliable means to our epistemic goals, in which case the traits would no longer qualify as intellectual virtues according to the present account. This shows that there is an internalist way of accommodating Driver's scenario, and thus that the scenario does not by itself motivate a reliability requirement on intellectual virtue.

7.2.2 *Hursthouse's naturalism*

In her important book *On Virtue Ethics* (1999), Rosalind Hursthouse defends the view that a "virtue is a character trait a human being needs for *eudaimonia*, to flourish or to live well." She divides this definition into three separate claims: (1) "The virtues benefit their possessor"; (2) "The virtues make their possessor a good human being"; (3) "[These] two features of the virtues are interrelated" (167). My focus here will be on (2), since this is the conceptual heart of her account.

Hursthouse elaborates on the claim that virtues make their possessor good qua human being, saying: "Human beings need the virtues in order to live well, to flourish *as* human beings, to live a characteristically good, *eudaimon*, human life" (167). As this makes clear, Hursthouse's account of virtue is a version of ethical "naturalism," which grounds ethical properties or concepts in an account of human nature. Hursthouse makes the further point that "'ethical naturalism' is usually thought of as not only basing ethics in some way on considerations of human nature, but also as taking human beings to be part of the natural, biological order of living things. Its standard first premise is that what human beings *are* is a species of rational, social animals and thereby a species of living things—which . . . have a particular biological make-up and a natural life cycle" (206).

In what sense, then, are virtues traits that make their possessor good qua human being? According to Hursthouse, the idea is (roughly) that virtues make

25 The belief in question need not be *explicit*; nor must its content be especially detailed or specific. The point is rather that the person in question cannot be *oblivious* to the (apparent) reliability of her virtue-relevant actions. Moreover, the requirement holds only for virtues that have a *positive* and *active* dimension (not for "negative" virtues that consist in dispositions *not* to engage in certain sorts of behavior or for "passive" virtues that are manifested in certain passive "noticings" or feelings). I explore these matters in considerably more detail in my manuscript "The Cognitive Demands of Intellectual Virtue".

their possessor good qua human being by facilitating characteristically human "ways of going on," which include individual and species survival, the experience of pleasure and avoidance of pain, and social organization and functioning (202). She adds that these ways are "rational" in the sense that "we can rightly see [them] as good, as something we have reason to do" (222). As this suggests, Hursthouse's notion of "characteristically human" is neither statistical nor purely descriptive. Rather, she says it is normative and that most human beings fail to do what is "characteristically human" in her sense. The emerging view is that a virtue is a trait of character that contributes to characteristically human ways of going on, which again are rational ways, or ways that can rightly be regarded as good or as something humans have reason to do.[26]

While a great deal more could be said about Hursthouse's account of moral virtue, its central features are as stated. And here again it is not too difficult to see how the account in question might be parlayed into an account of intellectual virtue. For instance, Hursthouse might add *learning* or *inquiry* to the relevant "ways of going on," and she might say that intellectual virtues are traits that allow one to engage in these activities in a "characteristically human" or "rational" way. In other words, she might think of intellectual virtues as character traits that facilitate "characteristically human" or rational modes of learning or inquiry.[27]

An account of this sort has at least one notable similarity with my own. It maintains that an intellectual virtue is a trait that makes its possessor good qua *human being*. Similarly, I claim that an intellectual virtue is a trait that makes its possessor good qua *person*. Yet the difference between our accounts, even on this point, is considerable. For while human beings are persons, my account makes no reference to any of the species-specific or biological considerations which Hursthouse thinks of as critical to her own account and to naturalism in general. Accordingly, my own account, unlike Hursthouse's, would not qualify as a version of naturalism.[28]

[26] For a similar naturalistic account of moral virtue, see Foot (2003).

[27] Hursthouse is less clear than one might like about whether the fact that virtues facilitate the relevant ends means that their exercise partly *constitutes* or is simply a *means* to these ends. Compare her comments on pp. 169, 172, and 173. We need not try to resolve this ambiguity here.

[28] In note 20 on p. 206, Hursthouse registers her preference for the concept of *human being* rather than *person*. Her objection to the latter is that it tends to be "thinly defined." I hope, however, that my elaboration of the notion of personal worth in Chapter 6 is sufficiently informative to overcome this worry.

While I do not wish to rule out the possibility that the relevant naturalistic account of intellectual virtue picks out a genuine type or concept of intellectual virtue, I think it has at least two significant problems. One problem concerns whether the account sheds sufficient light on the actual nature of a virtue. A second and related problem concerns the extent to which the account is genuinely naturalistic. I shall discuss each of these issues in turn.

Recall that on the model in question, a trait is an intellectual virtue just in case it facilitates *rational* intellectual activity or "ways of going on." The notion of rationality is the conceptual basis of this account, and yet it is itself—as Hursthouse herself admits—an explicitly *normative* notion. While Hursthouse does say a fair amount about how "rationality" might be understood, her discussion does not, by my lights, take us substantially beyond her initial explanation, according to which an activity is rational just in case it is rightly regarded as good, or as something that we have reason to do. And the problem, of course, is that to the extent that Hursthouse fails to unpack the concept of rationality, her account will fail to shed substantial light on the actual nature or basis of a virtue. A virtue is an excellence of character, so we should expect any philosophical account of virtue to shed substantial light on its nature or character *as* an excellence. The claim is not that an account of virtue (be it moral or intellectual) cannot reasonably appeal to any other normative concept, but rather that, whatever form the account takes, it must say something substantive and informative about how or why or in virtue of what the traits in question are valuable or excellent. Accordingly, to be sufficiently illuminating, the Hursthouse-inspired account of intellectual virtue must say more about what is or is not involved with something's being "rightly seen as good" or as something we "have reason to do."

A second worry is related to the first. Given the central and critical role that the appeal to rationality plays on Hursthouse's account, and given that she is thinking of rationality in normative terms, a question arises concerning the extent to which this account is genuinely *naturalistic*. As we have seen, carrying on in "characteristically human" ways, for Hursthouse, is not a matter of doing what human beings tend to do. It is rather a matter of carrying on in ways that human beings have *reason to think are good*. When understood in this way, however, to what extent is her account really grounded in or constrained by a conception of human nature? In what sense is it really a version of ethical naturalism?

Hursthouse is aware of this challenge. She gives expression to it and suggests a reply to in the following passage:

> But, it may be objected, if we introduce a normative notion of "a characteristic way of going on", how have we preserved any vestige of naturalism? Well, we have preserved the structure: it is still the case that human beings are ethically good in so far as their ethically relevant aspects foster the four ends appropriate to the social animal [viz. individual survival, species survival, experience of pleasure and avoidance of pain, and social organization and activity], in the ways characteristic of the species. And the structure—the appeal to just those four ends—really does constrain, substantially, what I can reasonably maintain is a virtue in human beings. I cannot just proceed from some premises about what it is reasonable or rational to do to some conclusion that it is rational to act in such-and-such a way, and hence that a good human being is one who acts that way. I have to consider whether the corresponding character trait... would foster or be inimical to those four ends. (224)

Hursthouse's response to the objection seems to be that her account is genuinely naturalistic because what it says about the nature of a virtue is necessarily constrained by the relevant ends or "ways of going on," and specifically, by ends or ways of going on that are "characteristic of the species."

But it is difficult to see how this response is supposed to solve the problem. First, the relevant ends or ways of going on are not themselves specific to the human species (indeed the first two are shared by all living things). And second, what Hursthouse means by "characteristic of the species," again, is not anything like how members of the species *tend* to act, live, or survive. It is more a matter of how they *ought* to act, live, or survive, or ways that can rightly be regarded as *good* or *appropriate* ways to carry on.

To get a better handle on the problem, let us consider an example that Hursthouse herself discusses in an effort to illustrate and support the reply just noted. She attempts to show that her appeal to various aspects of human nature is doing substantial explanatory work by showing how it might generate the claim that something like "impersonal benevolence"—which "knows no species-boundaries," "recognizes no special bonds of family or friendship," and which at least some philosophers seem to regard as a moral virtue—is *not* a genuine virtue (224).[29] The basic idea seems to be that if impersonal benevolence were widespread among the human species, this would be devastating to the social dimensions of human life. The reason is that a person with this trait will be "someone who does not think of 'That's a fellow human being' or 'She's my

[29] Hursthouse identifies Peter Singer (2001) as an advocate of the view that impersonal benevolence is a moral virtue.

child/parent/friend/partner' as [a compelling] reason for seeking another's good." Hursthouse adds:

> [W]e have to think of [a person with this trait] as someone whose emotions, being in harmony with her reason, do not particularly engage with her fellow human beings or her own children or parents, as someone who does not have close emotion-invoking attachments to other individual human beings that would make it difficult for her to act from this putative virtue. (225)

Hursthouse concludes that such a trait might well be inimical to a "characteristically human" way of going on and thus might fail to be a virtue on her view.

But this response seems questionable. While widespread impersonal benevolence might be inimical to standard or typical or familiar "ways of going on" for the human species, this does not settle the question of whether it would be inimical to "characteristically human" ways, which again are necessarily *rational.* It is easy to imagine a defender of impersonal benevolence—someone who, like Peter Singer (2001), thinks pleasure and pain are the central morally relevant factors and sees no grounds for distinguishing between human pain and the pain of other animals—immediately balking at the idea that our present ways of going on are "characteristically human" or "rational" in Hursthouse's sense. Indeed, insofar as this person has reasons in support of his position, and insofar as his position supports the widespread possession of impersonal benevolence, he is likely to regard the relevant social arrangements or practices as *irrational.*

Hursthouse attempts to resist something like this complaint by claiming that widespread impersonal benevolence would not just alter humanity's present "ways of going on" (in particular, the human species's characteristic ways of surviving and the social character of its existence), but in fact would *obliterate* them. Human beings, she seems to think, could not exist as a species, or at least as a social species, if impersonal benevolence were widespread among its members. She comments: "The onus is on those who recommend impersonal benevolence as a virtue to provide at least a speculation about how a species of rational animals who had brought themselves to care naught for their own children or each other's company might still be a species of *social* animals who, moreover, nurtured their young..." (226). But at this stage of her discussion, "impersonal benevolence" appears to be a much more extreme and radical trait than was suggested by her initial description of it: it apparently requires of its possessors that they "care naught for their own children or each other's company," that they devote very little to the nurturing of their young, and so forth.

One problem with understanding impersonal benevolence in these stronger terms is that very few people (philosophers or otherwise) would be likely to endorse an account of moral virtue according to which impersonal benevolence qualifies as a genuine virtue. Consequently, the fact that Hurthouse's account "rules against" impersonal benevolence understood in this way does not go very far toward supporting her claim that her appeal to human nature is doing interesting and substantive explanatory work. (Again, her aim was to show that her appeal to human nature has significant theoretical traction by showing that it might rule against certain traits that at least some philosophers regard as genuine virtues.) Moreover, the fact that virtually no ethical system or framework would endorse practices or the cultivation of traits that would obliterate the social dimension of human life further suggests that the relevant features of Hursthouse's account are "naturalistic" only in a relatively weak or thin sense.

This examination of Hursthouse's account reveals that the central and fundamental concept in Hursthouse's account of moral virtue—and in the corresponding account of intellectual virtue—is that of rationality, where this again is an explicitly and robustly normative notion. It also illustrates one of the most serious challenges for any avowedly naturalist account of moral or intellectual virtue. On the one hand, such an account must refrain from grounding the nature of a virtue strictly in human nature as we know it, for as already noted, this is bound to make for a skewed account. On the other hand, to the extent that a non-descriptive, normative element is introduced, the question arises as to whether or to what extent the account is genuinely naturalistic. Hursthouse claims to have found a way between the horns of this dilemma; but on careful inspection, it appears that her account falls prey to the second horn.

7.2.3 *Zagzebski's "motivational" account*

In *Virtues of the Mind* (1996), Linda Zagzebski constructs a theory of virtue intended to encompass both moral and intellectual virtue. She defends the following, general account: "A virtue, then, can be defined as a deep and enduring acquired excellence of a person, involving a characteristic motivation to produce a certain desired end, and reliable success in bringing about that end" (137). She says that a "motivation" is "a disposition to have a certain motive" and that a "motive" is "an emotion that initiates and directs action to produce an end with certain desired features" (136). As this initial characterization suggests, Zagzebski anchors her account of virtue in the concept of a good or virtuous *motive*; thus it is aptly labeled a "motivational" account of virtue.[30]

[30] See Michael Slote (2001) for a related but different "motivational" account of virtue.

This initial characterization also makes clear that on Zagzebski's view virtues have two main components: a motivational component and a reliability component. The motivational component itself also has two parts. For Zagzebski, to possess a given virtue is to be motivated to bring about a certain immediate end or goal for the sake of achieving some more ultimate end. More specifically, she thinks that each virtue has a characteristic aim and corresponding immediate motivation, and that virtues of the same general kind share a more ultimate aim and motivation. The end or goal proper to the class of intellectual virtues, on her view, is "cognitive contact with reality," which includes, but is not reducible to, knowledge (167).[31] Thus, for Zagzebski, to possess a particular intellectual virtue V is to be motivated to bring about a certain end characteristic of V out of a deeper or more ultimate motivation to achieve knowledge or "cognitive contact with reality." She illustrates her view as follows:

> We have seen that all intellectual virtues arise out of the motivation for knowledge and include an internal aim to operate cognitively in a way that is believed to be knowledge conducive, a way that is unique to each virtue. So the aim of open-mindedness is to be receptive to new ideas and arguments even when they conflict with one's own in order to ultimately get knowledge. The aim of intellectual thoroughness is to exhaustively investigate the evidence pertaining to a particular belief or a set of questions in order to ultimately get knowledge. The aim of intellectual courage is to defend one's belief or a line of inquiry when one has good reason to be confident that it is on the right track, and to fearlessly answer objections from others in order to ultimately get knowledge. (269)

But it is not sufficient for the possession of a virtue, Zagzebski thinks, that one be motivated in the relevant ways. She requires that one also be successful at *bringing about* the immediate and ultimate ends characteristic of the virtue in question—hence the need for a "reliability" requirement. For Zagzebski, a person who is motivated, say, to be fair and careful in inquiry out of a desire to acquire to knowledge, but who fails actually to inquire in fair and careful ways or to acquire knowledge as a result of her fair and careful inquiry, also fails to possess the virtues of intellectual fairness or carefulness. Again, to possess a given virtue V, one must be reliably successful at achieving both the immediate and ultimate ends characteristic of V. To summarize, an intellectual virtue is a "deep and enduring acquired excellence of a person" that involves being

[31] She notes that "cognitive contact with reality" might also include understanding, which (unlike knowledge) "includes the comprehension of abstract structures of realty apart from the propositional". Zagzebski is less clear, however, about the ends proper to moral virtue.

motivated to bring about the immediate and ultimate ends characteristic of this virtue together with reliable *success* at doing so.

My own account of intellectual virtue bears some importance resemblances to (and indeed has been influenced by) Zagzebski's. First, though Zagzebski does not give the notion of personal intellectual worth a central conceptual role in her account, she is clearly sympathetic to the idea that intellectual virtues make their possessor good qua person.[32] Second, on both accounts, the psychological basis of intellectual virtue is a certain positive orientation toward one or more intellectual goods. Third, Zagzebski and I largely agree about how to individuate intellectual virtues. We both maintain that intellectual virtues can be distinguished from each other on account of certain psychological elements unique to each individual virtue, and that these elements constitute a kind of immediate focus that is in some sense grounded in the more general orientation just noted.

But there are also some important differences between Zagzebski's account of intellectual virtue and my own personal worth account. Here I shall limit myself to a discussion of just one of these differences—a difference concerning our views of what exactly *makes* the traits in question intellectual virtues. Zagzebski believes that these traits are intellectual virtues because they are partially constituted by *intrinsically* valuable intellectual motives, and she subscribes to a strict account of intrinsic value, according to which something is intrinsically valuable just in case it has its value entirely "in itself," that is, its value is not in any way derivative from any other source of value (83; 203). On my view, the traits in question are intellectual virtues because they contribute to personal intellectual worth. As I shall get to below, while I think that such traits are intrinsically valuable, I do not think they are intrinsically valuable in Zagzebski's sense. And, at any rate, their being intrinsically valuable (in any sense) is not what *makes* them intellectual virtues on my account.

In the remainder of this section, I want to look more closely at two critical parts of Zagzebski's account of intellectual virtue and raise some concerns about them. Her account is what some philosophers (e.g. Driver 2001) have referred to as a "mixed" account of intellectual virtue, for it involves both an "internal" and an "external" component, the internal component being intrinsically valuable intellectual motives and the external component being reliable success at achieving the ends characteristic of these motives. While it may be that Zagzebski's mixed account picks out a genuine kind or concept of intellectual

[32] See, for example, pp. 85, 89, and 125. It is also clear, however, that she does not want to *define* intellectual virtue in terms of personal intellectual worth (see pp. 134 and 93f).

virtue, I want to suggest some reasons for doubting that this is the case, and specifically, for thinking that Zagzebski's account runs together two different and independent concepts of intellectual virtue.

Given the earlier discussion of Driver's account of intellectual virtue, the basis of this worry should be apparent. We have seen that a trait's contributing to personal intellectual worth is sufficient for its counting as an intellectual virtue in some robust and pretheoretical sense. And we have seen that a trait's being epistemically reliable (which is no guarantee of its contributing to personal worth) is sufficient for its counting as an intellectual virtue in an alternative but also legitimate and pretheoretical sense. Given the similarity between Zagzebski's motivational component of intellectual virtue and my own account of the basis of personal intellectual worth (again, something like a desire for truth or knowledge), the question arises whether Zagzebski's account is an attempt to wed what are in fact two distinct concepts of intellectual virtue.

It is not easy to know how to go about settling this question, but one natural strategy is to ask whether there is anything like an intuitive or reasonably pretheoretical notion of intellectual virtue that answers to Zagzebski's mixed account. Suppose a subject S satisfies the motivational requirements of a range of intellectual virtues but is prevented, unawares and through no fault of her own (by an evil demon, say), from successfully reaching the truth. The question is whether (1) there is an intuitively and reasonably pretheoretical notion of intellectual virtue according to which S has, as it were, satisfied only *one half* of its requirements and therefore fails to possess an intellectual virtue; or whether it is more plausible to think that (2) while S is genuinely virtuous in one legitimate (personal worth) sense, there is another distinct but still legitimate (consequentialist) sense in which S's traits fail to qualify as intellectual virtues. The possibility identified in (2) strikes me—and others, I would imagine—as considerably more plausible than the possibility in (1). This makes it look as if Zagzebski's account is indeed running together two distinct concepts of intellectual virtue.

Another way to come at this point is to note the difference in value between what Zagzebski regards as the two main components of an intellectual virtue: namely, the motivational component and the reliability component. As already noted, she thinks of the relevant motives as intrinsically valuable—and intrinsically valuable in a very strong sense. The value of epistemic reliability, however, is paradigmatically *instrumental*: a trait that is reliably productive of true belief gets (at least a substantial part of) its value from the value of truth itself. Recall that a virtue is an excellence: it is a trait of character that embodies a certain kind of value. My suggestion is that there is something at least initially counterintuitive about an account of virtue that locates the excellence or value of a virtue in two fundamentally different kinds of value. More plausible, it seems, is the view that the two different kinds of value are representative of two different kinds or concepts of virtue.

To be clear, my claim is not that a mixed account is incoherent or contradictory. Still less is it that a given trait or object cannot be both instrumentally and intrinsically valuable. The claim is rather that, other things being equal, there is something counterintuitive about the suggestion that two fundamentally different kinds of intellectual value might be definitive of a single kind of virtue. Given the central role that the notion of a virtuous motive plays in Zagzebski's account, and given her commitment to thinking of virtuous motives as intrinsically valuable, it seems that Zagzebski would do best to drop her reliability requirement on intellectual virtue.[33]

A second general worry also concerns Zagzebski's account of the value of an intellectual virtue. As we have seen, she thinks, first, that the motivational component of an intellectual virtue is intrinsically valuable in the strong sense that its value does not depend in any way on its relation to anything else of value. Second, she maintains, rather surprisingly, that the value of the reliability component of an intellectual virtue is derivative from the value of the motivational component (not, say, from the value of true belief). I find these claims, both of which are crucial to her overall account of intellectual virtue, problematic; and I shall address each one in turn.

Consider, first, the claim that the value of the motivation for knowledge (and related cognitive goods) is independent of the value of knowledge itself. Zagzebski says that "the intrinsic and primary value of the motivation for knowledge . . . is not derived from its connection with any other good, not even the good of knowledge" (203). This is a radical claim. Zagzebski is saying that the fact that knowledge is good plays no role in explaining why desiring or being motivated by knowledge is good.

Suppose, however, that knowledge were not good, or that we did not regard it as good. Would it still be plausible to think of a desire for knowledge as good? Presumably not. If we came to think of knowledge as a worthless or even

[33] Zagzebski's main reason for embracing a reliability requirement (see pp. 176–84) seems to be that *under normal circumstances*, we would reasonably expect an intellectually virtuous person to be reliable. But this is entirely consistent with a denial of the claim that reliability is *necessary* for intellectual virtue. Indeed, as already noted, it is precisely reflection on certain non-standard worlds (like those controlled by an evil demon) that generates doubt about a reliability requirement.

disvaluable or dangerous end, presumably we would no longer think well of persons who desired or pursued this end. What this suggests is that, contra Zagzebski, desiring or being motivated by the end of knowledge is valuable at least in part because knowledge itself is valuable.[34] The value of knowledge at least partially explains why desiring knowledge is a good thing.

This might be thought to lead to the conclusion that the motivation for knowledge is strictly *instrumentally* valuable. While I agree that such a motivation is instrumentally valuable (presumably its possession does make one more likely—within certain parameters—to acquire knowledge), this is not a full account of its value. Indeed it seems obvious that being motivated by or "loving" knowledge is good simply on account of the fact that knowledge itself is good. A love of knowledge is good, in other words, not just because of its causal relation to the goal of knowledge, but also because of its *intentional* relation to this goal. As Hurka claims, it is apparently good in itself to love what is good in itself (2001: 13). This suggests a weaker notion of intrinsic value than the one to which Zagzebski appeals. We may refer to this kind of value as "conditional" intrinsic value, since it is contingent on the value of some other object or end. It differs from "unconditional" intrinsic value, which does not depend for its value on any relation to anything else of value.

Finally, it is worth noting briefly that Zagzebski defends the idea that a motivation to acquire knowledge has unconditional intrinsic value by arguing against the claim that this motivation is strictly instrumentally valuable (203–9). As already noted, I agree with her that the motivation in question is not merely instrumentally valuable; and I think her arguments do a good job of showing why this is the case. But these arguments do not in any way favor thinking of the motivation to acquire knowledge as having unconditional rather than *conditional* intrinsic value.

I turn now to Zagzebski's claim that the reliability component of an intellectual virtue derives its value from the motivational component. Her argument for this claim is brief and reasonably straightforward. She advances as a "reasonable maxim" the claim that "reliable success in achieving the aim of a good motive is itself a good thing" and concludes that "the goodness of the reliability component of an intellectual virtue derives from the goodness of the motivational component" (209). If the conclusion here is intended to be that the

[34] Indeed consider kinds of knowledge the value of which is often questioned by epistemologists (for example, purely "trivial" knowledge). Presumably a "love" of knowledge about grains of sand, blades of grass, names in phonebooks, etc., is not very valuable (if it is valuable at all).

sole value of reliability is derivative from the motivational component of intellectual virtue, then it clearly does not follow from Zagzebski's maxim. For the central or at least most obvious value of epistemic reliability is the value it derives from the value of truth itself (which again Zagzebski wants to regard as independent of the value of virtuous motives). Reliable qualities or processes are valuable, in the most obvious or straightforward sense, because they are an effective means to truth. The value of reliability, in this sense, is instrumental to and derivative from the value of truth. If, however, the conclusion is supposed to be that the reliability component of an intellectual virtue derives *some* value from the value of a good motivation on account of its causal connection with the aim or end of this motivation, this seems plausible enough. It is reasonable, that is, to think that if a given motivational state M is valuable, and M aims at a given end or goal E, then anything that is reliably productive of E derives some value from M. Accordingly, it makes sense to think that if a desire for truth is valuable, then being reliably productive of truth derives some value from the value of this desire.

But a problem remains. Zagzebski maintains that the *full* value of an intellectual virtue (as such) is derivative from the value of its underlying motivation (which again is unconditionally intrinsic). She also maintains that reliability is an essential and defining feature of an intellectual virtue. We have just noted, however, that the main or most obvious value of reliability is straightforwardly derivative from that of truth or related epistemic ends. It follows that while Zagzebski might not *deny* that intellectual virtues are instrumentally valuable on account of their reliability, she must deny that this value is any part of what makes them intellectual virtues in her sense. Put another way, while Zagzebski thinks that reliability is an essential feature of an intellectual virtue, the most obvious *value* of reliability, on her view, is no part of the value of an intellectual virtue as such. This suggests that Zagzebski would do better to deny either that reliability is a defining feature of a virtue or that the full value of an intellectual virtue is derivative from the value of its motivational component.

7.3 *Conclusion*

Considerable ground has been covered in this chapter. My aim has been to situate my personal worth account of intellectual virtue vis-à-vis several other accounts of moral and intellectual virtue in the literature. We have found that my account is similar to recent accounts of moral virtue by Hurka and

Adams, but that it differs considerably from other accounts of either moral or intellectual virtue by Driver, Hursthouse, and Zagzebski. Finally, we have examined a range of problems with these alternative accounts, some of which seem to be fairly serious. In this regard, the present chapter adds to the case for the personal worth conception begun in Chapter 6.

Chapter 8

OPEN-MINDEDNESS

Open-mindedness appears at the top of nearly every list of intellectual virtues in the virtue epistemology literature.[1] Despite its status as an intellectual virtue par excellence, however, it is not at all clear what exactly open-mindedness amounts to. That is, it is unclear what sort of intellectual activity or orientation is essential to it. In fact, there are ways of thinking about open-mindedness that cast serious doubt on its status as an intellectual virtue.

Consider, for instance, the following description from Bob Roberts and Jay Wood (2007), of a "bright college freshman, taking an introductory course in philosophy." Given this student's "taste for ideas,"

> she treats the survey as a smorgasbord at which she partakes with an appetite. Within a course of sixteen weeks she may have been a Platonist, an empiricist, a skeptic, a Cartesian, a Kantian, a utilitarian, a social contractor, a mind-body dualist, a Berkeleyan idealist, a reductive materialist, a theist, an atheist, and an agnostic. Having scratched the surface of a debate, having followed for a few steps the flow of a dialectical exchange, she commits quickly to each theory, easily relinquishing its contrary, then passing on to the next. She is bright, but under the pressure of successive presentations of ideas, her intellectual character is too soft to hold onto a position. (188)

Roberts and Wood cite this as an example of intellectual "flaccidity," but it also serves to illustrate a (less than virtuous) kind or variety of open-mindedness—the kind, for instance, that tends to elicit utterances of the familiar (if cynical) maxim, "Don't be so open-minded that your brains fall out."

I see no reason to think that any trait that can aptly be labeled "open-mindedness" must be an intellectual virtue. Nonetheless, it is extremely

[1] Of intellectual *character* virtues, that is. See, for instance, Kvanvig (1992), Montmarquet (1993), Zagzebski (1996), and Roberts and Wood (2007). See Riggs (2010) for a discussion of why open-mindedness enjoys the status of a paradigmatic intellectual virtue.

plausible to think there exists a genuine and important intellectual virtue in the neighborhood of these traits. My aim in this chapter is to go some way toward uncovering the essential or defining character of this virtue. I take as my immediate focus that which is *distinctive* of this virtue as compared with other intellectual virtues—not the qualities that make open-mindedness an intellectual virtue per se or the qualities that open-mindedness shares with *other* intellectual virtues.[2] In addition to sketching an account of the basic nature and structure of open-mindedness, I also briefly address two other issues: first, the characteristic function of open-mindedness vis-à-vis other intellectual virtues; and second, the issue of when (or to whom or how much) an exercise of open-mindedness is intellectually appropriate or virtuous. While the latter question in particular merits a lengthier treatment than I can provide here, I hope to be able to shed at least some light on the largely practical concern that motivates it.

As this brief preview suggests, the focus of the book shifts in the present chapter from the concept of an intellectual virtue per se to the basic nature and structure of one intellectual virtue in particular. In the chapter that follows, I undertake a similar examination of intellectual courage. As pointed out earlier in the book, one broader aim of these chapters is to advance the case for "autonomous" virtue epistemology, which again is the view that reflection on intellectual character virtues and their role in the intellectual life can form the basis of a fruitful and interesting epistemological research program that is largely independent of traditional epistemology. This point is taken up in more detail in Chapter 10.

8.1 *Some initial characterizations of open-mindedness*

I begin by considering some initially attractive proposals concerning open-mindedness. I then point out ways in which these proposals are unsatisfactory. This sets the stage for an explanation of my preferred characterization of open-mindedness in the section that follows.

Whatever its fundamental nature or structure, it is tempting to think of open-mindedness as essentially relevant to situations involving intellectual conflict, opposition, challenge, or argument, and in particular, to situations involving a conflict between a person's beliefs, on the one hand, and an

[2] It should be clear, however, that the trait I profile here would be an intellectual virtue if accompanied and motivated by the general virtue-making qualities discussed in Chapter 6.

opposing position, argument, or body of evidence, on the other.[3] Here an open-minded person characteristically moves beyond or temporarily sets aside his own doxastic commitments in order to give a fair and impartial hearing to the intellectual opposition. He is willing to follow the argument where it leads and to take evidence and reasons at face value. He does not ignore, distort, or caricature opposing positions. He is not narrow-minded, dogmatic, or biased. While he may have many firm and dear convictions, his hold on them does not prevent him from giving serious consideration to the "other side."[4]

An example of open-mindedness thus conceived is the fictional protagonist of C. P. Snow's 1934 novel *The Search*. Arthur Miles is a young and ambitious Cambridge scientist conducting groundbreaking research in crystallography. At one point in the narrative, he appears to have made a major discovery that seems bound to catapult him into scientific stardom. Shortly thereafter, however, a critical piece of counterevidence appears on one of his x-ray films. Initially, Miles tries to resist the force of this new datum:

> I hunted round for another explanation: the film might be a false one, it might be a fluke experiment; but the look of it mocked me: far from being false, it was the only experiment where I had arrived at precisely the right conditions. Could it be explained any other way? I stared down at the figures, the sheets of results which I had forced into my scheme. My cheeks flushing dry, I tried to work this new photograph into my idea. An improbable assumption, another improbable assumption, a possibility of experimental error—I went on, fantastically, any sort of criticism forgotten. Still it would not fit. I was wrong, irrevocably wrong. I should have to begin again.

While Miles initially yields to the counterevidence, his surrender is incomplete, for he subsequently entertains the possibility of destroying the offending slide. Upon still further deliberation, he acquiesces to a nobler inclination:

> I was swung back... by all the forms of—shall I call it "conscience"—and perhaps more than that, by the desire which had thrown me into the search. For I had to get what I myself thought was the truth. Honour, comfort and ambition were bound to move me, but I think my own desire went deepest. Without any posturing to myself, without any sort of conscious thought, I laughed at the temptation to destroy the photograph. Rather shakily I laughed. And I wrote in

[3] This tends to be the focus of William Hare's (1979; 1985) excellent treatments of open-mindedness. However, as I explain below, Hare (rightly) allows that open-mindedness can also be exhibited outside such contexts.

[4] For a spirited tribute to and partial explication of open-mindedness thus conceived, see John Stuart Mill's *On Liberty* (1978: esp. ch. 2).

> my notebook: "Mar. 30: Photograph 3 alone has secondary dots, concentric with major dots. This removes all possibility of the hypothesis of structure B. The interpretation from Mar. 4–30 must accordingly be disregarded." (1958: 92–3)

Miles is no epistemic saint. He clearly feels the temptation to ignore, distort, even to destroy, evidence that runs counter to his hypothesis. In the end, however, he chooses to confront, take seriously, and alter his doxastic attitudes in light of this evidence. And he does so out of a motivation definitive of intellectual virtue: namely, a compelling or overriding desire to get to the truth.

This initial characterization suggests that open-mindedness is essentially a willingness or ability *to temporarily set aside one's doxastic commitments about a particular matter in order to give a fair and impartial hearing to an opposing belief, argument, or body of evidence.* Because it portrays a conflict between an open-minded person's beliefs and some alternative belief or source of information as essential to an exercise of open-mindedness, let us refer to this as the "conflict model" of open-mindedness.

While initially plausible, the conflict model is inadequate as a general account of open-mindedness. This is because an exercise of open-mindedness (1) need not involve the setting aside or suspending of any beliefs; and (2) it need not presuppose any kind of conflict or disagreement between an open-minded person's beliefs and the object of her open-mindedness. Both (1) and (2) are a function of the fact that open-mindedness can be manifested in situations in which the person in question is *neutral* with respect to the items being assessed.

Imagine, for instance, an honest and impartial judge preparing to hear the opening arguments in a given trial. The judge has no prior opinions or biases about any part of the case; nor does she have any stake in its outcome. There is, then, no conflict between the beliefs of the judge and the beliefs or arguments she is preparing to hear. Nonetheless, it seems that the judge might still listen to the arguments in an open-minded way or that she might conduct an open-minded inquiry into the case. The latter might look like giving a careful and protracted hearing to the relevant arguments prior to allowing herself to form an opinion or to be swayed in one direction or another.[5] If this is possible, then open-mindedness is not essentially or necessarily a matter of setting aside one's doxastic commitments in order to give a fair or impartial hearing to the intellectual opposition. For again, there is no doxastic conflict or disagreement

[5] See Hare (1979: 9 and 24 and 1985: 94) for a development of the point that an open-minded person can be "neutral" or "undecided" about the views toward which he is being open-minded.

between the judge and the arguments she is preparing to evaluate; she does not yet agree with, nor does she have an antecedent inclination to favor, one side or the other. In cases of this sort, open-mindedness is manifested instead in something like a willingness *to hear both sides of an issue, to follow the relevant arguments where they lead, and to refrain from making hasty or premature judgments.*

The difference between the two applications of open-mindedness considered thus far is evident in connection with the intellectual *vices* that correspond to each application. In the context of intellectual conflict or opposition, open-mindedness is the antidote to vices like narrow-mindedness, closed-mindedness, dogmatism, prejudice, and bias.[6] But such vices are less relevant to situations in which a person is neutral or undecided about the matter being assessed. The judge, for instance, is unlikely to be closed-minded, dogmatic, or prejudiced in her assessment of the relevant case, since again, she has nothing at stake in it. In this context, the corresponding vices include traits like intellectual hastiness, impatience, and laziness, for these defects may prevent a person from listening to both sides of an issue, taking each side seriously, or avoiding hasty or premature conclusions.

In a book on religious conversion, Emilie Griffin (1982) describes the initial stage of her own conversion in terms suggestive of the latter application of open-mindedness. She describes this period as involving an ongoing dialectic between atheistic and theistic arguments:

> Often, when I felt myself becoming convinced or persuaded by believers, I ran from that and deliberately plunged myself into the opposite point of view. I knew the emotional power which Christianity had for me, but I did not want to be overcome by that. So, from time to time, perhaps not consciously, I administered an antidote. When I went to the writings of atheists, it was not only for the sake of being fair-minded; the fact was that I did not know from which direction clarity or resolution of my difficult questions would come. (97)

On the one hand, given her admitted attraction to Christianity, Griffin may not appear very neutral with respect to the subject matter at issue. But if we take at face value her claim that she had not yet made up her mind and did not yet know what the outcome of her inquiry would be, her intellectual activity illustrates how open-mindedness can be exhibited outside a context of intellectual opposition or disagreement, and within that of open inquiry. Griffin

[6] For illuminating discussions of some of these vices, especially of closed-mindedness, see ch. 12 of BK. 4 of Locke's *Essay Concerning Human Understanding* (1996).

examines both sides of the issue, gives each serious consideration, and does not rush to judgment or draw premature conclusions.

We have seen that open-mindedness cannot be identified with a disposition to set aside one's beliefs in order to give a fair and impartial consideration to an opposing position, argument, or body of evidence. Nevertheless, both applications of open-mindedness considered thus far have at least two things in common which may be thought to take us some way toward a grasp of the essential character of open-mindedness. First, both involve intellectual conflict or opposition of one form or another. In the first case described above, the conflict is between the open-minded person's beliefs and some alternative belief or source of information. In the second, it is between two or more competing positions about which the open-minded person is presently neutral or undecided. Second, both of the relevant applications of open-mindedness involve some kind of rational assessment or evaluation of one or more of the conflicting items. Again, in the first case, an open-minded person assesses a belief or argument that stands in opposition to one of his beliefs. And, in the second, he assesses multiple competing positions, none of which he presently accepts or rejects. This suggests that open-mindedness is essentially a disposition *to assess one or more sides of an intellectual dispute in a fair and impartial way.* Call this the "adjudication model" of open-mindedness.[7]

While an improvement on the conflict model in some respects, the adjudication model is still too restrictive. This is because open-mindedness can also be exhibited (1) in situations void of any (relevant) intellectual conflict or disagreement and (2) in intellectual activity *other* than rational assessment or evaluation.

To begin to see how, imagine a physics teacher who has just led a group of bright high school students through a unit on Einstein's Special Theory of Relativity. Most of the students have managed to follow the teacher's lessons and thus have achieved a basic understanding of the theory. In the final part of the course, the teacher intends to push his students a significant step further by introducing them to Einstein's General Theory. This is bound to pose a major challenge for most of the students in the course. It will require an even more dramatic departure (compared with the Special Theory) from their usual ways of thinking about space, time, physical laws, velocity, frames of reference, and the like.

[7] This model raises the question of whether open-mindedness is anything over and above other virtues like intellectual fairness and impartiality. I defend an affirmative reply to this question in section 8.3 below.

Here again it is extremely plausible to think that the persons in question might benefit from a kind of open-mindedness. This trait might help the students "wrap their minds" around certain otherwise incomprehensible scientific or metaphysical proposals. Indeed, we can easily imagine the teacher saying to his students: "Okay, for this next unit, I need you to really *open your minds*—to loosen your grip even more on some of your ordinary and commonsense ways of thinking about the world around you." If this is right, then an exercise of open-mindedness does not presuppose any kind of intellectual dispute or disagreement. For Einstein's General Theory is not at odds or in competition with his Special Theory; rather, it is a natural (if complex and mind-bending) extension of it.

This example also shows that open-mindedness does not necessarily involve rational assessment. For the students are not attempting to assess or evaluate Einstein's General Theory. At this stage, they are simply trying to *follow* or *understand* it. This shows that open-mindedness, while at times bearing on the activity of rational assessment or evaluation, can also bear on other intellectual activities or operations: for instance, on the process of coming to understand or comprehend a certain foreign or challenging subject matter.

Nor is this the only alternative activity or operation on which open-mindedness might be brought to bear. Again, the students just described are attempting to follow their teacher's lead; while they do want to "understand for themselves," there is a clear sense in which they are not attempting to *think* for themselves. There is a fixed subject matter before them and their aim is to wrap their minds around it—to *grasp* it. By contrast, imagine a detective attempting to solve an especially confounding case. His investigation of the case is complete: he has examined the crime scene in painstaking detail, studied the forensics reports, interviewed all the witnesses, followed up on possible suspects, and so on; he is in possession of all of the relevant facts. And yet he is stumped. He cannot conceive of a coherent explanation of the full range of evidence. Some of the evidence points to a certain suspect and sequence of events, while other parts of the evidence seem to exonerate this suspect and to suggest an alternative sequence of events. At some level, the detective's aim is to understand what happened, to comprehend how the crime unfolded, who did what, and so on. Prior to achieving such understanding, however, the detective must do something else: he must attempt to *imagine* or *conceive* of a coherent explanation of the relevant data. He must engage in a kind of creative thinking, imagining, or hypothesizing. This is likely to require a kind of generative intellectual strength and autonomy that is not required of the physics students, who again are attempting merely to comprehend a body of information that has already been worked out and presented to them by their teacher.[8]

Such activity is clearly relevant to the practice of (if less so to the study of or attempts to comprehend) science and other disciplines. Success in these areas often requires rigorous, autonomous, and creative thinking.[9] Einstein himself described advances in scientific thinking as involving a quasi-artistic "sudden illumination" and "great forward leap of the imagination."[10] The more immediate point, however, is that activity of this sort might very well be facilitated or enhanced by an exercise of open-mindedness. Open-mindedness might help a person conceive of or imagine certain otherwise inscrutable or unidentifiable possibilities or explanations.

Griffin's (1982) discussion of religious conversion also provides an example of this application of open-mindedness. She describes the conversion process as often involving "fits and starts of insight and illumination":

> What seems to happen is that a number of ideas and arguments are collected from various sources; the mind works away at them; then, sometimes in a sudden burst of energy, a sorting and ordering occurs not sequentially, but all at once. Things fall into patterns. Even before the last piece is fitted into the jigsaw, the picture of the mountain can be seen taking shape. Then, with exhilaration, the mind rushes to complete the picture. (72)

Griffin illustrates this point with the conversion of the late Jesuit contemplative Avery Dulles:

> So in a brief moment—standing beside a tree on the rainy bank of the Charles—Dulles was able to integrate into one vision of reality much that he had already absorbed from the ancient philosophers—Anaxagoras, Plato, Aristotle—and from later thinkers, Augustine among them. But this moment of insight was rationally based; it came about after Dulles had been engaged for some time in

[8] The students will, of course, need to stretch their minds in order to grasp this information (this is why they might benefit from being open-minded). The difference between them and the detective is that the detective is also being called upon to *originate* or *creatively conceive* of a certain possibility or explanation. And the present suggestion is that this sort of intellectual activity might also be facilitated by an exercise of open-mindedness.

[9] For an interesting discussion of the place of open-mindedness in scientific inquiry, see Hare (1985: ch. 7).

[10] Isaacson (2007: 549). The context of this remark was a discussion with poet Saint-John Perse in which Einstein asked: "How does the idea of a poem come?" In response, Perse emphasized the role of intuition and imagination, to which Einstein replied with delight: "It's the same for a man of science."

> the dialectical process; now it became possible for Dulles to "see"—in a whole, clear vision—what till then he had only been thinking about. (74)

Griffin adds that it was "the *disposition of his mind*, its *openness*, which made the insight possible. It was his yearning that stirred the working of his mind and moved him towards the drawing of conclusions" (75; my emphasis). As Griffin describes it, Dulles's insight, his identification of a new explanatory framework, was made possible in part by his open-mindedness, which in turn was motivated by a deeper intellectual "yearning," presumably a yearning for knowledge or understanding.

To summarize, we have seen, first, that despite the initial plausibility of such a view, open-mindedness cannot be identified with a disposition to set aside one's beliefs about a particular issue in order to consider some opposing viewpoint or piece of evidence (the conflict model). This is because open-mindedness can be exhibited by individuals that are neutral or undecided about the views or arguments they are considering. Second, we have seen that neither is open-mindedness necessarily a matter of making a fair or impartial assessment of one or more sides of an intellectual dispute with respect to which one may be neutral (the adjudication model). For it can bear on situations in which there is no disagreement and on activity that is void of rational evaluation or assessment.

8.2 *Open-mindedness: a unified account*

The discussion up to this point has left us with a rather disparate range of applications and examples of open-mindedness. The main point of the chapter, however, is to shed light on the essential or defining character of open-mindedness. We must, then, confront the question of whether a unified account of open-mindedness is even possible. That is, we must attempt to determine what, if anything, the foregoing instances or applications of open-mindedness have in common that *make* them instances of open-mindedness.[11]

8.2.1 *The conceptual core of open-mindedness*

We can begin to answer this question by focusing on one reasonably salient feature of each of the cases of open-mindedness discussed above. In each case, a

[11] This is a critical task. For, if we cannot identify a common element in the various instances and applications of open-mindedness that we have considered thus far, it is likely to appear that in fact we have been concerned with a variety of fundamentally *different* traits.

person *departs* or *detaches* from, he or she *moves beyond* or *transcends*, a certain default or privileged cognitive standpoint.[12] Consider first the application of open-mindedness to situations involving intellectual disagreement or conflict. We said that here an open-minded person is (roughly) one who is able to set aside or loosen his grip on his belief that P in order to consider or take seriously the case for not-P. Intuitively, it is this cognitive "moving beyond" or transcending of the person's doxastic commitments, a willingness to consider things from the other side, that makes the activity in question an expression of open-mindedness.

Next consider the bearing of open-mindedness on attempts to understand or imagine. Recall, for instance, the physics students attempting to wrap their minds around Einstein's General Theory. To the extent that their attempts to understand the theory are facilitated by open-mindedness, this is likely to involve an ability to transcend familiar or default ways of thinking about the basic structure of reality. Recall as well the detective attempting to make coherent sense of a baffling and seemingly incoherent set of data. Again, open-mindedness might enable this person to be "open" to and hence to identify or conceive of explanations that would otherwise be out of reach.

This leaves the application of open-mindedness to situations involving "impartial adjudication," that is, to situations in which the person in question is adjudicating between two or more competing positions about which she is presently undecided or neutral. Here the relevant "departing" or "transcending," which I am claiming is the conceptual core of open-mindedness, is more complex and less apparent. To see why, recall the case of the open-minded judge preparing to hear a set of opposing arguments. We said that while the judge may not have anything at stake (cognitive or otherwise) in the outcome of the case, she might still listen in an open-minded way to the relevant arguments or conduct an open-minded assessment of them. Again, in situations like this, open-mindedness involves a willingness to listen to both sides of an issue, to follow the arguments or evidence where they lead, and to refrain from bringing the inquiry to a hasty or premature conclusion. But in what

[12] In *Character Strengths and Virtues* (2004), empirical psychologists Christopher Peterson and Martin Seligman explain that one way psychologists have been able to measure open-mindedness in their subjects is by testing for "integrative complexity," which is a function of two notions: "differentiation" and "integration." They explain these concepts as follows: "*Differentiation* refers to an individual's ability to apply different perspectives to a particular issue, and *integration* refers to a person's ability to see connections between and among these divergent perspectives" (148). Central to both of these notions is a kind of cognitive transcending or detaching that is at least similar to the kind just described.

sense, if any, does this involve moving beyond, detaching from, or transcending a default or privileged cognitive standpoint? And even if it were to involve as much, could this plausibly explain why the activity in question is an instance of open-mindedness?

There are, in fact, at least three distinct ways in which the activity in question might involve a kind of detaching from a default cognitive standpoint. First, to the extent that this activity is a matter of assessing the relative merits of two or more positions *neither of which one presently accepts*, it might involve entertaining or giving one's mind to a previously unconsidered possibility or standpoint, which in turn might require a kind of intellectual "opening" or transcending of one's present cognitive perspective. And where this is the case—for instance, where a person is assessing two competing positions in connection with an issue to which she previously has given very little thought—it is not implausible to think that the transcending or detaching in question might amount to a kind of open-mindedness.

Second, to adjudicate between two or more competing positions in an open-minded way, one must at a certain level be able to *move back and forth between the positions in question*—to compare and contrast their meaning, understand the logical relations between them, and assess their respective strengths and weaknesses. This opens up the possibility that one might get stuck or hung up in one's assessment of one or more of these positions. For instance, having focused intently on the merits of one set of arguments, the judge might find herself unwilling or unable to turn to or reorient her attention on the opposing set. And it is reasonable to think that this unwillingness or inability might be due to a lack of open-mindedness on the judge's part. This, then, suggests a second way in which the kind of cognitive detaching characteristic of open-mindedness might be manifested in the context of impartial adjudication.

A third way in which the kind of cognitive detaching characteristic of open-mindedness might be manifested in the context of impartial adjudication is evident in cases in which a person resists the temptation to make a hasty generalization or to draw a premature conclusion. For in doing so, this person is, as it were, keeping his distance from a certain (premature, hasty, or "closed") cognitive standpoint; he is "keeping an open mind." There are, however, some noteworthy differences between this expression of open-mindedness and the other two noted above. In the earlier two cases, for instance, open-mindedness is manifested in a kind of *positive* psychological activity. Where an open-minded adjudicator shifts, say, from focusing intently on one position to a consideration of a competing position, he *moves beyond* his present standpoint to entertain an alternative standpoint. In the third case, however, open-mindedness has a negative character: it consists in *refraining* from taking up an alternative cognitive standpoint (which again is the standpoint represented by the hasty or premature judgment). This illustrates the important point that while open-mindedness is often a matter of positively opening one's mind, it is sometimes a matter of *not closing it.*

This might initially seem counterintuitive. It might seem strange, that is, to think that open-mindedness could consist in resisting or refusing to take up an alternative cognitive standpoint. The explanation, however, lies with the fact that the *default* or *privileged* cognitive standpoint in this case is different from what it is in most other cases. In the typical case, the default standpoint is one that the person in question presently occupies or accepts; and indeed, it is the fact that the person occupies this standpoint that accounts for its default status. In the present case, however, the default standpoint is the one that the person is *tempted* by or *inclined* to take up. And it is this fact—the fact that the person is tempted or inclined to take up the standpoint in question—that makes the standpoint a default or privileged one. The result is that open-mindedness, in cases like this, consists in detaching (or remaining detached) from a forward-looking or hypothetical standpoint rather than a standpoint that one already occupies.[13]

Before turning to offer a definition of open-mindedness based on the preceding characterization, it is important to add that whether a particular instance of cognitive "detaching" or "transcending" counts as an instance of open-mindedness depends in part on the immediate *motivation* behind it. Imagine a person who sets aside or moves beyond one of his beliefs in order to assess an argument against this belief, but who has no real intention of making an honest or fair assessment of this argument (he just wants to get the attention of his interlocutor, say). Intuitively, this person is not genuinely open-minded. And the reason, it seems, is that he is not committed to *taking seriously* the opposing argument. This suggests that where open-mindedness involves assessing one or more competing views, it necessarily involves doing so with the aim of giving these views a "serious" (i.e. fair, honest, objective)

[13] When understood as a kind of transcending of one's cognitive limits, biases, and the like, open-mindedness bears an interesting relation to two epistemic/ethical virtues discussed at length by Miranda Fricker (2007): namely, testimonial justice (ch. 4) and hermeneutical justice (ch. 7). See e.g. pp. 7, 91–2, 169–71, and esp. 122. Both virtues are correctives to varieties of what Fricker describes as "epistemic injustice."

hearing or assessment. This reveals that a certain immediate motivation is partly constitutive of open-mindedness.[14]

8.2.2 *A definition of open-mindedness*

We are now in a position to consider a more general and formal characterization of open-mindedness. I propose the following account:

> (OM) An open-minded person is characteristically (a) willing and (within limits) able (b) to transcend a default cognitive standpoint (c) in order to take up or take seriously the merits of (d) a distinct cognitive standpoint.

Parts (b) through (d) of the definition mainly summarize the key points of the discussion up to this point and thus I will not elaborate on them here.[15]

Part (a), however, deals with an aspect of open-mindedness that we have yet to consider. Specifically, it concerns the question of whether open-mindedness should be understood as a disposition of the *will* or to what extent it might also involve a kind of reliable *ability* or *capacity*. That open-mindedness is at least partly constituted by a disposition of the will seems clear enough. If a person is able, say, to set aside her commitment to P in order to assess some prima facie compelling evidence for not-P, but is *unwilling* to do so, then presumably she is not open-minded. It may be thought, in fact, that open-mindedness is nothing more than a willingness to engage in the intellectual activity in question. But this is not quite right. Suppose that a person has been brainwashed by her community concerning a particular matter in such a way that while she is willing, and perhaps *thinks* herself able, to detach from the "accepted" way of thinking about this matter and to assess it in an impartial and objective way, she is in fact constitutionally incapable of doing so; despite her willingness, she

[14] Cf. Hare (1979) and (1985). Note that the present concern is distinct from a concern with an open-minded person's *ultimate* motivation for engaging in open-minded activity. Someone who consistently sets aside his beliefs in an effort to give a fair and honest hearing to the "other side," but who does so for entirely non-epistemic reasons (e.g. to better his reputation), might be open-minded, even if not virtuously so.

[15] A different, but not unrelated, definition of open-mindedness is defended by Hare in (1979) and (1985). He describes open-mindedness as "a willingness to form and revise one's own views as impartially and as objectively as possible in the light of available evidence and argument" (1985: 3). While there is much to be said in support of this definition (and considerable convergence between it and the definition just stated), I think it fails to identify the characteristic element of open-mindedness: namely, the "cognitive transcending" or detaching described above. In fact, as Wayne Riggs (2010) has suggested, Hare's account seems to equate open-mindedness with rationality *simpliciter* or with the entire "package" of intellectual virtues.

simply cannot think "outside the box." This person cannot be considered open-minded.[16]

Now consider a person who is willing to set aside her usual way of thinking about something in order to consider an opposed way, whose cognitive constitution does not rule this out, but who nonetheless is prevented from doing so on account of certain "external" factors (perhaps her community has destroyed all information concerning the opposed way of thinking and will severely punish anyone suspected of trying to learn about it). This person, I take it, can reasonably be regarded as open-minded.

The difference between these two cases lies with the source of the agents' inability to think in the relevant way. In the latter case, this inability is entirely (or at least relevantly) external to the person's agency. In the initial case, however, the corresponding inability, while not the agent's fault, is a *function* of her agency, at least in the sense that presently, on account of her own cognitive or psychological constitution, she is unable to think or reason in the way in question.[17] Accordingly, we should think of open-mindedness as constituted both by a willingness and an ability, but only where the ability is understood in the relevant "internal" terms.

Two additional issues concerning (OM) need to be addressed. The first is a potential objection. In certain cases, it may seem possible for a person to satisfy the conditions of (OM) while failing to instantiate the character trait of open-mindedness. Suppose, for instance, that while looking through some of my family's genealogical materials, I run across some counterevidence for my belief that my paternal grandparents migrated from Germany to Wisner, Nebraska. The evidence suggests instead that they migrated to nearby Wayne. Is confronting the evidence in this case likely to make demands on my intellectual character? Is it likely to require an exercise of open-mindedness on my part? This is at least questionable.[18] If nothing is riding on this issue for

[16] Hare (1979: 8) makes a similar point. This indicates a kind of reliability requirement on open-mindedness. This requirement is very different, however, from the truth-connected reliability requirement that I argued against in Chapter 7.

[17] Thus there is a sense in which the ability essential to open-mindedness is immune to luck. But this does not mean that it is completely immune to luck, for a person's cognitive or psychological constitution can itself be a matter of luck. For more on the role of luck in the possession of moral and intellectual virtues, see my (2007).

[18] Similarly, we can imagine cases in which the adjudication of two competing theories or arguments is simple and straightforward (one theory is obviously false, the other clearly correct) so that anything like "open-minded inquiry" would be irrelevant. And presumably the process of coming to *comprehend* or of *conceiving* of an explanation—processes which, as we saw above, can involve an exercise of open-mindedness—do not always or necessarily do so.

me, and if I immediately (with little or no thought or deliberation) change my mind about the matter, then presumably there will not be anything particularly "open-minded" about my doxastic activity.

This suggests a further requirement of open-mindedness. It might be thought, say, that (OM) should be supplemented with a proviso to the effect that the kind of activity it describes is expressive of open-mindedness only when it occurs within the context of an intellectual *challenge*. Alternatively, we might say that open-mindedness is a matter of transcending a default cognitive standpoint *where doing so makes a significant demand on the person's agency*. On the other hand, it is important not to set the bar for an exercise of open-mindedness (or any other character trait) too high. More specifically, it is important to allow for relatively easy and spontaneous displays of open-mindedness, particularly because such displays are likely to be especially common among those who are most open-minded (that is, those for whom open-minded intellectual activity is most natural or a matter of "second nature").

I will not attempt to settle this matter here. At issue is the very difficult question of how to understand the minimal demands of an exercise of a character trait or virtue. My own view is that an exercise of an intellectual virtue necessarily makes certain demands on its possessor's agency. But exactly what these demands are (and whether they are met in the kind of case noted above) is far from obvious. Accordingly, I shall leave it an open question whether (OM) should be modified in the suggested way.[19]

A second issue concerns a rather different way in which a person might satisfy the conditions of (OM) while failing to be genuinely open-minded. Here the worry is limited to cases that involve rational assessment or adjudication of one or more competing views. In cases of this sort, open-mindedness seems necessarily to range, not just over the assessment itself, but also over the open-minded person's doxastic *response* to this assessment. Suppose I am willing and able to set aside or detach from my commitment to P in order to assess the case for not-P, that as a result of this assessment I conclude that the case for not-P is stronger than I thought and the case for P weaker, but that I fail to adjust my belief or confidence levels accordingly. While I might have the "beginning" of open-mindedness or a small degree of it, surely I am not genuinely or completely open-minded. Accordingly, (OM) must be supplemented by the proviso that *where open-mindedness involves rational assessment or evaluation, it also necessarily involves adjusting one's beliefs or confidence levels according to the outcome of this assessment.*

[19] See Foot (2002: 9–14) for a related discussion.

This is not, however, a completely general requirement on (or necessary condition for) an exercise of open-mindedness. For in contexts void of rational assessment, there is no question as to whether the person has shown a proper or open-minded doxastic response to such assessment. Where a person exhibits open-mindedness in an attempt merely to understand a foreign or difficult subject matter, for instance, the question does not arise as to whether he has adjusted his beliefs or confidence levels accordingly. He has not sought to assess this subject matter; thus no such response should be expected of him. The additional requirement is, then, applicable only to a limited range of cases.[20]

8.3 *Open-mindedness and other cognitive excellences*

At various points in the chapter, we have had occasion to refer to cognitive excellences other than open-mindedness. These include virtues like intellectual fairness, impartiality, and honesty, as well as certain cognitive abilities or faculties like comprehension, conception, and imagination. We have seen, for instance, that in the face of intellectual opposition or conflict, an open-minded person is likely to move beyond her own convictions to give a serious, fair, and honest assessment to an opposing viewpoint; or that she is likely to be in a better position than someone who lacks open-mindedness to grasp a foreign or abstruse subject matter or to conceive of an explanation of a puzzling collection of evidence.

These connections between open-mindedness and other intellectual excellences give rise to two questions. First, is open-mindedness really anything over and above a disposition to exercise these other excellences? And second, assuming that it is, what exactly is the relationship between open-mindedness and these other traits? I shall address each of these questions in turn. Doing so will provide an even more perspicuous account of open-mindedness and its role in the cognitive economy.

[20] Wayne Riggs (2010) identifies two other qualities as partly "constitutive" of open-mindedness: namely, "self-knowledge" and "self-monitoring." While I will not stop to develop the point here, my own view is that these are better understood as *preconditions* for the possession of the actual intellectual *virtue* of open-mindedness. In other words: (1) Open-mindedness is not itself a matter of knowing oneself or monitoring one's beliefs (though to be open-minded in the right *way*, one's open-mindedness must operate against the "backdrop," so to speak, of the kind of self-awareness these things bring about); and (2) A person can be "open-minded" in a relevant (even if less than fully virtuous) sense even if she lacks much self-knowledge or doesn't engage in much cognitive monitoring (recall the open-minded college student described at the outset of the chapter).

It should be fairly clear at this point that open-mindedness cannot be reduced to any other intellectual virtue, a mere cognitive capacity, or any nexus thereof. To be sure, open-mindedness is closely related to virtues like intellectual fairness, honesty, impartiality, empathy, patience, adaptability, and autonomy; it is also importantly related to various cognitive capacities or faculties. We have seen, however, that it can be distinguished from these other qualities because it involves a certain willingness and ability to transcend a particular cognitive standpoint, and to do so with the aim of "taking up" or "taking seriously" an alternative cognitive standpoint. While the transcending in question is often accompanied by activity characteristic of other virtues or abilities, it is ultimately distinct from this activity. Intellectual empathy, for instance, involves a willingness or ability to view things from the standpoint of another person, to "get inside another's head." In certain cases, a person may be unable to do this if he lacks open-mindedness, since open-mindedness might comprise the breaking free or departing from his own cognitive standpoint that is necessary before he can hope to take up the standpoint of the other. But the "breaking free" and the "taking up" are distinct activities or phenomena, the former being proper to open-mindedness and the latter to intellectual empathy. Similarly, creativity, understood either as a character trait or hardwired capacity for conceiving of new possibilities, concepts, approaches, or the like, is often aided by, and for its successful operation can even require, an exercise of open-mindedness. But here again the actual conception of the new thought or possibility is the work of creativity, while the antecedent cognitive detaching or abstracting, which amounts to a kind of *preparation* for creative activity, is the work of open-mindedness. Open-mindedness thus occupies its own characteristic niche within the cognitive economy. It is not entirely parasitic on or reducible to other intellectual excellences.

What more can be said about the relationship between open-mindedness and these other, closely allied virtues and abilities? Several of the examples of open-mindedness discussed above, together with certain remarks just made, suggest that open-mindedness plays something of a *facilitating* role vis-à-vis other cognitive excellences—that it allows its possessor to employ or make effective use of these excellences. This is evident, first, in the immediate motivation of open-mindedness, as specified by (c) and (d) of (OM). An open-minded person, we have seen, is one who transcends a certain standpoint in order to "take up" or "take seriously" a different standpoint. The latter notions implicate some of the virtues and abilities in question. "Taking up" a cognitive standpoint, for instance, can amount to *comprehending* or *conceiving* of it; and taking such a standpoint "seriously" requires giving it a *fair, honest,* and *objective* hearing. This shows that other intellectual virtues and capacities enter into the specific motivational conditions of open-mindedness (even if open-mindedness itself is not reducible to these other qualities).

Two additional points concerning the relation between open-mindedness and these other excellences are worth noting. First, open-mindedness can *initiate* a cognitive process on which these other qualities are subsequently brought to bear. For instance, my open-mindedness might be what initiates or explains my decision to engage in honest dialogue with one of my intellectual opponents. Or it might fundamentally be what allows me to "think outside the box," to conceive of an explanation of an apparently incoherent set of facts. Second, open-mindedness can *sustain* or *support* other virtues or abilities already in operation. Again, suppose my open-mindedness leads me to enter into a rational, honest dialogue with an intellectual adversary. It might also be essential to keeping the dialogue going, since I may, after a few minutes of discussion, be tempted to terminate the conversation. The continuation or sustaining of honest, fair dialogue sometimes requires keeping an open mind. Alternatively, suppose my curiosity about an issue (rather than my open-mindedness) leads me to assess the relative merits of two competing theories. Upon realizing that the theories, or their logical relationship, are more complex or rigorous than I expected, I may need to exercise open-mindedness if I am to avoid bringing the inquiry to a premature conclusion or drawing a hasty conclusion. In short, the initiation of virtuous or otherwise excellent cognitive activity may require an exercise of open-mindedness; in other cases, open-mindedness may be necessary for sustaining such activity.

Open-mindedness, then, is largely or often a "facilitating virtue." By freeing the mind, or keeping it free, by allowing the mind to detach or remain detached from a default position or standpoint, it creates the "psychological space" for other virtues and faculties to perform their respective functions.

8.4 *When to be open-minded?*

In this final section, I turn to one of the more pressing questions for a philosophical account of open-mindedness: namely, when (or under what conditions or toward which views) is it appropriate to exhibit or exercise open-mindedness? While an important and challenging question, I can do little more at this point than offer an initial sketch of an answer. But the discussion will, I hope, shed at least some worthwhile light on the relevant structural and practical dimensions of open-mindedness.

My immediate focus will be a slightly (though importantly) narrower version of the question just stated. I shall consider under what circumstances it is *intellectually* (versus, say, morally) virtuous to engage in the kind of cognitive transcending or detaching that I have argued is characteristic of open-mindedness.[21] This question presupposes that an exercise of open-mindedness is not always intellectually virtuous and thus (potentially at least) that open-mindedness itself is not always an intellectual virtue. But this assumption is all to the good, for as indicated at the outset of the chapter, there are ways of being open-minded, and ways displaying open-mindedness, that are less than intellectually virtuous—and indeed that might even be intellectually vicious. My aim, then, is to begin to identify what distinguishes an intellectually virtuous exercise of open-mindedness from a non-virtuous one.

It should be no surprise that an answer to this question might be derivable from the overall goal or end of intellectual virtue. As explained in Chapter 6, this goal includes a range of epistemic goods. For present purposes, it will be helpful to limit our attention to the preeminent good in question: namely, the goal of truth or true belief.[22] Once we restrict our attention in this way, the following reply to our question naturally presents itself:

> (R1) A person S's engaging in the activity characteristic of open-mindedness under circumstances C is intellectually virtuous just in case S's engaging in this activity in C would be helpful for reaching the truth.

While initially plausible, (R1) is problematic, particularly if we are concerned with anything like a "personal worth" account of intellectual virtue, that is, if we are thinking of intellectual virtues as traits that bear favorably on their possessor's intellectual goodness or badness qua *person*. Specifically, as indicated at various points in Chapters 6–7, this reply is at once too strong and too weak. It is too strong because it would prevent us from regarding as intellectually virtuous the open-minded activity of, say, a systematically deceived (but fully internally rational) victim of a Cartesian demon. And it is too weak because it would

[21] In taking up this question, we are addressing a more normative aspect of open-mindedness, that is, we are concerning ourselves with open-mindedness as an intellectual *virtue* in a way that we have not up to this point in the chapter. But even an exhaustive answer to the present question would not yield a complete "picture" of the actual intellectual virtue of open-mindedness, since it would not address the underlying or fundamental *motivation* of open-mindedness (a matter which, as I argued in Chapter 6, is essential to its or any trait's status as an intellectual virtue).

[22] For a related truth-oriented account of open-mindedness, see Adler (2004: 130 and 139).

deem intellectually virtuous the truth-conducive open-minded activity of a person who has *no reason whatsoever* to think that this activity really *is* truth-conducive—or, even worse, who has reason to think that the activity is likely to lead an increase in *false* beliefs.

A related but more promising suggestion (also alluded to in Chapters 6–7) is as follows:

> (R2) A person S's engaging in the activity characteristic of open-mindedness under circumstances C is intellectually virtuous just in case it is reasonable for S to believe that engaging in this activity in C may be helpful for reaching the truth.[23]

This reply to our question rules correctly in connection with both sorts of cases noted above.[24] It also permits us to make sense of many other familiar and commonsense judgments about open-mindedness. Suppose, for instance, that I have extremely good reasons in support of a proposition P and no direct or indirect evidence for not-P, but that some person whom I know to be highly irrational accepts not-P and would like for me to give an open-minded hearing to his favorite arguments against P. It likely would not be intellectually virtuous for me to engage in open-minded inquiry concerning this person's reasons for accepting not-P.[25] One plausible explanation of this is that it would be unreasonable for me to think that doing so might be epistemically profitable or get me any closer to the truth regarding P. Alternatively, suppose my grounds for P are relatively weak, that I tend to be biased and hasty in my thinking about P (and am aware of this tendency), and that I have a great deal of respect for the intellectual abilities and character of the person asking me to consider the case for not-P. Here I take it that it likely would be intellectually virtuous for me to be open-minded. And again one plausible explanation of this is that it is entirely

[23] This formulation could easily be extended to cover other normative dimensions of open-mindedness. We might say, for instance, that it would be intellectually virtuous for S to exhibit a certain *amount* of open-minded activity or to show open-mindedness toward a particular *idea* or *person* just in case it is reasonable for S to think that doing so may be epistemically profitable.

[24] Specifically, it "rules in" the victim of the Cartesian demon, since it is entirely reasonable for this person to believe that his open-minded activity may be helpful for reaching the truth; and it "rules out," for an even more obvious reason, the person who lacks any reason at all for thinking the same.

[25] Recall that we are concerned strictly with what would be *intellectually* virtuous. Depending on the person, my relationship to him, and so forth, it might very well be *morally* virtuous (even virtuous all-things-considered) for me to give an open-minded hearing to the case against P.

reasonable for me to think that doing so may be helpful for reaching the truth about P.

While I think (R2) is on the right track, more needs to be said about it. For instance, it might be wondered whether (R2) is too weak. The principle stipulates that for an exercise of open-mindedness to count as intellectually virtuous, it must be reasonable for the person in question to think (merely) that this exercise *may* be helpful for reaching the truth. Doesn't this threaten to cast the net of open-mindedness too broadly? Wouldn't following this rule lead to excessive exercises of open-mindedness—to a wasteful or otherwise inappropriate allotment of our epistemic resources?

This concern is well-placed and indeed calls for a modification of (R2). Before getting to this modification, however, it is important to note that there is at least some motivation for thinking of the standard at issue in relatively weak terms. For suppose that we were to maintain instead that S's engaging in open-minded activity regarding P in C is intellectually virtuous just in case it is reasonable for S to think that engaging in this activity in C is *likely* to be helpful for reaching the truth regarding P. This would limit the class of intellectually acceptable or virtuous exercises of open-mindedness in an objectionable way. For presumably it is sometimes intellectually worthwhile or virtuous to give an open-minded hearing to the case against a particular belief given the mere *possibility* that this belief is mistaken and thus that an open-minded inquiry may get one closer to the truth.[26]

The obvious solution at this point is to treat the condition specified by (R2) as necessary but not sufficient. Suitably modified, (R2) becomes:

> (R3) A person S's engaging in the activity characteristic of open-mindedness under circumstances C is intellectually virtuous *only if* it is reasonable for S to believe that engaging in this activity in C may be helpful for reaching the truth.

(R3) is considerably weaker and less ambitious than (R2). I assume, however, that it captures one central condition that must be met in order for an exercise of open-mindedness to count as intellectually virtuous.

[26] In certain cases, this is likely to be due to certain *pragmatic* stakes (as with belief in God, say). But the stakes might also be *epistemic*. Suppose that some things are epistemically more worth knowing or having true beliefs about than others. Relative to a particular belief about one of these epistemically "significant" or "worthy" subject matters, an open-minded consideration of a counterargument might be warranted given the mere *possibility* that it is mistaken. Here what hangs in the balance is a straightforwardly epistemic good. This is a notable point of intersection between my inquiry in this book and the burgeoning field of epistemic value theory (for more on the latter, see Pritchard 2007).

One additional issue worth considering concerns what exactly might be involved with its being "reasonable" for a person to think that the activity characteristic of open-mindedness may be truth-conducive in the relevant sense. This issue could be approached from a variety of different angles.[27] My own approach will be a fairly modest one. I will not attempt to specify anything like necessary and sufficient conditions for the relevant concept of reasonability. Rather I will address the issue of which factors are likely to govern the applicability of this concept.

Imagine, then, a person S in circumstances C who accepts a proposition P but is considering giving an open-minded hearing to an argument or evidence against P. My suggestion is as follows:

> Its being "reasonable" for S to think that being open-minded in C may be helpful for reaching the truth is generally a function of the comparative strength of S's grounds concerning: (1) P itself; (2) S's own reliability relative to the propositional domain to which P belongs; and (3) the reliability of the source of the argument or evidence against P.[28]

Therefore, as suggested earlier, if S has very strong reasons in support of P, is reliable in his judgments concerning P and related matters (and is aware of this fact), and has reason to doubt the credibility of the source of the alleged counterevidence, then presumably it will not be reasonable for S to believe that being open-minded in the present circumstances may be helpful for reaching the truth. But, again, if S's reasons for P are weak, S knows himself to be sloppy or careless or otherwise unreliable in making judgments concerning P and related matters, and has reason to trust the source of the alleged counterevidence to P,

[27] We might seek to identify necessary and sufficient conditions for this notion. Or we might ask about the required *strength* of a "reasonable" person's grounds or evidence. Or about whether "reasonability" should be understood in fully "internal" (or partially "external") terms.

[28] Three brief remarks are in order. First, it might be thought that (2) and (3) would collapse into (1), that is, that if I have reason to think that a reliable source denies P, this bears on my evidence for "P itself." While this may be right, I am thinking of (1) in terms of evidence or reasons that bear in a more direct or immediate way on P. I assume this idea is sufficiently intuitive. Second, this formulation applies only to the context of intellectual conflict or dispute; thus it does not say anything about what "reasonability" might amount to in some of the other contexts to which open-mindedness is relevant (e.g. that of trying to *comprehend* a foreign subject matter or to *conceive* of an explanation for some perplexing data). Third, even relative to the context of intellectual disagreement, the account is only "generally" correct given that in certain cases there may be evidential considerations that bear upon what is "reasonable" but that do not fit into any of the three categories just delineated.

then presumably it will be reasonable for S to believe that being open-minded in the present situation may be helpful for reaching the truth.[29]

This reply is limited in some important ways. Again, it does not actually specify *when* it is reasonable for a person to hold the relevant sort of belief. Rather, it attempts merely to identify the factors relevant to making such a determination.[30] Nonetheless, the formulation still sheds some light on when it is reasonable for a person to think that the activity characteristic of open-mindedness may be helpful for reaching the truth, and thus, when conjoined with (R3), on when it is intellectually virtuous to engage in such activity.[31]

8.5 *Conclusion*

We have examined several aspects of open-mindedness. We began, in sections 8.1–8.2, by looking closely at the internal structure of this trait. I argued that open-mindedness is fundamentally a kind of cognitive detaching from or transcending of a default cognitive standpoint. In section 8.3 we looked closely at the relation between open-mindedness and other intellectual virtues, making the observation that while open-mindedness is a distinct intellectual virtue, it often plays a facilitating role vis-à-vis other virtues. And in section 8.4 we considered the question of when, from an intellectual standpoint, it is appropriate or virtuous for one to exercise open-mindedness.

[29] Riggs's (2010) discussion of the role of self-knowledge and self-monitoring, discussed briefly in note 20, is clearly relevant to an assessment of (2) above. To exercise open-mindedness appropriately or virtuously, one must have a good sense of one's own reliability with respect to the subject matter at issue. The kind of self-knowledge and self-monitoring that Riggs describes is critical for bringing this about. Also relevant here are the discussions by Adler (2004) and Riggs (2010) concerning the importance to open-mindedness of a second-order awareness of one's cognitive *fallibility*.

[30] To convert the formulation into an account of when it is reasonable for a person to hold the relevant belief, we would (at a minimum) need a way of assigning relative weights to the various parameters identified in (1)–(3).

[31] It is worth noting briefly that the present account of open-mindedness apparently satisfies the various desiderata identified by Riggs (2010) for an acceptable philosophical treatment of open-mindedness: it provides a reasonably "thick" characterization of open-mindedness; it portrays open-mindedness as a distinctive cognitive excellence that is inherently *personal*; it does not leave the nature or value of open-mindedness looking paradoxical; and it sheds some light on when it is appropriate or intellectually virtuous to be open-minded.

Chapter 9

INTELLECTUAL COURAGE

In the previous chapter, we examined an intellectual virtue concerned with detaching from or transcending one's default cognitive perspective. Here we turn our attention to a virtue concerned with sticking to or persisting in this perspective. The virtue in question is intellectual courage. Like open-mindedness, intellectual courage is at once (1) a paradigm instance of an intellectual virtue and yet (2) a trait that obviously can go awry. My primary aim here is to identify the "characteristic psychology" of intellectual courage, that is, the features of intellectual courage that distinguish it from other intellectual virtues. The discussion will also, I hope, go a considerable way toward resolving the tension between the two features of intellectual courage just noted.

9.1 *Intellectual courage vs. moral courage*

It will be helpful to begin by marking a distinction between intellectual courage and courage *simpliciter* or moral courage.[1] One natural way of drawing this distinction is in terms of the ultimate end or object aimed at by each type of courage. Specifically, it might be said that if a person's courage aims ultimately at a *moral* end—if she is motivated to do something courageous out of, say, an intrinsic concern for social justice—then she possesses moral courage, while if her courage aims ultimately at an *intellectual* end—at the acquisition of knowledge or understanding—then she possesses intellectual courage.

It would seem, however, that a person can be intellectually courageous in a genuine sense while lacking an ultimate concern with knowledge or related ends. Imagine, for instance, an investigative journalist who, despite serious and

[1] Any such distinction is bound to be somewhat artificial given that few persons are likely to have one kind of courage but not the other. Nevertheless, given that our primary concern is *intellectual* virtue, I think the distinction is still worth attempting to draw.

pointed threats to his well-being, persists in researching and writing about the appalling human rights record of an oppressive dictatorial regime. The journalist's ultimate motivation, however, is strictly to win a Pulitzer Prize and gain the professional status and other benefits that come therewith. Thus while the journalist has an immediate concern with discovering and reporting the truth about his subject matter, he has no *intrinsic* interest in it: he is not curious about the relevant states of affairs; nor does he have any intention of doing anything to alleviate the relevant suffering. It is reasonable to think that while the journalist would not be intellectually (or morally) *virtuous*, he might still be intellectually *courageous*.[2] Again, he regularly puts himself in harm's way out of an immediate and focused concern with getting at and reporting the truth. This suggests that an ultimate concern for truth or knowledge—a concern for truth or knowledge *as such*—cannot be what distinguishes intellectual courage from moral (or other kinds) of courage.

A more plausible view, suggested by the case just considered, is that intellectual courage can be distinguished from moral courage on account of its involving an *immediate* concern with intellectual or epistemic ends. As I explain below, and as is more or less evident from common sense, courage of any sort involves responding in a certain way to a conflict between the achievement of a particular good and one's own safety or well-being. With intellectual courage, I am suggesting, the good in question is necessarily an intellectual one, while with other forms of courage some other kind of good is at stake. Put another way, an intellectually courageous person is immediately moved or motivated by certain distinctively intellectual ends like knowledge, truth, justification, and understanding. I will have more to say about this distinction below, but I take it that it provides at least an initially plausible way of capturing the difference between intellectual courage and its non-intellectual counterparts.

9.2 *Some examples*

Let us begin our inquiry into the nature and structure of intellectual courage by considering a few "real life" examples of the trait.

[2] He would not, at any rate, be intellectually virtuous in the "personal worth" sense discussed at length in Chapter 6. Some might take issue with the suggestion that a person could be genuinely intellectually courageous without being intellectually virtuous, that is, that intellectual courage might fail to be an intellectual *virtue*. I address this question at length in section 9.6.1 below.

1. Perhaps more than any American journalist, Edward R. Murrow stands out as one who was willing to put himself in harm's way for the sake of reaching the truth. His dogged pursuit of Senator Joseph McCarthy is but one example. Another is his famous rooftop coverage of the London Blitz. Murrow also regularly demonstrated intellectual courage in his interactions with his employer, the Colombia Broadcasting System (CBS), and with the media industry at large.

For instance, in a 1958 address to the Radio-Television News Directors Association, Murrow issued an excoriating critique of the general drift of these media. He began on the following ominous note: "At the end of this discourse a few people may accuse this reporter of fouling his own comfortable nest, and your organization may be accused of giving hospitality to heretical and even dangerous thoughts. But the elaborate structure of networks, advertising agencies, and sponsors will not be shaken or altered. It is my desire, if not my duty, to try to talk to you journeymen with some candor about what is happening to radio and television" (Edwards 2004: 130–1). Murrow proceeded to lambaste television's "decadence, escapism, and insulation from the realities of the world in which we live," adding that "[i]f this state of affairs continues, we may alter an advertising slogan to read: Look Now, Pay Later. For surely we shall pay for using this most powerful instrument of communication to insulate the citizenry from the hard and demanding realities which must be faced if we are to survive" (132). He declared that he was "frightened by the imbalance, the constant striving to reach the largest possible audience for everything; by the absence of a sustained study of the state of the nation" (134). And he offered the following proposal: " Why should not each of the twenty or thirty big corporations which dominate radio and television decide that they should give up one or two of their regularly scheduled programs each year, turn the time over to the networks, and say in effect, 'This is a tiny tithe, just a little of our profits. On this particular night, we aren't going to try to sell cigarettes or automobiles; this is merely a gesture to indicate our belief in *the importance of ideas*'" (134–5; my italics). This was an extremely bold move on Murrow's part; and, unsurprisingly, it led to further deterioration of his relationship with CBS and the broadcasting industry at large.

While the motivation behind Murrow's critique was mixed,[3] there is little reason to doubt that among these motives was a desire to shed light on certain truths or realities that many others in the industry preferred to let remain in the

[3] The attack was at least partly motivated by Murrow's sense that CBS had wronged him by cancelling his famous *See It Now* television program.

dark. Longtime National Public Radio reporter Bob Edwards (2004) describes Murrow thus: "Most of all, Murrow was absolutely fearless. His favorite commentator, Elmer Davis, used to say, 'Don't let the bastards scare you.' Nothing scared Murrow—not bombs, dictators, generals, members of Congress, sponsors, corporate executives, or Joseph McCarthy. Murrow could not be muscled, bullied, bought, corrupted, or intimidated" (155).

2. In 1989, United States Supreme Court Justice Sandra Day O'Connor found herself with the opportunity to dramatically alter the legal standing of one of the most controversial moral issues of our time. The Court had taken up the case of *Webster v. Reproductive Health Services*, which concerned several restrictions passed by the Missouri state legislature on a woman's ability to receive an abortion. O'Connor, who possessed the swing vote in the case, faced intense pressure from several corners to decide the case in a way that would satisfy the interested parties—and to do so quickly.

Within the court, for instance, she faced pressure from Justice Blackmun (the author of the Court's 1973 opinion in *Roe v. Wade* legalizing abortion) to uphold a lower court's ruling overturning the Missouri law. Joan Biskupic (2005), one of O'Connor's biographers, notes that Blackmun "had a habit of challenging new justices to be with him or against him on abortion rights. He saw no middle ground" (218). O'Connor also faced intense pressure from Chief Justice Rehnquist and Justice Scalia, both of whom apparently saw *Webster* as an opportunity to overturn *Roe* and strategized carefully to get the necessary cooperation from O'Connor (224–5). The pressure from outside the court was even more intense. An unprecedented number of "friend of the court" briefs were filed by "physicians, historians, elected officials, women's groups, and religious organizations on both sides . . . Thousands of letters were also being delivered, most addressed to Justice O'Connor. Some of the mail was graphic, including photographs of aborted fetuses and of coat hangers, the latter a symbol of illegal abortions" (225). Furthermore, in the preceding months, hundreds of thousands of pro-life and pro-choice advocates had taken to the National Mall in an effort to influence the Court's ruling. Add to this that O'Connor was a woman, mother, and the first female Supreme Court Justice in U.S. history, and the stakes and pressure in the case can appear nearly unbearable. Even to *consider* or *think* about the merits of the case in the required dispassionate and objective way must have required considerable intellectual courage on O'Connor's part.

O'Connor also demonstrated intellectual courage in two other ways. First in the *time* it took her to draft and issue an opinion. O'Connor was well-known within the Court for expedient deliberation: "Usually, O'Connor was the picture of efficiency. She liked to get her opinions out quickly and let her views be known so that she could affect the process" (228). The pressure to do so in the present case was especially intense. But despite this pressure and her penchant for expediency, O'Connor took her time in formulating her position, waiting until the last minute to issue an opinion. Second, O'Connor proceeded to issue an opinion that was bound to prove unsatisfactory to the most invested and vocal members of the Court and the American public on either side of the issue. Contra Blackmun and many pro-choice advocates, she voted to uphold most of the Missouri restrictions on abortion; on the other hand, contra Rehnquist, Scalia, and many pro-life advocates, she refused to support any decision that would amount to an overturning of *Roe*. Given the enormous stakes at issue, it is difficult not to regard O'Connor's deliberation and decision in the case as requiring a substantial amount of intellectual courage.[4]

3. A third illustration comes from some recent history in astrophysics. In the late 1960s, John Bahcall and Raymond Davis collaborated on an experiment designed to confirm the "Standard Solar Model," according to which the "sun shines" by converting hydrogen into helium and a small amount of extra mass into a substantial amount of extra energy. Using this model, Bahcall calculated the number of neutrinos likely to be present on the earth's surface. Davis proposed to test these predictions using a large vat of cleaning fluid housed deep underground in a South Dakota gold mine and designed to register the presence of the relevant particles. Davis's proposal was as unconventional as it sounds, largely because he was attempting to substantiate claims in particle physics on the basis of results in radiochemistry. The outcome of the experiment was disappointing to both parties, as it detected only one-third of the expected number of neutrinos, suggesting that either Bahcall's calculations or Davis's measurements were mistaken.[5]

Over the next 30 years, despite considerable pressure within the profession to alter or abandon their views, Bahcall stood behind and continued to refine his calculations and Davis did the same with his measurements. Of their predicament, Bahcall remarks: "[E]very year for 30 years I had to look at different processes that people would imaginatively suggest that might play a role in

[4] This is something that all parties to the debate should be able to agree on, particularly because the question is strictly whether O'Connor demonstrated intellectual *courage*, not whether her courage was intellectually or morally *virtuous*. More on this distinction below.

[5] For an account of this recent episode in the history of science, see Hargittai and Hargittai (2004).

the sun, and it didn't matter how convinced I was that they were wrong. I had to demonstrate scientifically that these processes were not important in order to convince people [that] yes, the expectation from the sun was robust and therefore you should take the discrepancy seriously."[6]

Around the turn of the century, the work of Bahcall and Davis was vindicated, as new experimental data revealed that the discrepancy between Bahcall's calculations and Davis's experiments was attributable, not to any error on their part, but to previously unknown properties of neutrinos: in particular, to the fact that they have mass and therefore can change forms upon coming into contact with matter. This insight explained Davis's failure to detect the full number of neutrinos predicted by Bahcall: the remaining neutrinos had changed form (from electron neutrinos to muon and tau neutrinos) and were therefore undetectable by Davis's mechanism.

The perseverance and courage required for "sticking to his guns" for over three decades is evident in how Bahcall describes his response to the recent findings: "For three decades people had been pointing at this guy and saying this is the guy who wrongly calculated the flux of neutrinos from the sun, and suddenly that wasn't so. It was like a person who had been sentenced for some heinous crime, and then a DNA test is made and it's found that he isn't guilty. That's exactly the way I felt" (ibid.). Bahcall also testifies to the intellectual courage of his friend and colleague Davis, who received a Nobel Prize in 2002 for his work on solar neutrinos: "In the early days, the 1960s and the 1970s and into the early 1980s, all of the people who were seriously committed to solar neutrinos could, and frequently did, ride in the front seat of Ray's car. Only Ray and I were committed in the sixties and seventies. I rode with Ray because I had confidence that Ray could do a reliable experiment, one that would justify my spending so much time on making precise theoretical calculations. Only Ray was willing to take the risk and devote himself to such an exotic experiment. And probably, only Ray had the set of talents and the character to make it work."[7] The intellectual activity of Bahcall and Davis illustrates nicely the defining character and potential epistemic benefits of intellectual courage and related excellences.

[6] This and the quotation that follows are taken from the transcript of a *Nova* segment called "The Ghost Particle," a copy of which is available at <http://www.pbs.org/wgbh/nova/neutrino/>. It can reasonably be asked whether Bahcall *ought* to have "stuck to his guns" in this way. But this again is the question of whether his cognitive activity was intellectually *virtuous*—not whether it was (merely) intellectually *courageous*. See section 9.6.1 below for more on this point.

[7] Hargittai and Hargittai (2004: 246–7).

9.3 *The "context" of intellectual courage*

The foregoing examples suggest the following characterization of intellectual courage: namely, that intellectual courage is (at least roughly and generally) a matter of (1) pursuing an intellectual good (2) despite the fact that doing so involves a certain threat or potential harm to oneself. We can begin to refine our grasp of this trait by exploring both parts of this characterization in more detail. I begin with (2), which pertains to what we might think of as the essential "context" of intellectual courage, that is, to the conditions or circumstances under which the positive substance of intellectual courage can be manifested.

In what sort of context or situation, then, does an intellectually courageous person characteristically exhibit or exercise his courage? One prima facie plausible response is that he does so in situations involving *fear*. Indeed it can be tempting to equate courage of any sort with an ability to respond to or to manage one's fears in a certain rational or appropriate way.[8]

The experience of fear, however, is not a precondition for an exercise of intellectual courage. To see why, suppose that after years of standing up to powerful figures in the interest of reaching and conveying the truth, doing so no longer evokes any fear on Murrow's part. Rather, in the relevant circumstances, his confidence and perseverance kick immediately into gear. While *aware* of the harm that might befall him, this harm no longer registers at an affective or emotional level. Murrow fearlessly confronts his subjects and pushes to have the truth about them made public. While perhaps an unlikely scenario, surely it is not impossible. Moreover, it is reasonable to think that the fearless Murrow might still be intellectually courageous, despite his lack of fear. If so, then an exercise of intellectual courage does not presuppose or require an experience of fear. In a discussion of intellectual courage and caution, Robert Roberts and Jay Wood (2007) make similar observation: "A person who has repeatedly faced down fear and thus become courageous may have become fearless in some of the circumstances in which he acts courageously. Despite the absence of actual fear, we still call him courageous" (218).[9]

In response, it might be argued that while present or psychologically occurrent fear is not an essential precondition for an exercise of intellectual courage,

[8] Aristotle, for instance, gives the notion of fear (more specifically, of *fearlessness*) a very prominent role in his account of courage. See *NE* 1115a–1117b.

[9] Foot (2002) also argues that "the emotion of fear is not a necessary condition for the display of courage" (12).

an experience of fear still figures necessarily in this domain. One possibility is that fear must be present in the etiology of the relevant trait. For instance, it might be said that while it is not essential that Murrow continue to experience fear in the context of confronting powerful media figures, it is essential that he previously experienced fear in this context. Alternatively, it might be thought that fear is essential to the context of intellectual courage in the sense that the relevant threat or danger must be one that human beings *generally* find fearful (even if in isolated cases they do not).[10] While I acknowledge some initial plausibility in both of these suggestions, I think both are mistaken. We will be in a better position to see why this is the case, however, once we have considered some other aspects of the "context" of intellectual courage. Thus I shall return to these suggestions later in the chapter.

An alternative but also prima facie plausible way of thinking about the preconditions for an exercise of intellectual courage is in terms of the presence of certain threats or risks, regardless of whether these engender any fear on the part of the agent. But this proposal is also problematic. For it is easy to imagine situations in which a person persists in a belief or inquiry under circumstances that are *in fact* dangerous, say, but who (like the extremely near-sighted Mr. Magoo) is entirely unaware of the danger at hand. I take it that even where such a belief or inquiry involves an immediate concern with truth or knowledge, it cannot be said to involve an exercise of intellectual courage.

Perhaps the right position, then, is that an exercise of intellectual courage necessarily involves an actual threat or danger *together with* an awareness of it. This is also too demanding, however, for a person can exhibit intellectual courage even if she is mistaken about the presence of any threat or danger. A biologist conducting research on a particular species of venomous snake might exhibit intellectual courage even if the particular specimen he is handling has a genetic defect that has rendered it harmless. Thus there is in no genuine threat to the biologist's well-being. Nonetheless, it seems clear that if his activity is motivated by an immediate desire for truth or knowledge, it might well count as an exercise of intellectual courage.

This suggests the following account of the "context" of intellectual courage: an intellectually courageous person is one who engages in a certain sort of activity despite the *appearance* of a threat or harm, and more specifically, despite a *judgment* or *belief* to the effect that the activity in question is dangerous or threatening. This judgment amounts to a precondition for an exercise

[10] Roberts and Wood (2007: 218) seem to endorse both of these possibilities.

of intellectual courage—it comprises the background against which the positive "substance" of intellectual courage is manifested. Along these lines, James Wallace (1978) remarks: "An agent, in performing a courageous act, need not feel any fear at all, nor need he feel the act difficult. We admire the courage of someone who does something very dangerous so coolly it appears to be easy for him. It is necessary, however, in order for his act to be courageous, that he be *aware* of the danger and that he recognize it *as* a danger" (80; my emphasis).

We are now in a position to return to the reply noted above according to which intellectual courage requires the presence of fear either in the psychological etiology of the intellectually courageous person or such that the circumstances in question are generally feared by human beings. Assuming the necessity of the sort of belief or judgment just identified, these further requirements turn out to be otiose. Consider again the utterly fearless version of Murrow. Suppose he were psychologically hard-wired so that he does not presently and indeed never did experience fear in the course of the relevant confrontations (perhaps he suffers from a psychological defect that prevents him from experiencing a range of emotions including fear). If in fact Murrow perceives the situations in question as dangerous or threatening, if he is sensitive to their dangerous or threatening features, and if he proceeds with the relevant activity despite this appearance, then presumably he can be considered intellectually courageous. Likewise, suppose that human nature were to evolve in such a way that we no longer had the relevant affective or fearful response to dangerous or potentially harmful situations. Surely this state of affairs would not make intellectual courage obsolete or undermine its status as a virtue. Again, inasmuch as we continued to *recognize* the potential dangers involved with getting to the truth or acquiring knowledge, intellectual courage would still have application.

This account of the context of intellectual courage is further supported by the fact that if either of the two conditions just discussed were to obtain, but the relevant perception or judgment were absent, then the activity in question intuitively would not count as an exercise of intellectual courage. Suppose, for instance, that the biologist conducting research on poisonous snakes becomes so accustomed to and skilled at interacting with the snakes that he no longer has *any* sense of the danger they pose. The dangerous features of the situation are entirely beyond his ken. He simply proceeds with his research in a careful and meticulous manner, completely oblivious to the risks he is taking. This person would not appear to be intellectually courageous. This does not entail that his character is *defective*; he may, in fact, be "beyond courage" or possess a kind of "super-courage."[11] The claim is rather that without any appearance of danger or risk, the concept of intellectual courage has no application. Moreover, this would be true even if early on in his career the biologist did sometimes experience fear under similar conditions; or if humans generally experienced fear under these conditions. This is further reason to think that fear is not a necessary precondition for an exercise of intellectual courage.

Finally, note that the *sort* of harm a subjective perception of which is essential to an exercise of intellectual courage can take either a positive or a negative form. An intellectually courageous person may risk social, political, professional, or bodily *injury*; or she may risk the *loss* of a considerable good along these lines. Concerning the latter, we might imagine that by resisting pressure from her fellow Justices to rush her decision in *Webster* or to cast her vote in a particular way, O'Connor risked a certain comfort level or measure of respect from one or more of her colleagues. It is a stretch to regard such a loss as a potential positive harm to O'Connor (clearly none of her fellow Justices were in a position to threaten her job security, her basic power or authority, her compensation, or the like). And yet the potential loss might still have been significant enough to demand an exercise of intellectual courage.

9.4 *The "substance" of intellectual courage*

Given what we have seen of the defining "context" of intellectual courage, we can revise our initial characterization of this trait as follows. Intellectual courage is a matter of (1) pursuing an intellectual good (2′) despite the fact that doing so involves an apparent threat or potential harm to oneself. In the present section, I turn to examine and refine (1). Again, our main focus here is the "positive substance" of intellectual courage, since we are attempting to specify just what an intellectually courageous person characteristically does under the conditions specified by (2′).

We can begin by noting that at a certain level there is no answer to this question, for the substance of intellectual courage is to a significant extent

[11] Cf. Aristotle *NE* 1145b. Similarly, a person might experience fear upon her first several trips on an airplane and might show courage by proceeding to fly. Over time, however, she might become so accustomed to flying that she no longer thinks about or has any real sense of the danger involved with doing so. At this point, it is doubtful that we would regard her decision to fly as courageous.

indeterminate.[12] To say of someone that she has acted in an intellectually courageous way is not by itself to provide any indication of what this person has actually done, of what sort of activity she has engaged in. In this respect, intellectual courage apparently differs from several other intellectual virtues. Attentiveness, for instance, necessarily involves a certain mental focusing or attention, intellectual patience a kind of waiting or enduring, and open-mindedness a kind of intellectual detaching or transcending. The defining character of intellectual courage, by contrast, is open or formal in a way or to an extent that the defining character of many other virtues is not. This illustrates the further point that intellectual courage, like open-mindedness, is a "facilitating virtue," in that it often serves to make possible or sustain the operation of one or more other virtues.[13] Indeed, as suggested by Peter Geach (1977: 150–5), given that an exercise of any other virtue could, under the right conditions, be both intellectually appropriate but also dangerous or threatening in the relevant sense, it follows that intellectual courage can play a supporting or facilitating role in connection with *any* other intellectual virtue. This does not mean, however, that intellectual courage is restricted to a facilitating role. For it can also bear directly on the operation of a cognitive faculty. It might take intellectual courage, for instance, to *observe* a certain threatening state of affairs or to *conceive* of a certain undesirable possibility.[14]

While the positive character of intellectual courage is open or formal in the sense just noted, can anything substantive or illuminating be said about it? For instance, what more can be said about the goods that an intellectually courageous person characteristically sees fit to pursue? Or about the sorts of intellectual activities on which intellectual courage might be brought to bear? One fairly obvious answer to the latter question is that intellectual courage can be applied to the activity of *inquiry*, or a course of action undertaken to reach the truth about some issue. As suggested by several of the examples above, an intellectually courageous person might initiate or follow through with an inquiry that she deems intellectually worthy despite the fact that doing so involves an apparent threat to her well-being. Note, however, that she might

[12] On this point, see Wallace (1978: 76–7), Roberts (1984), Rorty (1988: 302–3), and Roberts and Wood (2007: 17). Some of these authors think this allows us to draw a deep distinction between courage (and some similar virtues) and other more "substantive" virtues. On my view, the indeterminateness is rather a matter of *degree*, with all virtues being indeterminate to a greater or lesser extent.

[13] For more on the idea of facilitating virtues, see section 8.3 of Chapter 8.

[14] See the discussion of open-mindedness in Chapter 8 for a related point. Rorty (1988: ch. 15) also provides an illuminating discussion of some of these facets of courage.

also *call off* or *suspend* an inquiry. If, for instance, she judges that the inquiry is an epistemic dead end, then she might, despite a potential loss of admiration from her colleagues or funding for her research, choose to abandon the inquiry. This illustrates, perhaps in contrast with a certain intuitive or commonsense way of thinking about intellectual courage, that this virtue is not always a matter of *pressing on* or *moving forward* with some prior intellectual endeavor. It has certain negative applications as well.[15]

Inquiry is not the only intellectual activity on which intellectual courage might be brought to bear. An intellectually courageous person might also, it seems, adopt or maintain a *belief* that he regards as intellectually credible or justified despite the fact that doing so involves a certain risk or potential harm. And here as well the bearing of intellectual courage can be positive or negative. One might, in an exercise of intellectual courage, *suspend judgment* about some matter or *refrain* from accepting a tempting but ill-supported conclusion. We saw above, for instance, that Justice O'Connor likely exhibited intellectual courage in resisting certain conclusions that several of her fellow Justices thought she clearly ought to embrace.

There is, however, a notable objection to the idea that intellectual courage might bear on belief. Many epistemologists (e.g. Alston 1988) regard belief as largely, if not altogether, *involuntary*. Yet it is also widely thought that an exercise of any character virtue must be voluntary, at least in the sense that it involves choice or agency (that is, that it is not a passive or mechanistic psychological occurrence in the way that belief-formation often is).[16] But if an exercise of intellectual courage must be voluntary in this sense, can it really be said to bear on belief as such? Can one really believe (or disbelieve) something "out of" intellectual courage?

This is a challenging question, and one that I cannot address at length here. Thus I shall make just a few remarks. My own position is that intellectual courage can bear on belief in at least two main ways. First, it can do so in a quasi-indirect way. Suppose my epistemic community accepts that P, that I am presently on good terms with the other members of this community, but that they would frown upon me if I came to reject P. I have, however, arrived at what seem to me to be genuinely cogent reasons in support of not-P. My situation is

[15] Richard White's (2008) discussion of courage brings this point out nicely. He argues (against Aristotle's predominantly "martial" conception of courage) that *pacifism* is actually a proper expression of the virtue of courage. See especially pp. 35–41.

[16] To say that an exercise of a character virtue must "involve" agency or choice is not to say that it must involve a deliberate or conscious choice to *do* something or to perform some action. For more on the possibilities here, see Chapter 2.

lamentable. I have a lot to lose by embracing not-P; nonetheless, I recognize that accepting not-P is the only intellectually respectable course, and in the face of intense pressure to ignore or to try to forget about my reasons for not-P, I proceed instead to countenance these reasons, to bring them before my mind, to focus on them, reminding and reassuring myself of their logical force. The immediate result is that I come genuinely to accept not-P. Clearly this process might involve intellectual courage. It might even be plausible to regard my belief as a product of my intellectual courage. And yet the connection between these things is not immediate: my courage bears directly on the activity of countenancing, focusing on, or appreciating certain reasons, which in turn gives rise to my belief.[17]

The question remains, however, whether intellectual courage might also bear in a more direct way on belief. It seems to me that it might. For, in certain cases at least, to believe something is fundamentally to *endorse* or *accept* a proposition. And this, it seems, can be a direct product of agency and consequently of intellectual courage. In the case just discussed, for example, we might imagine that my newly acquired reasons for not-P are not so powerful as to compel my assent, but that on the basis of these reasons I proceed to *affirm, judge,* or *conclude* that not-P. It is reasonable to think that this activity might amount to an acceptance of or a belief that not-P and that it might involve an exercise of intellectual courage.[18] Similarly, even where a person's initial acceptance of a proposition is involuntary (one simply "finds oneself" with the belief), the *maintaining* of this belief might largely be voluntary and thus a product of a character trait like intellectual courage. My continued acceptance of not-P, for instance, the cost of which is ongoing estrangement from my community, might involve or even require a volitional endorsement or acceptance of the proposition in question. In this case, intellectual courage might explain why I still accept not-P, that is, why I have not given in to the pressure to repudiate this belief.

Finally, *suspending judgment* about a given proposition can also be an immediate effect of agency and thus of intellectual courage. To modify the above case, suppose that despite my newly acquired evidence for not-P, I initially feel compelled to continue believing P; the repudiation of P strikes me as unthinkable. After further thought and reflection, I might, though still unable to accept

[17] Clearly there are other even *less* direct ways that intellectual courage might bear on belief, for instance, where one engages in intellectually courageous inquiry which eventually (over a long period of time, say) yields new knowledge.

[18] See Ginet (2001) and Zagzebski (2001) for more on such possibilities.

not-P, nonetheless decide or choose to suspend judgment concerning P. I might voluntarily bring about a kind of agnosticism concerning P. This much, it seems, might be under my immediate voluntary control; and again, given other features of the situation, it is plausible to think that my suspension of judgment regarding P might instantiate intellectual courage.

A third kind of intellectual activity on which intellectual courage might bear is the *transmission* or *communication* of knowledge or related epistemic goods. Edward Murrow, for instance, jeopardized his career and personal well-being in the interest of exposing and communicating the truth about Senator McCarthy's witch hunt. In this domain as well intellectual courage might be manifested in either positive or negative ways. A teacher or other purveyor of information might, out of "respect for the truth," or concern for his hearers' intellectual well-being, *refuse* to share or transmit a body of information that she believes is "beyond the pale." If the situation is such that doing so involves an apparent threat to her well-being, the activity in question may constitute an exercise of intellectual courage.[19]

These examples illustrate the further and related point that intellectual courage need not be *egoistically* motivated.[20] While intellectual courage does necessarily involve a concern with an apparent threat to one's own well-being, and while it can be egoistic in the sense that one can act out of intellectual courage to further one's own share in the epistemic goods, the examples show that it is also possible to exercise intellectual courage out of a concern with or respect for the intellectual well-being of *others*. Again, in exposing the misbehavior of powerful figures or pursuing a firsthand account of the situation on the battlefield, Murrow presumably was concerned at least in part with something like the American public's intellectual welfare or right to know.

The foregoing discussion sheds some initial light on the positive substance of intellectual courage. We have seen that intellectual courage can be brought to bear on the domains of inquiry, belief, and communication. And we have seen that within these domains, an intellectually courageous person might, despite an apparent threat to her well-being, initiate, follow through with, or call off an inquiry, accept or reject a proposition, suspend judgment about an issue, communicate the truth, refrain from communicating misinformation, and more.

[19] Another possibility here is the bearing of intellectual courage on the activity of "proclaiming" or "bearing witness" to the truth. Here the aim need not be to *produce* true beliefs in others (though of course it may be this as well); instead it might be to "respect" or "take a stand on behalf of" the truth. Someone (a religious martyr, say) might do this in a way that manifests intellectual courage without any hope or expectation of convincing anyone of his message.

[20] See Wallace (1978: 77–8), Kawall (2002), and the Appendix for related discussions.

9.5 *Intellectual courage: a definition*

This way of thinking about intellectual courage suggests, contra (1) above, that intellectual courage need not involve "pursuing" an intellectual good. A person who, out of intellectual courage, clings to or retains a certain well-supported conviction is not pursuing an intellectual good as much as she is trying to *hold on* to one. A more plausible formulation begins with the idea that intellectual courage becomes "relevant" or that the need for intellectual courage arises when a person has judged, first, that a particular state or course of action is intellectually good or appropriate or required, and second, that this state or activity also brings with it a certain threat or potential harm. An intellectually courageous person, then, is one who *persists* in the relevant state or with the relevant activity. She is undeterred by the danger or threat; her concern with the intellectual good at stake "wins out" over any fear or appearance of danger. It bears repeating, however, that this good need not be positive in character. Again, an intellectually courageous person might, having decided that this is the intellectually appropriate course of action, persist with calling off an inquiry or repudiating a belief.

Accordingly, I propose the following general account of intellectual courage:

> (IC) Intellectual courage is a disposition to persist in or with a state or course of action aimed at an epistemically good end despite the fact that doing so involves an apparent threat to one's own well-being.

Several remarks concerning (IC) are in order. First, (IC) is not aimed at capturing all that is necessary for possessing the full *virtue* of intellectual courage or for intellectual courage *qua* intellectual virtue. A person could, for instance, satisfy the requirements of (IC) while failing to possess the kind of positive orientation toward epistemic goods which in Chapter 6 I argued is an essential characteristic of any intellectual virtue (at least where intellectual virtues are conceived as "personal excellences").[21] Alternatively, possessing the virtue of intellectual courage in its fullness might require having certain feelings or other affective states not required by (IC). It might, for instance, require that one exhibit a certain level of confidence or not experience a high degree of fear as one persists

[21] A related point is that, strictly speaking, the formulation should read that an intellectually courageous person necessarily aims at an *apparent* epistemic good, since, under certain circumstances, this person might be mistaken about the normative status of the end in question while nevertheless remaining intellectually courageous.

in or with the relevant state or course of action. (IC) is aimed, instead, at capturing the characteristic psychology of intellectual courage per se, that is, the features of intellectual courage that distinguish it from other intellectual virtues. My suggestion is that it does accomplish this much.

Second, the "disposition" referred to in (IC) should be understood as involving both a certain *willingness* on the part of the agent together with a certain (limited) *ability*. That is, an intellectually courageous person is one who is both willing and (within limits) able to proceed or carry on in the relevant way. For a more in depth discussion of this and related points, see the corresponding discussion of open-mindedness in section 8.2.2 of Chapter 8.

Third, (IC) makes reference to both a "state" and a "course of action" in order to cover the full range of cases discussed above. Specifically, the notion of "state" is meant to cover cases of intellectually courageous belief, while "course of action" is a more apt description of courageous inquiry or communication.

Fourth, it bears emphasizing that the goodness or appropriateness of the relevant state or course of action must be *epistemic* in nature. For as noted at the beginning of the chapter, this is what distinguishes intellectual courage from other kinds of courage. If, by contrast, a person's immediate concern, or the immediate good on behalf of which the person is acting, is, say, a moral one, then presumably whatever courage this person demonstrates will be moral as well.

Finally, it is worth considering what more can be said concerning the psychological basis of the disposition described in (IC). What exactly does this disposition consist in? One fairly obvious reply is that it consists in a certain psychological *toughness* or *imperviousness*. The intellectually courageous person is not deterred or overcome by fear or apparent danger in her pursuit of epistemic goods. While she may be fearful, and while she may be aware of the relevant danger or threat, these things are not what move or control her.

But what explains or underlies this imperviousness? In principle, it is explainable in terms of any number of motivations or motivational structures. For present purposes, however, I shall limit my attention to "virtuous" instances of intellectual courage, and more specifically, to intellectual courage that is ultimately supported or motivated by the sort of positive orientation toward or "love" of epistemic goods described in Chapter 6. On this conception, an intellectually courageous person might be moved to persist with an apparently dangerous but intellectually promising course of action because she desires to reach, maintain, or convey the truth. This in turn suggests that the psychological imperviousness in question consists in a certain motivational or desiderative structure wherein a desire for epistemic goods is *dominant* vis-à-vis other motivations.[22] The latter include things like the desire to be well liked, an aversion to physical pain, or a tendency toward a kind of intellectual laziness or inertia. To sum up, we can say that a person with the virtue of intellectual courage characteristically persists in or with an intellectually appropriate but threatening state or course of action on account of a motivational structure wherein a motivation for truth and related epistemic goods occupies an appropriately dominant position.[23]

9.6 *Challenging cases*

In the present section I turn to examine two kinds of cases that present some challenging questions about the basic nature and structure of intellectual courage. The first concerns the claim made above that ill-motivated intellectual courage is still genuine courage (even if not a genuine intellectual *virtue*). The second concerns the "demandingness" of an exercise of the virtue of intellectual courage. Specifically, the question here is whether a person who overcomes certain fears that we would likely deem questionable or irrational can still be said to possess the virtue of intellectual courage.

9.6.1 *Ill-motivated courage?*

Many moral philosophers have pondered the possibility of a "courageous villain," that is, of an agent who displays many of the qualities characteristic of courage (e.g. overcoming fear or persisting in the face of danger) but in the pursuit of an evil or otherwise morally problematic end (theft, murder, etc.). The main questions raised by such cases are whether the person in question can really be said to be courageous; and, if he can, whether his courage can be considered a genuine moral *virtue*. Accordingly, analyses of such cases tend to fall along the following lines: (1) the courageous villain is not genuinely courageous (and therefore not virtuously courageous); (2) the courageous villain is genuinely courageous, but his courage is not a genuine moral virtue; and (3) the courageous villain is genuinely courageous and his courage is a genuine virtue (even if he is still defective in some other respect).[24]

[22] Roberts and Wood (2007: 217) make a similar point about intellectual courage, as do Wallace (1978: 77) and Rorty (1988: ch. 15) about courage proper or moral courage.

[23] For a more in depth account of the kind of dominance in question, see Roberts (1984).

[24] See Zagzebski (1996: 92f) for a related discussion.

The case of the courageous villain has obvious epistemic counterparts. One is the fame-motivated reporter mentioned briefly in section 9.1 above. I claimed there (based partly on corresponding discussions in Chapters 6–7) that this person—whose intellectual courage, it was stipulated, is motivated ultimately by a desire for a Pulitzer Prize—could reasonably be considered intellectually courageous, but that his courage would not be a genuine intellectual virtue. Given the corresponding discussions in ethics, it is likely that some would object to my diagnosis, claiming either that I have been too liberal in my assessment of the case (that the reporter is not genuinely courageous) or that I have been too conservative (that he is courageous and that his courage is a genuine intellectual virtue). Let us refer to the views in question as the "conservative" view (the reporter is not courageous at all), the "liberal" view (he is courageous and his courage is a virtue), and the "moderate" view (he is courageous, but his courage is not a genuine intellectual virtue).

I cannot give these views the full attention they deserve here. Instead I shall limit myself to just a few remarks against the conservative and liberal positions and in favor of the moderate position.[25]

The conservative view of the fame-motivated reporter has at least some appeal. The reporter clearly is deficient from an intellectual or epistemic standpoint. And there may be some plausibility in the suggestion that, given his questionable motivation, he is not "truly" or "fundamentally" intellectually courageous.[26]

On closer inspection, however, the conservative view appears too restrictive. Note that this view maintains, not merely that a fleeting or unstable propensity to face fears or dangers in an intellectual context is insufficient for intellectual courage, but also that a *stable, entrenched* disposition to do so is insufficient as well. For, ex hypothesi, the fame-motivated reporter has such a disposition. While this disposition is ultimately rooted in his desire for journalistic fame, it is, we may assume, a central and integral part of his psychology; again, he *habitually* places himself in harm's way with the (immediate) aim of uncovering and exposing the truth about various corrupt regimes. Surely it would be wrong to deny that this person might be courageous in some genuine (even if not virtuous or fully virtuous) sense. This point can also be illustrated in connection

[25] Geach (1977: 160) suggests that the difference between the moderate and conservative views is merely terminological and therefore insignificant. However, the problems with the conservative view identified below suggest otherwise.

[26] Geach (1977) is a representative of the conservative view. Aristotle (*NE* 1115a–1117b) also seems to favor something like this view of courage.

with traits like intellectual carefulness and patience. Suppose the reporter were also to engage in the activity characteristic of these traits on an habitual basis: he routinely scrutinizes the reliability of his sources, checks all his facts, refrains from making any unwarranted assumptions or hasty generalizations, and so on. Again, despite the fact that he is ultimately motivated by professional status, it would be implausible to deny that the reporter might be intellectually careful or patient in some genuine sense.[27]

Let us, then, turn to the other end of the dialectical spectrum. The liberal view of the fame-motivated reporter says that this person is genuinely intellectually courageous and that his courage is a genuine intellectual virtue.[28] We have seen that the liberal view is right to embrace the former claim. In fact, given a certain "externalist" understanding of intellectual virtue, the view as a whole may be unobjectionable. For, as I argued in Chapter 7, there is a kind or concept of intellectual virtue for which epistemic reliability or truth-conduciveness is both necessary and sufficient. Accordingly, provided that the reporter's courage is cognitively reliable, we may conclude that it is also an intellectual virtue in the relevant externalist sense.

Nonetheless, as explained in previous chapters, my main concern in the book is a broadly "internalist" conception of intellectual virtue. Let us, then, restrict our attention to the corresponding way or ways of thinking about intellectual virtue. Once we do this, problems with the liberal view quickly emerge. Suppose that in the latter part of his career the reporter experiences a kind of intellectual conversion, such that the fundamental motivation of his work (including his consistently courageous reporting) is no longer fame, but rather a desire to know and report the truth for its own sake (or, perhaps, a respect for his readership's "right to know"). He now sees a kind of final or intrinsic value in the goal that for so many years he regarded as a mere means to journalistic fame. Consequently the reporter's intellectual courage now springs from something like a desire for truth. If the liberal view is correct, the quality of this person's intellectual courage is not relevantly enhanced subsequent to his

[27] A related way of drawing out the problem is to note that a defender of the conservative view presumably would not deny that a person without a good epistemic motivation can perform *acts of intellectual courage* (that is, can do what an intellectually courageous person would characteristically do in the situation); nor, indeed, that such a person might do so *habitually*. This apparently commits the defender of the conservative view to the implausible claim that a person can habitually perform acts of intellectual courage (can habitually do what an intellectually courageous person would do) while not—in any respect—being intellectually courageous herself.

[28] Defenders include Zagzebski (1996: 91–7) and Adams (2006: 31–5 and 174–9).

conversion: it is no more of an intellectual virtue, no more intellectually virtuous, than it was when its source was a mere desire for fame. But this, I take it, is an implausible implication. Surely his truth-motivated intellectual courage is more virtuous, or enjoys a greater claim to intellectual virtue, than his previous, fame-motivated courage.[29]

Many sympathetic to an "internalist" account of intellectual virtue would also allow for an important connection between intellectual virtue and "personal worth," or one's goodness or badness qua person. While I argued for a conceptual connection along these lines in Chapter 6, one need not accept that account in order to agree that a possession of intellectual virtues has *some* significant (though perhaps non-definitional) bearing on personal worth.[30] But such a connection is very difficult to make sense of on the liberal view. This point can be developed on either a theoretical or an intuitive level. Again, I argued in Chapter 6 for the claim that personal worth—one's goodness or badness qua person—is a function of the value of what one "loves"; and, more precisely, that personal *intellectual* worth is (roughly) a function of the extent to which one "loves" distinctively intellectual or epistemic goods like knowledge, truth, and understanding. If this account is correct, it follows that the fame-motivated reporter is not intellectually virtuous, and thus that the liberal view is mistaken. This point can also be made in a more immediate and intuitive way. Given that the reporter's ultimate motivation is strictly that of fame, that he is not in any way motivated by knowledge or any other worthy end, it seems implausible to think that he is an intellectually good or better *person* on account of his intellectual courage. Therefore, to the extent that intellectual virtues enhance personal worth, the liberal view should be rejected.

The present objection is even more compelling vis-à-vis cases in which a person is ultimately motivated by an obviously epistemically *bad* or *inappropriate* end, for example, that of mass deception. Imagine, along these lines, that our reporter has come into the service of one of the corrupt regimes which he previously railed against, that he has been tasked with gathering information that this government can use to deceive the masses about some matter, that this dubious end has become "his own," and that carrying out this work has repeatedly required a show of intellectual courage (much of the sought after information, we might imagine, is in the possession of dangerous persons

[29] See Geach (1977: 160) for a similar point.

[30] Zagzebski (1996: 85, 89, and 125) and Roberts and Wood (2007: 65), for instance, point to important connections between intellectual virtue and personal worth, but do not endorse a personal worth conception of intellectual virtue per se.

hostile to the government). Here the reporter's intellectual courage is ultimately grounded in a desire to *deceive*: to distort the truth, bring about ignorance, and so on.[31] While we have seen that the reporter might still be intellectually courageous in some sense, his intellectual courage clearly is not an intellectual virtue in the relevant internalist sense.

We have seen that the conservative and liberal views of the fame-motivated reporter are problematic. There is, however, an obvious middle ground here: namely, the moderate view, according to which the reporter is genuinely intellectually courageous but his intellectual courage is not a genuine intellectual virtue. The moderate view has the advantages of the conservative and liberal views identified above and none of their weaknesses. Like the conservative view, the moderate view does justice to the fact that the reporter is deficient in a way that intuitively is relevant to intellectual virtue. Like the liberal view, it allows that, despite the limitations of his character, the reporter can still be considered intellectually courageous in some sense. Finally, the moderate position fits very well with the account of the nature and structure of intellectual virtue defended in Chapters 6–7. While, again, accepting the moderate view does not require accepting that account, to the extent that the account is plausible, it is an advantage of the moderate view that it coheres with it.[32]

9.6.2 *Easy courage?*

The philosophical literature on courage proper or moral courage also betrays considerable disagreement concerning the "demandingness" of this trait. On one end of the spectrum are those who think of courage as rather commonplace or mundane, and thus as reasonably easy to attain. On the other end are those

[31] For more on this sort of case, see my paper (2010) on the vice epistemic malevolence.

[32] Zagzebski (1996) voices the following worry about the moderate analysis of the courageous villain: "This position seems to me to raise some difficulties about the identities of traits. If the virtuous trait of courage is distinct from the nonvirtuous trait of courage, this difference can have nothing to do with motivations, beliefs, attitudes, or dispositions to act... Alternatively, if the virtuous trait of courage is the same trait as the nonvirtuous trait of courage, it follows that whether a trait is a virtue or a vice is an accidental feature of it. I find these two alternatives undesirable...." (92). I confess that I do not see the difficulty here. My suggestion is that we draw a distinction between, as it were, "perfected" and "unperfected" intellectual courage. Both have certain motives, attitudes, beliefs, dispositions, and the like in common (viz. the motives, etc., characteristic of intellectual courage per se); the central difference between them is that virtuous or "perfected" intellectual courage involves a proper or virtuous underlying *motivation* (e.g. a desire for truth).

who think of courage as more or less heroic.[33] This debate also has several aspects and iterations; and here again I am able to address only one of the relevant issues, and to do so only in a rather cursory way. I shall argue that in one notable respect, the virtue of intellectual courage is not very demanding, and specifically, that its exercise is consistent with a certain kind of *irrationality*.

To orient the discussion, consider the case of "Shy Di," an exceedingly shy individual whose extreme fear and anxiety about social interactions with anyone but her closest of intimates conflicts with her serious and deeply felt desire to obtain a first-rate university education. Di realizes that, given the options available to her, the kind of education to which she aspires will require a range of interactions with students, professors, and other persons outside her immediate social circle, interactions which she finds terrifying and fears may even precipitate a psychological breakdown. Nevertheless, out of a deep and firm love of knowledge, Di proceeds to set aside her fears and enroll at the university.

Let us stipulate that Di's pursuit of knowledge will not lead to the unraveling of her psyche and that she ultimately lacks grounds or reasons for her belief to the contrary. Thus Di's fear is irrational. One question we can ask is whether Di's decision to enroll might nevertheless be intellectually courageous. I think it is obvious that it might and thus will not bother defending this claim here. A separate question is whether this decision can be viewed as an exercise of a genuine intellectual *virtue*.

Any case for thinking that Di's intellectual courage should *not* be regarded as a genuine intellectual virtue presumably will rest on something like the following principle:

> A person S's pursuing an epistemic good despite an apparent threat to S's well-being is intellectually virtuous only if the appearance in question is *rational* or *reasonable*.

If this principle were correct, Di's actions, while perhaps intellectually courageous, would not be intellectually virtuous. But this principle is too demanding. Di clearly exhibits a kind of cognitive deficiency. Intuitively, however, the fact that her fear is irrational would not appear to make her "conquering" or overcoming of it any less an instance of intellectual courage; nor would it appear to make her intellectual courage less than intellectually *virtuous*. Di's pursuit of

[33] In the former camp is Geach (1977: ch. 8). Aristotle's discussion of courage in *Nicomachean Ethics* suggests the latter view, as does Foot's discussion (2002: 8–13). See Rorty (1988: ch. 15) for more on this dichotomy.

knowledge is still very admirable; it still reflects well on her personal intellectual worth.

This suggests that the question of whether a given instance of intellectual courage qualifies as a genuine intellectual virtue is independent of the rational status of the corresponding fear or other threatening appearance. Put another way, it suggests that whether intellectual courage is a virtue depends on how one *responds* to certain perceptions of danger—regardless of whether these perceptions are themselves rational.[34] Again, this does not mean that Di or similar persons are free of cognitive defect. Rather, my claim is merely that the irrational character of her fear does not prevent her from being genuinely intellectually courageous, nor her intellectual courage from being a genuine intellectual virtue.

To pursue this issue a bit further, consider a slightly modified version of the case. Suppose Di were *also* irrational in thinking that her decision to enroll at the university would advance her epistemic goals. Suppose, for instance, that her community is geographically very isolated and that the only university education available to her is a manifestly poor one (she clearly would do better to educate herself than to enroll at this school). Here I take it that while we might still regard Di's educational efforts as "intellectually courageous" in some sense, they are sufficiently irrational or quixotic not to be intellectually *virtuous*.

Accordingly, while I reject the principle noted above, I think the following related principle is correct:

> A person S's pursuing an epistemic good G despite an apparent threat to S's well-being is intellectually virtuous only if it is reasonable for S to think that doing so may be helpful for securing G.[35]

This suggests that the virtue of intellectual courage involves a certain rational perspective on the activity expressive of intellectual courage that is not necessarily involved with the intellectually courageous person's apprehension of the

[34] This is not to say that the overcoming of just *any* fear is virtuous. Aristotle (*NE* 1115a–1117b), for instance, claims that the overcoming of fears about things unrelated to virtue or about things that are entirely beyond our control is not true courage. Similarly, where a person overcomes a fear that is irrational, the *source* of this irrationality may be important to whether we can regard this person's courage as a genuine virtue. See Wallace (1978: 66–70) and Foot (2002: 12) for related discussions.

[35] This is the counterpart of the principle I defended in Chapter 8 regarding open-mindedness. Note that it is limited to the bearing of intellectual courage on the *pursuit* of an epistemic good—rather than, say, on the *maintenance* or *retaining* of such a good. I limit the focus in this way so as to make the discussion here and in the section that follows more manageable.

danger or threat her courageous activity aims to overcome. Or, a certain rationality constraint applies to the virtuously courageous agent's perspective on the connection between her courageous activity and her epistemic goal that does *not* apply to her initial judgment about the corresponding threat.[36]

9.7 *When to be intellectually courageous?*

The principle just articulated has obvious bearing on the question of when (or to whom or in what amount, etc.) it is intellectually appropriate or virtuous to engage in the activity characteristic of intellectual courage. In the present section I want to consider this issue in a bit more detail.

While the principle stated above identifies a necessary condition for its being intellectually virtuous to exercise intellectual courage, this condition is not sufficient. To see why, consider the following, much stronger principle:

> A person S's pursing an epistemic good G despite an apparent threat to S's well-being is intellectually virtuous *if and only if* it is reasonable for S to think that doing so may be helpful for securing G.

Counterexamples to this principle are abundant. First, the epistemic end in question might be only very minimally epistemically good, with the result that even if it were reasonable for one to think that exposing oneself to the relevant threat "may" result in one's securing this end, doing so would not be intellectually virtuous. This might be the case, for instance, where the good in question is an item of relatively trivial (though not entirely worthless) knowledge. A second and closely related possibility is that the value of the good in question might be minimal by *comparison* with the disvalue of the corresponding harm. If the potential harm were that of death or torture, say, then even if the epistemic good at stake were of a somewhat higher grade than trivial knowledge, it is at least questionable whether an intellectually courageous pursuit of this end would be intellectually virtuous. Third, if an intellectually courageous pursuit of an epistemic good were to rule out other, more worthy epistemic pursuits (at present or down the line), then such a pursuit presumably would not, on the whole, be intellectually virtuous. If, for instance, an intellectually courageous pursuit of a certain minimal epistemic good G_1 would, owing to limitations of time or epistemic resources, rule out the subsequent pursuit of

[36] For more on the constraint in question, see my (2007), Chapters 6 and 7, and my "The Cognitive Demands of Intellectual Virtue" (manuscript).

some other far more valuable epistemic good G_2, then presumably it would not be intellectually virtuous to engage in this pursuit.

What more can be said, then, about the conditions under which an exercise of intellectual courage is intellectually virtuous? Or under which an intellectually virtuous person characteristically exercises intellectual courage? The cases just cited suggest that an answer to this question depends at least in part on the *comparative normative significance* of the relevant epistemic good and potential harm in question. For instance, if, in a particular situation, the epistemic good to be gained by inquiring in an intellectually courageous way is minimal and the potential harm is great, then it will not be intellectually virtuous to exhibit intellectual courage in that situation. On other hand, if the epistemic end is extremely valuable and the potential harm comparatively mild, then it likely will be intellectually virtuous to proceed with the inquiry.

The concept of *phronesis* or practical wisdom obviously is relevant to the discussion at this point. This concept is often appealed to in response to the question of when or under what conditions it is virtuous to exhibit the qualities characteristic of a particular character virtue.[37] The idea, roughly, is that it is virtuous to exhibit the relevant qualities just in case doing so is called for by phronesis, or just in case the "phronimos" or person of practical wisdom would exhibit these qualities under similar conditions. Such appeals, while perhaps correct, are of limited theoretical value. For, presumably, when the phronimos chooses a particular end or course of action, she does so on the *basis* of certain normative considerations or factors. And it is these considerations that we are after here, for they are more likely to shed positive light on when it is intellectually virtuous to exercise intellectual courage and why. So let us consider whether something more can be said, beyond an appeal to phronesis, about the normative dimensions of intellectual courage.[38]

While I cannot, with the limits of this (already lengthy) chapter, go too much beyond what has already been said, the principle stated near the end of the previous section suggests one additional factor relevant to our question:

[37] Aristotle's discussion of *phronesis* in the *Nicomachean Ethics* (esp. his discussion of its role in connection with the doctrine of the mean at 1106a15–1110a25) is an obvious example. See also Zagzebski (1996: 180, 219–31, and 239–40). This point is relevant to discussions of courage in particular (whether intellectual or moral) given that a substantial normative *conflict* (between a particular good and the well-being of the agent) is built into the very idea courage.

[38] Jim Hanink's paper "Courage, Cowardice, and Conscience" does a nice job of illustrating the potential normative complexity of such judgments. This paper was given at a 2008 conference at Viterbo University on the topic of courage (a copy is available at <www.viterbo.edu/ethics>).

namely, the apparent *probability* or *likelihood* that the good and harm in question will come to fruition. Consider the following four variations on a situation in which the pursuit of an epistemic good would involve subjecting oneself to a potential harm and thus potentially call for an exercise of intellectual courage. (1) The epistemic good at stake is substantial and the corresponding potential harm is fairly minimal. Further, one has reason to think that a pursuit of the good is very likely to be successful and that the corresponding harm is only somewhat likely to obtain. (2) The epistemic good at stake is substantial and the corresponding potential harm is fairly minimal. However, one's grounds suggest that, if one pursues the good, one is only somewhat likely to secure it, and the corresponding harm is very likely to materialize. (3) The epistemic good at stake is minimal and the corresponding potential harm is very substantial. Nonetheless, one has reason to think that a pursuit of the good is very likely to be successful and that the harm, while severe, is only minimally probable. (4) The epistemic good at stake is minimal and the corresponding potential harm is very substantial. Further, one's grounds suggest that, if one attempts to secure this good, one is not very likely to succeed, and the corresponding harm is very likely to come about.

I take it that it clearly would be intellectually virtuous for a person to exercise intellectual courage in (1), but that it is less clear whether doing so would be intellectually virtuous in (2). Likewise, it is reasonable to think that it would not be intellectually virtuous to exercise intellectual courage in (4), but that it might in (3). The lesson to be drawn is that part of what determines whether an exercise of intellectual courage is intellectually virtuous is the apparent likelihood that the relevant good and corresponding potential harm will actually come to pass.

The foregoing scenarios and corresponding judgments support the following, further proposal:

> Its being intellectually virtuous to engage in the activity characteristic of intellectual courage is a function (minimally) of (1) the comparative normative weight or significance of the epistemic good and potential harm at issue, as well as (2) the apparent likelihood that the good and harm will actually obtain.

This hardly amounts to a formula for determining when it is or is not intellectually virtuous to exercise intellectual courage. Nor does it go too far beyond the appeal to phronesis noted above, for it is widely agreed that a large part of what distinguishes the phronimos from other persons is precisely her ability to accurately or effectively weigh the normative factors in a situation in light of their apparent probabilities. It does, however, bring into at least somewhat sharper focus the factors most relevant to making the kind of determination in question.

By way of conclusion, I want briefly to address one further issue. Thus far I have been deliberately unspecific about the *sorts* of potential harms relevant to determining when an exercise of intellectual courage would be intellectually virtuous. In particular, I have left it open whether the harms in question must be *epistemic* in nature (or whether they might be of, say, a strictly *moral* variety). It might be wondered, however, whether the answer to this question could have important implications for some of the claims made above. Recall, for instance, my claim that the principle laid down at the end of the previous section specifies a necessary but not a sufficient condition for when it is intellectually virtuous to exercise intellectual courage. In support of this claim, I adduced a case in which the epistemic good to be gained is minimal by comparison with the corresponding potential harm. Similarly, in scenarios (2) and (4) above, I indicated that owing to the likelihood of certain harms (and minimal likelihood of any epistemic benefits), an exercise of intellectual courage apparently would not be intellectually virtuous. It might be argued, however, that insofar as the conflict in such cases is between epistemic goods and *non*-epistemic harms, it *would* actually be intellectually virtuous (even if not morally virtuous or virtuous all-things-considered) to exercise intellectual courage under the circumstances.

At issue here is the interesting but tricky question of whether non-epistemic or non-intellectual normative considerations can play a role in determining whether an exercise of intellectual courage is *intellectually* virtuous. It is at least prima facie odd to think that they might. For we tend to think of intellectual character and virtue as character and virtue "as it pertains to" strictly epistemic values or norms—the latter are thought to constrain the normative parameters of intellectual virtue. And yet it also seems strange to consider, say, a person who exhibits intellectual courage in scenario (4) above as virtuous in *any* sense. This again is a person who pursues a minimal epistemic good even though she has reason to think, first, that doing so is only somewhat likely to secure the good in question, and second, that it is very likely to bring about significant (and what we may now suppose is a non-epistemic) personal harm.

To bring this issue further into focus, imagine a person who is considering subjecting himself to a certain extremely severe non-epistemic harm (torture, lifelong imprisonment, etc.) for the sake of an equally minimal epistemic good (knowledge, say, of a very minor but difficult to ascertain detail of some ancient battle).[39] While, in a different context, a pursuit of such knowledge might

[39] Let us assume, further, that the harm in question is not *indirectly* epistemic. We might imagine, for instance, that even if this harm were to obtain, the person in question would still

exhibit various intellectual virtues, is it reasonable to think that it might do so in the present context? Specifically, would it be intellectually virtuous (even if morally or otherwise foolish) for this person to exercise intellectual courage by pursuing the knowledge in question? My own inclination is to think that it would not, at least insofar as we are thinking of intellectual virtues as *admirable* traits of character. For I find it difficult to consider the person in question admirable in *any* respect—whether intellectual or otherwise. Rather, he seems foolish through and through. Put another way, it strikes me as counterintuitive to think that a person in whom intellectual courage is a genuine intellectual virtue would not *as such* give any normative weight or concern to any non-epistemic aspects of his well-being.[40]

That said, there is admittedly something strange about the idea that whether a particular exercise of intellectual courage should count as intellectually virtuous might depend at all on certain inherently non-epistemic or non-intellectual normative factors. Alternatively, there is something prima facie very *plausible* about the view that the domain of intellectual virtue can be demarcated from other normative domains relative to certain distinctively epistemic or intellectual values, in such a way that anything that makes an exercise of intellectual courage intellectually virtuous must itself be epistemic in nature. Because I cannot, within the space allotted here, begin to resolve this issue, I shall leave it an open question whether the sort of harm relevant to determining when it would be intellectually virtuous to exercise intellectual courage is strictly epistemic, or whether it might also include moral or other kinds of harm.

be granted the same level of access to epistemic opportunities and goods that he would have enjoyed had the harm not occurred.

[40] In this regard, the present case differs from some cases discussed in the Appendix in which it does seem possible to abstract away from certain (negative) moral considerations and to identify in the subject an intellectual orientation that is genuinely intellectually admirable. A possible explanation of the difference (and of the intuition just invoked in the text) lies with the fact that if we were, in the present case, to bracket the relevant moral considerations, we would no longer be concerned with an exercise of intellectual *courage*.

Chapter 10

THE STATUS AND FUTURE OF CHARACTER-BASED VIRTUE EPISTEMOLOGY

A great deal of ground has been covered in the preceding nine chapters. We began by surveying the landscape in contemporary virtue epistemology (Chapter 1) and considering the relationship between intellectual virtues and a range of other cognitive excellences (Chapter 2). Next we turned to consider what role the concept of intellectual virtue might play in a philosophical analysis of knowledge. I argued that while virtue-based analyses of knowledge face formidable problems (Chapter 3), the concept of intellectual virtue nevertheless merits a limited role in connection with both reliabilist (Chapter 4) and evidentialist (Chapter 5) theories of knowledge or epistemic justification. Our attention then shifted from relatively traditional epistemological concepts and concerns to intellectual virtues considered in their own right. I sketched a "personal worth" conception of intellectual virtue (Chapter 6) and situated this conception vis-à-vis other accounts of intellectual and moral virtue in the literature (Chapter 7). Finally, we looked carefully at the basic nature and structure of two individual virtues: namely, open-mindedness (Chapter 8) and intellectual courage (Chapter 9).

The discussion has, I hope, gone a considerable way toward enriching our understanding of intellectual virtues and their role in the broader cognitive economy. If so, it has achieved one of the main goals of the book as a whole. A second main goal, however, is meta-epistemological: it is to clarify the role that reflection on intellectual virtues should play within epistemology proper. Again, the concern here is with what *work* there is for epistemologists to do in connection with these traits—with the sorts of issues, questions, puzzles, or problems that might occupy them. The discussion in the preceding chapters also has important implications relative to this goal. My aim here is to explore these implications. I begin with a brief reiteration of the classification of approaches to character-based virtue epistemology introduced in Chapter 1, a classification that turns on how approaches in question construe the relation between the concept of intellectual virtue and the issues and questions of traditional epistemology. I then turn to assess each view in light of the arguments of the preceding nine chapters. The result is a systematic account of the present status and probable trajectory of character-based virtue epistemology.

10.1 *Four varieties of character-based virtue epistemology*

As noted in Chapter 1, character-based approaches to virtue epistemology have tended to take one of two general forms. Proponents of *Conservative* VE invoke the concept of intellectual virtue to address traditional epistemological issues like the analysis of knowledge and justification, skepticism, and the internalism/externalism debate. By contrast, defenders of *Autonomous* VE see intellectual virtues as epistemologically interesting in their own right. That is, they tend to focus on questions and issues pertaining to the intellectual virtues and their role in the cognitive life as such—questions and issues that are largely independent of the quarry of traditional epistemology.

Both Conservative and Autonomous VE admit of two subtypes. Among defenders of Conservative VE, there are those (e.g. Zagzebski 1996) who think the concept of intellectual virtue merits a *central* and *fundamental* role within traditional epistemology. In their minds, the most promising replies to traditional epistemological questions and problems are virtue-based. This is Strong Conservative VE. But not all defenders of Conservative VE are this optimistic about the importance of intellectual virtue to traditional epistemology. Some (e.g. Baehr 2006b and 2009) think that the concept of intellectual virtue merits a mere *background* or *supporting* role in connection with one or more issues in traditional epistemology. Unlike defenders of Strong Conservative VE, these philosophers do not regard a turn to intellectual virtue as having a major impact within traditional epistemology. Accordingly, they subscribe to Weak Conservative VE.

Autonomous VE also admits of stronger and weaker varieties. According to Strong Autonomous VE (e.g. Kvanvig 1992), an immediate theoretical focus on intellectual virtues and their role in the cognitive life should *replace* or *supplant* traditional epistemology. That is, epistemologists should cease trying to address the sorts of issues and questions they have long been occupied with and turn instead to matters of intellectual character and virtue considered in their own right. But here too there are stronger and weaker alternatives. Defenders of Weak Autonomous VE (e.g. Roberts and Wood 2007) agree with defenders of Strong Autonomous VE that intellectual virtues considered in their own right are a fitting object for broadly epistemological reflection. They maintain, however, that this "autonomous" concern with intellectual virtue is a suitable complement to—not a replacement for—a more traditional approach.

10.2 *Assessing the alternatives*

I turn in this section to consider what the preceding nine chapters suggest about the viability of each of the four approaches just identified. Again, this will shed light, not merely on the present state of character-based virtue epistemology, but also on the form it is likely to take in years to come.

10.2.1 *Strong Conservative VE*

Chapter 3 was aimed at casting significant doubt on the viability of Strong Conservative VE. I argued, first, that for Strong Conservative VE to succeed, the concept of intellectual virtue must figure prominently in a plausible analysis of knowledge, that is, in a plausible specification of the necessary and sufficient conditions for knowledge. I then proceeded to argue against this possibility, focusing in particular on Linda Zagzebski's (1996) well-known virtue-based account of knowledge, but also showing why an equally pessimistic conclusion is likely to hold for *any* virtue-based analysis.[1] The conclusion of the chapter was that the prospects of Strong Conservative VE are poor.

10.2.2 *Weak Conservative VE*

While there are compelling reasons for doubting the viability of Strong Conservative VE, these reasons do not immediately extend to Weak Conservative VE. Indeed, in Chapters 4 and 5, we saw that while the concept of intellectual virtue may not figure prominently in an analysis of knowledge, it does merit a notable background or peripheral role.

The focus of Chapter 4 was reliabilist accounts of knowledge. Reliabilists maintain (roughly) that knowledge is true belief arrived at via reliable or truth-conducive processes or qualities. While the qualities that reliabilists typically

[1] That is, any virtue-based analysis on which intellectual virtues are conceived as character traits. This leaves open whether "virtue reliabilist" or faculty-based accounts of knowledge might be successful. For more on this distinction, see Chapter 1.

appeal to in this regard are cognitive *faculties* like vision, memory, and introspection, I argued that they must expand their repertoire of knowledge-making attributes to include various intellectual *character* virtues. This requirement stems from the fact that, relative to certain domains of knowledge, epistemic reliability is a matter of virtuous intellectual character—not (principally) of well-functioning cognitive faculties. While this does not mean that reliabilists must adopt anything like a "character-based" analysis of knowledge, it does reveal their need to rely in a more limited way on the concepts of intellectual character and virtue. Toward the end of the chapter, I explained why adding intellectual character virtues to the reliabilism's repertoire of knowledge-conferring traits generates new and challenging philosophical questions and problems with which any comprehensive reliabilist epistemology must reckon.

In Chapter 5, I offered additional support for Weak Conservative VE, in this case focusing on evidentialist accounts of epistemic justification. Evidentialists maintain (roughly) that a person S is justified in believing a given proposition P at time T just in case S has good evidence in support of P at T. I argued that in a range of cases (mainly involving the neglect or distortion of evidence) the satisfaction of this condition is insufficient for justification. I then proceeded to argue that evidentialists need not abandon the thrust of their account in order to get around this objection; rather, they need only supplement this account with a virtue-based "background constraint," according to which S's belief that P is justified on evidentialist grounds *provided that*, if S's agency was centrally involved with the formation of this belief, S functions in an intellectually virtuous manner. Here too the suggestion was that while the concept of intellectual virtue does not deserve pride of place within the relevant account of justification, it does merit a notable secondary or background role. The upshot of this and the preceding chapter was that Weak Conservative VE is viable indeed.

10.2.3 *Strong Autonomous VE*

Strong Autonomous VE is the view that a more immediate focus on matters of intellectual virtue should *replace* the focus of traditional epistemology—that epistemologists should abandon their concern with the nature, structure, sources, and limits of knowledge in favor a concern with intellectual virtues considered more or less in their own right. As this description suggests, the challenge for Strong Autonomous VE is twofold. Its defenders must make good on the claim, first, that there are in fact broadly epistemological issues and questions concerning the intellectual virtues that are largely independent of traditional epistemological issues and questions and that might form the basis of an alternative epistemological research program. A second and more formidable challenge is to support the claim that an autonomous, virtue-based epistemology should *displace* or *supplant* traditional epistemology. Specifically, the defender of Strong Autonomous VE must identify some flaw or defect in traditional epistemology that warrants its repudiation but that is absent from whatever virtue-based approach is offered in its place.

The former, positive challenge is also the central challenge for Weak Autonomous VE. Therefore I will postpone a discussion of it to the discussion of Weak Autonomous VE below. In the remainder of this section, I will focus instead on the latter, negative challenge for Strong Autonomous VE.

In principle, any number of arguments could be given in support of the claim that traditional epistemology ought to be abandoned, which makes anything like a comprehensive assessment of the negative dimension of Strong Autonomous VE difficult. But this challenge is mitigated by the fact that within the virtue epistemology literature, only one unequivocal defense of Strong Conservative VE has been advanced.[2] This defense is a core component of Jonathan Kvanvig's *Intellectual Virtues and the Life of the Mind* (1992).

Kvanvig's book is an expansive and sophisticated inquiry into the role that reflection on intellectual virtues should play in epistemology. Its defense of Strong Autonomous VE begins with a meta-epistemological requirement according to which any plausible epistemology must bear a substantial connection to our cognitive experience and provide us with a kind of doxastic guidance. Kvanvig comments: "What we really want from an epistemologist is an account of the cognitive life of the mind that addresses our cognitive experience and helps us understand how to maximize our potential for finding the truth and avoiding error" (vii). On Kvanvig's view, traditional—or what he calls "modern" or "Cartesian"—epistemology falls well short of this standard. He describes the yield of traditional epistemology as "a maze of complexities surrounding the analysis of knowledge and justification from which no route into the promised land seems possible" (ibid.). Kvanvig contends that a virtue-based approach to epistemology is likely to fare much better in this regard: "Virtue theorists promise a happier ending. If we would but begin ... epistemology from the standpoint of the virtues, the results of our inquiry would yield significant insight rather than mere complexity; if we would concentrate on appropriate traits of character, our sorrow will be turned to joy" (ibid.). Kvanvig proceeds, over the

[2] Some authors (e.g. Code 1987 and Roberts and Wood 2007) at times seem tempted by this position, but ultimately stop short of endorsing it; and none offers anything like a compelling argument for Strong Conservative VE.

course of several chapters, to consider various ways in which the concept of intellectual virtue might play a central and fundamental role within traditional epistemology. After examining and assessing these possibilities at length, he concludes that none is plausible, and thus that traditional, Cartesian epistemology should be rejected (see esp. pp. viii, 150, 157–8, and 168).

This conclusion does not lead Kvanvig to despair about the entire epistemological enterprise, however, for it leaves open the possibility that there is a viable virtue-based approach to the discipline the theoretical substance of which is largely independent of that of traditional epistemology. In the final chapter, Kvanvig outlines an approach of this sort.[3]

In contrast with the "time-slice" orientation of traditional epistemology, Kvanvig's alternative approach is socially and diachronically oriented: it focuses on knowers within their epistemic communities and takes account of their cognitive histories and futures (9–10, 150). At the heart of this approach are questions about how "one progresses down the path toward cognitive ideality," the significance of "social patterns of mimicry and imitation" and "training and practice" in human intellectual formation, the acquisition of the sort of "know-how" involved with searching for and evaluating explanations (170–3), the relative merits of different kinds of epistemic communities and the bodies of knowledge these communities generate (176), and the evaluation of "structured chunks" of information (vs. discrete propositions) (182–6). Given the prominent role that Kvanvig envisions for the concept of intellectual virtue on this approach, and given his pessimistic assessment of traditional epistemology, he seems clearly to be a proponent of Strong Autonomous VE.

My concern here is not with the substance of Kvanvig's suggested alternative to traditional epistemology. Rather it is with his rejection of traditional epistemology. As the foregoing discussion suggests, his argument against traditional epistemology takes the following general form: (1) Any plausible epistemology must provide "an account of the cognitive life of the mind that addresses our cognitive experience and helps us understand how to maximize our potential for finding the truth and avoiding error" (vii); (2) Traditional epistemology fails to satisfy this requirement; (3) Therefore, traditional epistemology should be abandoned.

On one reading of premise (1), it is unobjectionable. An epistemology that did *nothing* to address our cognitive experience or that provided no indication

[3] See especially pp. 169–88. Kvanvig says of this theoretical alternative that it "jettisons the attempt to explain the virtues in terms of the role the virtues play in justification and knowledge. Instead, it holds that the importance of the virtues in not reducible to, or explicable in terms of, these traditional epistemological concepts, but is independent of them" (150).

whatsoever as to how we might go about achieving the epistemic ideal would indeed be unacceptable. It is also clear, however, that traditional epistemology is not a complete failure in this regard. Traditional epistemological questions arise from some fairly straightforward and intuitive ways of thinking about our cognitive situation.[4] While epistemologists' responses to these questions have, perhaps, tended toward the abstract and technical, they are not entirely void of the kind of practical value referred to in premise (1). Specifically, it is reasonable to think that these responses go at least some way toward providing an understanding of the cognitive ideal and how we might go about achieving it.

This point is worth dwelling on. Suppose that owing to certain pivotal events in my life it has suddenly become important to me to evaluate and seek to improve the quality of my cognitive life. Thinking that the so-called "theory of knowledge" might provide me with some guidance in this regard, I decide to familiarize myself with some of the literature in traditional epistemology. What, if anything, am I likely to gain from my inquiry? I would suggest that while my investigation may prove frustrating and tedious in various ways, it will not be futile. To begin, it will provide me with useful information concerning which *parts* or *aspects* of my intellectual life I ought to begin attending to: for instance, the evidential basis of my beliefs, the logical relations among these beliefs, how these beliefs were formed, what presently motivates or explains my acceptance of them, and the overall quality of my cognitive faculties and intellectual character. It will also provide me with a range of principles, structural models, and other standards that can be used to evaluate these aspects of my intellectual life: for example, various "internalist" criteria and principles, detailed foundationalist and coherentist models of the structure of epistemic justification, accounts of epistemic reliability and proper cognitive function, models of the so-called "basing relation," and descriptions of intellectually virtuous inquiry. My suggestion is that traditional epistemology is a source of a wide range of carefully worked out accounts of various *normative* epistemic concepts—accounts that can be applied in the assessment of one's beliefs, but that also speak to the question of what, in general, one should aim for or value in the pursuit of a good intellectual life.[5]

[4] See BonJour (2002) for a recent account of the straightforward and plausible intellectual origins of the traditional epistemological research program. See BonJour and Sosa (2003) for a debate about some of the main issues in traditional epistemology.

[5] For more on this point, see Alston (1993) and (2005). Alston also makes clear that while some of the principles and models just noted tend to be offered as competing theories, they need not be understood in this way. Thus a foundationalist, for instance, can agree that doxastic coherence is an epistemically good thing, even if she denies that it is part of the logical *basis* for

In response, Kvanvig might assert that this kind or level of epistemic "applicability" or "practicality" is too minimal—that the theories in question are, say, still objectionably abstract or detached from ordinary cognitive life. This move, however, would substantially weaken the plausibility of premise (1) of Kvanvig's argument. Suppose, for instance, that this premise should instead be understood as saying that any plausible epistemology must be applicable to the intellectual lives of ordinary cognizers in a very *immediate* and *straightforward* way; or, alternatively, that no plausible epistemology can contain abstract or technical content that does not have some kind of practical payoff.[6]

The problem with premise (1) understood in either of these ways is that it asserts an implausible view of how to handle the tension between the practical and theoretical desiderata applicable to theory-construction in epistemology. Surely *part* of what we hope for from epistemology is simply an accurate reflective or theoretical account of knowledge—an account, for instance, of its essential nature, structure, sources, and limits. But given the inherent difficulty and complexity of such matters, this desideratum is likely to conflict at various points with the more practical desideratum that apparently interests Kvanvig. That is, an intellectually satisfying philosophical account of knowledge is bound to be rigorous, complex, and abstract in ways that may have little immediate practical payoff. My claim, then, is that when these different kinds of desiderata conflict, there is no reason to think that practical considerations should always win out. If a particular theory of knowledge clearly fares well with respect to the goal of providing a deep, intellectually satisfying account of knowledge, but is also technical or complex in ways that have little "practical" benefit for ordinary cognizers, this need not be grounds for its dismissal.

Where does this leave Kvanvig's argument? We have seen that on a certain reading of premise (1) of this argument, the premise is plausible, but that premise (2) is not. Further, we have seen that if we modify premise (1) in order to make premise (2) more acceptable, premise (1) then becomes dubious. In either case, Kvanvig's argument apparently fails to vindicate the negative and more radical element of Strong Autonomous VE.

knowledge or justification; likewise for a reliabilist's perspective on having good evidence or reasons for one's beliefs. There is, then, nothing to prevent one's being guided by or learning from a rather wide range of epistemic models and principles.

[6] One hears notes in this objection of the sort of "action-guiding" complaint that is commonly leveled against virtue ethical accounts of right action. See Hursthouse (1995) and (1999: ch. 1) for helpful discussions of this objection.

The shortcomings of Kvanvig's argument do not, of course, establish that Strong Autonomous VE is beyond all hope. But given how radical this view is, the burden clearly falls on the *defender* of Strong Autonomous VE to offer a compelling defense. And, given that Kvanvig's is the only defense of Strong Autonomous VE to date, we can reasonably draw a pessimistic conclusion about the prospects of this approach.

10.2.4 *Weak Autonomous VE*

We come now to the fourth and final variety of character-based virtue epistemology. Like Strong Autonomous VE, Weak Autonomous VE asserts that philosophical reflection on intellectual virtues can form the basis of an "alternative" epistemological research program, one that revolves around theoretical issues and questions that are largely distinct from the issues and questions of traditional epistemology. This approach is "weak" because it regards an autonomous concern with intellectual virtue as merely *complementing*—not replacing—traditional epistemology. Thus Weak Autonomous VE calls for expanding the borders of epistemology proper, not for a total overhaul of the field.

The central challenge for Weak Autonomous VE is to make good on the claim that there are in fact theoretical—and indeed broadly *epistemological*—issues and questions that virtue-minded epistemologists might pursue but that are largely independent of traditional epistemological issues and questions. Elsewhere I have referred to this as the "theoretical challenge" for any autonomous variety of virtue epistemology.[7] While none of the preceding chapters has been directly or explicitly aimed at overcoming this challenge, several contain good grounds for thinking that the challenge is indeed surmountable. In particular, Chapters 2 and 6–9 illustrate in considerable detail the sorts of philosophical questions and issues that virtue epistemologists might address once they begin to focus on matters of intellectual virtue and character in their own right. By way of review, I will briefly note a range of questions proper to five different areas of autonomous, virtue-based inquiry that have been touched on in one form or another earlier in the book:

[7] See my (2008: 485–7). That discussion makes clear that the challenge is indeed a genuine one, and that the work of some virtue epistemologists in recent years has failed to overcome it. An analogous challenge exists for those virtue ethicists who think that moral virtues should be an important focus of ethics but who eschew any attempt to ground an account of right action in terms of an exercise of such traits. See Louden (1997) on this point.

(1) *Intellectual virtues and other excellences.* How are intellectual character virtues related to other cognitive excellences like intellectual skills, talents, temperaments, and faculties? Is the concept of an intellectual virtue *reducible* to that of (say) an intellectual skill?[8] If not, how exactly do intellectual virtues and skills differ? And how do they depend on each other? Which (if any) intellectual skills must an intellectually virtuous person possess and why? How are intellectual virtues related to *moral* virtues? Are they a subclass of moral virtues? Or are intellectual virtues somehow fundamentally distinct from moral virtues?[9]

(2) *The nature of an intellectual virtue.* There is widespread agreement that traits like open-mindedness, fair-mindedness, intellectual carefulness, thoroughness, courage, and tenacity are intellectual virtues. But what exactly *makes* these traits intellectual virtues? Is it something about their epistemic efficacy or reliability?[10] If so, how exactly is this feature to be understood? Or is it rather something about the traits' internal or psychological character considered in its own right?[11] If so, what is this character and why exactly does it make the relevant traits intellectual virtues? Finally, must there be a single right answer to the question of what makes something an intellectual virtue? Or might there multiple viable concepts of intellectual virtue?

(3) *The psychological elements and structure of an intellectual virtue.* Which (if any) psychological states or qualities are required for intellectual virtue?[12] Is something like a "love of truth" required?[13] If so, how exactly is this notion to be understood? For instance, should the "love" in question be understood in purely affective terms? Or does it also have *cognitive* dimension? If so, what does this dimension amount to, and how is it related to the other psychological elements of intellectual virtue?[14]

[8] See Annas (2003) for a defense of the view that intellectual virtues are intellectual skills. See Battaly (2011) and Chapter 2 for arguments against this claim.

[9] I take up the distinction between intellectual and moral virtues in the Appendix. See also Driver (2003) and Pouivet (2010).

[10] See Driver (2000; 2003) for an affirmative reply.

[11] This claim was defended in Chapter 6. See also Montmarquet (2000).

[12] Driver (2003) claims that there are no specific psychological requirements on intellectual virtue. This is because she thinks of cognitive reliability—a quality that can, in principle at least, be realized by a wide and diverse range of psychological states—as the *sole* defining feature of an intellectual virtue. For more on her view, see the Appendix.

[13] For affirmative replies, see Chapter 6 and Zagzebski (1996).

[14] This issue was touched on briefly at various points in Chapters 6–9. It was clear in those discussions, however, that considerably more needs to be said about the cognitive dimension of intellectual virtue.

(4) *The nature and structure of individual intellectual virtues*. How exactly are we to understand the nature and structure of various *individual* intellectual virtues like open-mindedness, intellectual courage, creativity, or originality? What are the core psychological elements or processes involved with an exercise of these traits? What is to display these traits at the right time, toward the right person or belief, for the right reason, and so on? What are the unique roles of these traits within the cognitive economy?[15] How are they are related to other virtues? Which intellectual *vices* correspond to these virtues? And how exactly are they related?[16]

(5) *Applied virtue epistemology*. Several of the examples and illustrations of intellectual virtue in the preceding chapters suggest that there are fixed and generic domains of human activity (e.g. journalism, law, science, and education) success in which makes substantial and reasonably systematic demands on a person's intellectual character.[17] These demands would appear to be traceable and worth exploring and understanding from a philosophical standpoint. For instance, for any of the relevant domains, we might consider: What exactly is the (intellectual character-relevant) structure of this domain? What sorts of demands does success in this domain make on a person's intellectual character? Which intellectual virtues are relevant to meeting these demands? And how exactly are they relevant? Are there potential *conflicts* between the requirements of intellectual virtue and the requirements for success in this domain? If so, how should they be understood and adjudicated? Because it involves applying the concepts and standards of intellectual virtue to various domains of human activity, this approach is aptly referred to as "applied virtue epistemology."[18]

This is but a quick and cursory sketch of a few of the issues and questions that might comprise the theoretical basis of a version of Weak Autonomous VE.[19]

[15] These and related questions were taken up in Chapters 8 and 9. Roberts and Wood (2007) is another fine example of this approach.

[16] For accounts of intellectual vices, see Battaly (2010) and my (2010).

[17] See, among many others, the illustrations of intellectual courage discussed at the beginning of Chapter 9.

[18] An excellent example of this approach is Miranda Fricker's *Epistemic Injustice* (2007). Fricker examines the role of moral and intellectual character in the context of evaluating *testimony*. She identifies a virtue she calls "reflexive critical openness" as the characterological antidote to the sorts of injustices that tend to occur in this domain. Another good example is Battaly (2006), which looks at the bearing of intellectual character virtues on the practice of teaching. See also Schmitt and Lahroodi (2008) for a discussion of curiosity and its role in education.

[19] There may be some overlap between these issues and questions the theoretical substance of Kvanvig's proposed alternative (1992) to traditional epistemology note above. However, as I touch on in my (2004), it is not clear to me that the concept of intellectual virtue would figure

While a great deal more could be said about these and related projects, I take it that what has been said, especially when viewed in light of the discussion in Chapters 2 and 6–9, lends considerable plausibility to the idea that there is philosophically substantive and interesting work to be done in connection with intellectual virtues and their role in the cognitive life that is largely distinct from the kind of work that has traditionally been central to the epistemological enterprise.

10.2.5 *A final objection*

One further objection must be considered. It might be said of the theoretical avenues just sketched that they are not really *epistemological* and thus that what I have been describing as a character-based approach to epistemology is really a contribution to virtue ethics, moral psychology, or some other philosophical discipline. One might, in other words, adopt a "purist" or "exclusivist" conception of epistemology proper, maintaining that while there is some interesting philosophy to be done in connection with the intellectual virtues, this work falls outside the purview of epistemology.

This may seem like a merely terminological matter. Whether it is or not, the matter is still worth considering. For it is plausible to think that epistemologists are especially well-suited to address some of the philosophical issues in question—that their expertise, methods, categories, and so on, can be employed to shed unique and valuable light on matters of intellectual character and virtue. The very perception, however, that an exploration of these issues is proper, say, to ethics but not to epistemology is likely to stymie if not prevent such research.[20] Therefore, I will briefly discuss some reasons for thinking that the sort of theoretical program sketched above does indeed fall under the purview of epistemology proper. This will bring the chapter and book to a natural close.

Consider a conception of epistemology according to which this field is concerned *strictly* with the nature, structure, limits, and sources of knowledge, that is, with the subject matter of traditional epistemology. One problem with this conception is that it is likely to put "beyond the pale" a considerable

properly into a lot of the main questions, problems, and projects that Kvanvig identifies as central to his approach.

[20] Likewise, there may be a danger (albeit one that I think is less realistic) of thinking of the philosophical work in question as strictly epistemological, for there are likely to be other important aspects of this work that ethicists in particular are uniquely well-suited to carry out. Therefore, as I suggest below, perhaps the most fitting perspective on the matter is that the theoretical territory in question is one in which the domains of ethics and epistemology *overlap*.

amount of philosophical work that virtually no one would deny is proper to epistemology. This includes many recent discussions of epistemic *justification*, for a number of authors who have done important work to illuminate this concept (e.g. Plantinga 1993a and Alston 1988) have nonetheless argued at length that justification is *not* an essential feature of knowledge.[21] A similar point can be made about certain accounts of epistemic *rationality*, for example, those defended by Richard Foley (1987; 1993). Foley argues with considerable plausibility that rationality as he conceives of it is not an essential ingredient of knowledge. But, again, it would be manifestly implausible to suggest that Foley's work on rationality does not really qualify as epistemology. Finally, the same can be said of recent work on the concept of *understanding* (e.g. Zagzebski 2001 and Grimm 2010). Here again, while virtually no one would deny that this work falls within the purview of epistemology, few would maintain that understanding as these authors conceive of it is part of the very nature or essence of knowledge.

A second way of rebutting the objection is to point out that while the immediate focus of any version of "autonomous" virtue epistemology is different from that of traditional epistemology, many of the concepts central to the latter are also central to the former. This includes concepts like truth, knowledge, rationality, and understanding. Indeed, the very chapters in this book that illustrate the promise of Weak Autonomous VE are replete with appeals to these concepts. Again, an intellectually virtuous person, on the view defended here, is one with a positive psychological orientation toward truth, knowledge, understanding, and other distinctively epistemic goods. Further, I have argued at a couple of points that intellectual virtues involve a kind or element of epistemic rationality or reasonability.[22] It is, then, not much of an exaggeration to say that intellectual virtues are "all about" knowledge and related epistemic ends. This in turn suggests that while the sort of philosophical territory sketched above may *overlap* with that of virtue ethics or moral psychology, it also fits very comfortably within the boundaries of epistemology broadly conceived.

On these and related matters I enthusiastically endorse some remarks by the late William Alston (2005). After identifying various problems with adopting

[21] Of course these authors could simply be wrong—it could be that justification as they think of it *is* an essential ingredient of knowledge. Nevertheless, it is implausible to think that they would *have* to be mistaken in order for their treatments of justification to be proper to epistemology.

[22] See Chapters 6 and 7 and, to a lesser extent, the final sections of Chapters 8 and 9.

the sort of overly narrow conception of epistemology noted above, Alston proposes the following account:

> Against this background, what can be said on the subject of what does and does not count as epistemology? I think the best we can do is the following. What we call "epistemology" consists of some selection from the problems, issues, and subject matters dealt with by philosophers that have to do with what we might call the cognitive side of human life: the operation and condition of our cognitive faculties—perception, reasoning, belief formation; the products thereof—beliefs, arguments, theories, explanations, knowledge; and the evaluation of all that. And so a very broad conception of epistemology would be *philosophical reflection on the cognitive aspects of human life*... (2–3; his emphasis)

On this conception, a philosophical research program aimed primarily at illuminating the basic nature and structure of intellectual virtues and how these traits figure in the overall cognitive economy clearly would count as a contribution to epistemology.

In fact, Alston himself, who was no virtue epistemologist, identifies precisely this sort of approach as one that epistemologists can and should give their attention to. He points out that in recent centuries, epistemologists have been preoccupied with skeptical considerations and related matters, but that "exclusive attention to these matters has been challenged recently from a variety of directions." He adds that "we can see these challenges as reflecting one or another neglected segment of [a] larger territory...one or another stretch of that territory that was overlooked in the rush to respond to skeptical worries." He continues:

> One such segment comprises the "intellectual virtues", such as open-mindedness, a disposition to consider reasons against one's own position, carefulness, and so on—virtues the exercise of which are conducive to success in attaining our cognitive goals. Flushed by the discovery of a subject matter that has not been overworked by recent epistemology, and encouraged by the recent revival of "virtue ethics", a number of thinkers have been vigorously cultivating the soil of "virtue epistemology." The more modest of these enthusiasts simply take the intellectual virtues to be one topic among others to be explored by epistemologists, an activity that is in no way incompatible with or in competition with other epistemological topics. But bolder partisans of the new look, well represented by Zagzebski 1996, present the intellectual virtues as the center of a new sort of complete epistemology. Zagzebski and others seek to provide an analysis of, for example, knowledge and justified belief in terms of the virtues and their exercise. I find these more imperialist pretensions to be unconvincing, but there is no doubt that the intellectual virtues are among the important objects of

> philosophical reflection on the cognitive aspect of our lives. And their neglect by epistemology in the last few centuries needs to be remedied. (3–4)

Alston's remarks map nicely onto some of the major aims and conclusions of this book. He expresses warranted skepticism about Strong Conservative VE and appropriate enthusiasm about something like Weak Autonomous VE. My hope is that the present inquiry has gone some way toward providing the sort of remedy that Alston says is sorely needed.

Appendix

ON THE DISTINCTION BETWEEN INTELLECTUAL AND MORAL VIRTUES

At several points in the preceding chapters, the question has arisen as to how we should understand the relationship between intellectual virtues, conceived as character traits, and what we typically think of as moral virtues. This is a natural and pressing question given that both intellectual and moral virtues are excellences of personal character and that we employ a common terminology to refer to both sets of traits (we speak, for instance, of honesty proper and intellectual honesty, of moral courage and intellectual courage, of fairness and fair-mindedness, etc.). In this appendix, I deal directly with the relationship between intellectual and moral virtues. My concern is what, if any, relatively deep or principled distinction can be drawn between the two sets of traits.[1]

It will be helpful, at least initially, to frame the discussion in terms of the following three theses:

> *Reductive thesis*: No principled distinction can be drawn between intellectual and moral virtues. Intellectual virtues just *are* or are "reducible" to moral virtues. While, in ordinary thought and language, we distinguish between "intellectual virtues" and "moral virtues," this distinction is superficial and lacks any ultimate basis.

[1] I shall not be concerned, therefore, with any potential *unity* between intellectual and moral virtues, that is, with whether the possession of any (or all) intellectual virtues requires the possession of any (or all) moral virtues, or vice versa. Further, because we are conceiving of intellectual virtues as character traits, many otherwise potentially promising ways of marking a distinction between intellectual and moral virtues fall by the wayside. This includes the idea that moral virtues are acquired by habituation and practice while intellectual virtues are not, that moral virtues are susceptible to voluntary control while intellectual virtues are not, and so on.

Subset thesis: Intellectual virtues are a species or proper subset of moral virtues. While intellectual virtues are moral virtues, they are unified in a way that sets them apart from other, more familiar moral virtues.

Independence thesis: Intellectual virtues are not a proper subset of moral virtues. Rather, they are fundamentally distinct from moral virtues.[2]

Later we will find that the actual relation between intellectual and moral virtues is considerably more complex than is suggested by this threefold distinction. This is, however, an intuitive and convenient way to begin thinking about the issues. My plan is to argue for a view of the relation between intellectual and moral virtues that falls somewhere between the subset thesis and the independence thesis.

A.1 *Belief vs. action*

One initially attractive way of defending the independence thesis makes use of a familiar and intuitive distinction between "the theoretical" and "the practical," or between belief and action. It might be argued that intellectual virtues are fundamentally different and distinct from moral virtues on the grounds that intellectual virtues bear primarily on the domain of *belief* (theoretical), while moral virtues bear primarily on the domain of *action* (practical). For instance, it might be said that to be intellectually virtuous is to *believe* or to *form beliefs* in a certain appropriate or excellent way, while to be morally virtuous is to *act* in a comparable way.[3]

This argument betrays a misunderstanding of intellectual virtues. As we have seen at various points in previous chapters, intellectual virtues do not bear primarily on the domain of belief—to possess or exercise the traits in question is not primarily a matter of believing or forming beliefs in any particular way. This is not to say that intellectual virtues never have bearing of this kind, for it does seem possible to believe something in an intellectually virtuous way or to

[2] For some similar theoretical options, see Pouivet (2010: 5). Clearly these are not the only possible ways of marking the distinction. We might, for instance, wonder whether moral virtues are reducible to intellectual virtues. This is at least suggested by the Socratic thesis that "virtue is knowledge" and by the idea that *phronesis* is at once a "master virtue" and an intellectual virtue. I doubt, however, that many readers will be tempted by the view that moral virtues just are intellectual virtues—at least not in any sense that *conflicts* with the position I plan to defend here. Thanks to Liz Murray for raising this point.

[3] This possibility is gestured at, though not ultimately endorsed, in Pouivet (2010: 9–10).

believe something "out of" intellectual virtue. Nonetheless, we have seen that intellectual virtues, like moral virtues, bear principally on rational *activity*.[4] This is evident in their central bearing on the process of inquiry, which involves activities like reading, interpreting, judging, assessing, reflecting, listening, and communicating. Belief, on the other hand, is best understood as a product of inquiry, and thus as a kind of indirect or mediate (though by no means accidental) result of the operation of intellectual virtues and vices. The independence thesis, then, is not supported by a distinction between belief and action or between theory and practice.[5]

A.2 *A unifying principle for intellectual virtues*

While intellectual virtues do not typically bear directly on beliefs, it is not implausible to think of them as *aiming* at certain sorts of beliefs or related psychological states.[6] Indeed, we saw in previous chapters that it makes sense to think of an intellectually virtuous person as one who is deeply and fundamentally motivated by epistemic ends like knowledge and understanding. We might, then, attempt to distinguish intellectual virtues from other kinds of virtues (moral virtues included) on the grounds that intellectual virtues aim uniquely at distinctively epistemic ends of the sort just noted.

Indeed, this way of thinking about intellectual virtues is widely embraced in the virtue epistemology literature, even by writers who, like Linda Zagzebski (1996), take considerable pains to highlight the fundamental similarities

[4] In Chapter 9, we saw that a person might believe something "out of" intellectual courage. In Chapters 2 and 8, however, we saw that intellectual virtues bear more commonly and immediately on intellectual activities of various sorts.

[5] Neither, then, will it do to distinguish between intellectual and moral virtues on the grounds that, say, intellectual virtues bear immediately on "mental" activity while moral virtues bear immediately on overt *behavior*, since many of the intellectual activities noted above involve overt behaviors (not to mention that many moral virtues have a robustly cognitive or "mental" dimension as well). Alternatively, it might be held that intellectual virtues bear characteristically on *intellectual* activities or practices, while moral virtues bear characteristically on *moral* activities (see e.g. Roberts and Wood 2007: 59 and 225). The obvious question here is how to distinguish between the kinds or varieties of activity in question. One fairly natural reply is that they differ in terms of their respective *ends* or *goals*, which suggests a teleological distinction between intellectual and moral virtues. I consider a view like this in section A.3 below.

[6] Similarly, it might be plausible to think of them as *causing* or as being *productive* of such states. Much of what I say below could easily be reformulated to address this alternative suggestion.

between intellectual and moral virtues. Zagzebski argues at length against Aristotle's sharp division between intellectual and moral virtues (137–58).[7] But she maintains that intellectual virtues nonetheless have a common and distinctive intentional object, which she refers to as "cognitive contact with reality," a notion that incorporates a range of familiar epistemic goods, including knowledge, understanding, wisdom, and the like (166–7).[8]

I take it that Zagzebski's basic point here is a plausible one—that it is reasonable to think of intellectual virtues as aimed uniquely at distinctively epistemic ends. While more could be said to demarcate epistemic ends from other kinds of ends, the basic distinction should be intuitive enough, and I will not elaborate on it here. Assuming that we are right to think of intellectual virtues in this way, we are now in a position to rule out one of three main theoretical options identified above: namely, the reductive thesis, according to which *no principled distinction* can be drawn between intellectual and moral virtues.[9]

A.3 *A teleological account*

But this way of thinking about intellectual virtues does not, by itself, yield a sufficient understanding of the relation between intellectual and moral virtues. For, while it clarifies the distinctive feature of intellectual virtues vis-à-vis other kinds of virtues, it does not clarify the difference between intellectual virtues and moral virtues in particular. It does not, for instance, help us adjudicate between the possibility that intellectual virtues are a proper *subset* of moral virtues (distinguishable from other moral virtues on account of their epistemic orientation) and the possibility that they are rather somehow fundamentally different or distinct from moral virtues. Accordingly, it prevents us from being able to adjudicate between the subset thesis and the independence thesis.

The suggested account of intellectual virtues does, however, point in the direction of a potentially more illuminating way of drawing the distinction. Specifically, it might be thought that moral virtues, like intellectual virtues, can

[7] See also Montmarquet (1993: 109–10) and Roberts and Wood (2007: 59–60).

[8] Zagzebski's view is that intellectual virtues are a kind of moral virtue—that "cognitive contact with reality" is a part of the broader whole at which moral virtues aim. Thus she defends the subset thesis.

[9] Defenses of the reductive thesis are, in fact, difficult to come by. Roberts and Wood (2007: 60) flirt with the thesis, but in the end seem pretty clearly to endorse a version of the subset thesis (309–11).

be understood teleologically, or in terms of their ultimate aim or goal, such that we can think of intellectual virtues as personal qualities aimed at distinctively epistemic ends and of moral virtues as personal qualities aimed at distinctively moral ends.[10]

While an initially plausible suggestion, a great deal depends, of course, on how exactly we are to understand the moral ends in question. Presumably they include things like pleasure, the absence of pain, autonomy, justice, love, respect, friendship, and the like. Note, however, that these ends represent a rather diverse lot. This in turn raises the important question of what (if anything) the ends have in common in virtue of which they are distinctively *moral* in nature. Consider, for instance, pleasure and autonomy. It is at least prima facie reasonable to think of both of these ends as morally significant, and in a more or less basic or fundamental way. But what is meant by "morally" here? What do we mean when we say that pleasure or autonomy or any of the other ends noted above have *moral* significance? I take it that the answer to these questions is far from obvious.[11]

One option at this point is to deny the need for any further account of the moral. Perhaps we should rest content with an enumerative specification, that is, with thinking of moral ends simply as ends *like* pleasure, justice, autonomy, love, friendship, and so on. There are, however, at least three problems with this suggestion. First, barring further clarity about the underlying notion of morality, the very distinction we are attempting to get at between intellectual and moral virtues will remain less than precise. Second, and more importantly, the possibility will remain open that the list of (apparently) moral ends does not, in fact, pick out a unified group at all. Again, the ends in question are extremely diverse, such that, in the absence of a more illuminating account of the moral, it can reasonably be wondered whether they represent more than one *kind* or *variety* of ends, rather than a single "moral" variety.[12] Third, the relevant lack of

[10] Zagzebski, who endorses the subset thesis, apparently does so on something like this basis (1996: 139, 256). Driver also defends a view along these lines (2000: 126; 2003: 114–15), though she thinks of the relations to the relevant ends in causal rather than intentional terms. We will consider her view below. Finally, a teleological account is also suggested briefly by Fricker (2007: 120).

[11] Nor does the problem disappear for, say, the pure Kantian or the pure utilitarian. For we can still ask: what does the former mean by "moral" when she says that pleasure does not have any intrinsic moral significance? Or what does the latter mean when he says that pleasure alone is of ultimate moral importance?

[12] I take it that the prima facie heterogeneity of these ends is substantially greater than that of the relevant intellectual ends (in terms of which we identified intellectual virtues above). That is, it is considerably more plausible to think of knowledge, understanding, insight,

clarity prevents us from being able to adjudicate between the subset thesis and the independence thesis. For, while knowledge and related epistemic ends do not appear on the relevant list of (ostensibly) moral goods, the list obviously is not intended to be complete. And, without a further account of the operative or underlying conception of the moral, it is reasonable to wonder whether these epistemic ends might turn up on a complete version of the list, that is, whether knowledge, understanding, and the like are also "moral" ends in the relevant sense, and thus whether intellectual virtues can viewed as a subset of moral virtues.

What is needed, then, is what might be referred to as a "substantive" conception of the moral that could underwrite the claim that moral virtues aim at distinctively moral ends or goods while intellectual virtues aim at distinctively epistemic ends. The difficulty, again, is that is far from clear what such a conception might amount to.[13]

Perhaps an appeal to the concept of human *well-being* or human *flourishing* would be helpful at this point. Suppose, for instance, that we think of moral virtues as personal qualities that aim at human flourishing, or at a well-lived human life, and of the relevant (putatively) moral goods noted above as (partly) *constitutive* of human flourishing. This is, at any rate, one fairly natural way of attempting to specify a reasonably substantive and unified conception of the moral, a conception that might in turn yield a more illuminating account of the relation between intellectual and moral virtues.[14]

Note, first, that if this suggestion is correct, it rules out the independence thesis. For true belief, knowledge, understanding, and related states are also partly constitutive of human flourishing. That is, part of what it is to flourish as a human being is to enjoy a stake in these goods. This is evident, among other ways, in the considerable (and not merely instrumental) value we tend to ascribe to the receipt of a good *education*. And it is likely to follow from any account of human flourishing that gives a central role to the uniquely human capacity of *reason* or *rationality*, since knowledge, understanding, and the like are a primary and non-accidental product of this capacity. If a share in the

wisdom, and so on, as representing a unified set (or picking out a kind of unified whole) than it is to think of ends like pleasure, justice, and freedom in this way. Therefore, while we could do more to spell out the intentional object of intellectual virtues, the challenge is not as pressing as it is in the case of moral virtues.

[13] Driver (2003: 107) emphasizes a similar point. As does Zagzebski (1996: 256).

[14] Here again the view could also be formulated in causal terms, so that moral virtues are conceived as traits that *contribute* to or *bring about* human flourishing (see e.g. Driver 2000 and 2003). The objections I raise below have equal force against an account of this sort.

epistemic goods in question is in fact partly constitutive of human flourishing, then intellectual virtues, which aim at these goods, presumably would be among the moral virtues; they would not be fundamentally distinct from them.

While inconsistent with the independence thesis, the suggested account of the moral yields an obvious strategy for defending the *subset* thesis. For if we think of moral virtues as personal qualities that aim at human flourishing, of the epistemic goods in question as partly constitutive of human flourishing, and of intellectual virtues as personal qualities that aim (uniquely) at epistemic goods, then we can reasonably think of intellectual virtues as a proper subset of the full range of moral virtues.

But is this a plausible conception of moral virtue? There are good reasons for thinking that it is not. To begin, note that we often appeal to the notion of the moral or of morality in order to pick out a certain kind or dimension of value that is apparently distinct from other kinds or dimensions of value that nonetheless are relevant to human flourishing. This is the case, for instance, with certain judgments about a person's athletic or artistic excellence. We sometimes make judgments to the effect that "So-and-so may be an excellent athlete or musician or chef, but he's a complete *jerk*," where the latter, I am suggesting, is at least sometimes equivalent to "he's *morally* rotten."[15] There is little reason to doubt that while the subjects of such judgments are defective from a moral standpoint, their athletic or artistic abilities still aim at and contribute to some aspect of their flourishing as human beings. While they may not be flourishing on the whole, and are not flourishing morally, presumably they still exhibit a distinctively human variety of excellence or enjoy a distinctively human kind of well-being. If so, then we cannot think of moral virtues merely as personal qualities aimed at human flourishing.[16]

A likely reply to this objection is that while these persons may have certain talents or skills that contribute to their flourishing, any concern with moral or intellectual virtues is necessarily a concern with certain *character* traits, and the relevant talents or skills presumably are not character traits. I doubt that the sorts of judgments at issue are always judgments about mere talents or abilities—that they never pertain to any character traits of the relevant subjects. But we need not settle this matter here, for we can easily identify other cases that clearly

[15] See Chapter 6 for an elaboration of this point.

[16] One could hold, of course, that aiming at human flourishing is a necessary but not a *sufficient* condition for moral virtue. But then the challenge would be to identify the relevant additional necessary feature or features. And this, I take it, is no less challenging than (and perhaps no different from) what we are already attempting to do.

do involve character traits aimed at athletic, artistic, or other seemingly morally irrelevant aspects of human flourishing.

Imagine, for instance, an athlete who habitually shows determination, persistence, patience, courage, or the like in his attempts to win. It is not unreasonable to think that the following might be true of such a person: his determination and so forth are genuine character traits; these character traits are aimed at the realization of his distinctively human athletic potential and thus at his flourishing as a human being; and yet he is extremely morally deficient. At a minimum, there would appear to be a familiar and intuitive sense of "moral" according to which such judgments might make good sense, and thus according to which the present conception of moral virtue is objectionably broad.

To drive this point home, let us consider the hypothetical case of Smith, whom at t_1 we learn is cold-hearted toward his wife, severely neglectful of his children, and consistently unfriendly to his neighbors. Accordingly, we make the judgment that Smith is a morally deficient or unvirtuous person. Suppose, however, that at t_2 we learn of Smith that, despite the flaws just mentioned, he is genuinely committed to achieving his artistic potential and regularly makes significant sacrifices and takes many pains in the service of this goal. While we might at t_2 regard Smith as having a certain characterological drive and determination that contribute to some dimension of his well-being qua human being, we would not, I take it, be very tempted to revise our *moral* assessment of him.[17]

An objection might be that Smith and similar characters described above are, on account of their aesthetically or athletically oriented character traits, in fact morally virtuous at least to some extent, but that our sense of this virtue is "swamped" by our awareness of their more substantial and salient moral *vices*. While a possibility like this is difficult to rule out, there is at least some reason to be dubious about it. For suppose that at some still later time, t_3, we learn of Smith that despite being a jerk to those closest to him, he does have a "heart" for the victims of remote suffering and evil (victims of natural disasters that he learns about on the evening news, say). The pain and suffering of these people genuinely moves Smith. I submit that while Smith might be a morally rotten person on the whole, the information we receive at t_3 could reasonably cause us to revise our moral assessment of him at least slightly. We might plausibly

[17] This bears an obvious similarity to Bernard Williams's Gauguin case (1981). Also relevant here is Susan Wolf's (1982) discussion of "moral saints," which underscores the apparent normative weight of certain non-moral traits and abilities.

conclude, for instance, that Smith is somewhat less morally vicious than we had thought him to be at t_2. This suggests that Smith's "artistic virtues," as we might refer to them, are not genuine moral virtues, and thus, again, that moral virtues cannot be defined as character traits aimed at human flourishing.

We began this section with the hope of marking a distinction between intellectual and moral virtues on the grounds that intellectual virtues aim at distinctively intellectual or epistemic ends while moral virtues aim at distinctively "moral" ends. We observed, however, that the latter sorts of ends are an extremely diverse lot, and that for the proposed distinction to prove defensible and illuminating, more would need to be said about the underlying concept of the moral. We have found that this is a very challenging task, and that an appeal to human flourishing is unlikely to mitigate this challenge. Again, what we have been unable to identify is a *substantive* conception of the moral that might underwrite the proposed distinction between intellectual and moral virtues. While I do not want to abandon hope that such a conception is available, I am at a loss as to what it might be, and thus will turn now to explore a rather different way of thinking about morality and about the distinction between intellectual and moral virtues.[18]

A.4 *An alternative proposal*

Let us begin anew our attempt to understand this distinction by considering a further iteration of the Smith case discussed above. Recall that at t_1 we learn of Smith that he is cold-hearted toward his wife, severely neglects his children, and is routinely unfriendly to his neighbors. We rightly conclude that Smith is a moral wretch. Suppose, however, that at t_2 we learn of Smith that he is also an accomplished biologist with a genuine thirst for knowledge and understanding of the natural world, and that this desire leads him to engage in scientific inquiry that is systematically careful, thorough, fair-minded, rigorous, and tenacious. I can see little problem with inferring that Smith might, on this account, be genuinely intellectually virtuous. Nonetheless, given his orientation toward those closest to him, I fail to see that we are in a position to revise

[18] As this suggests, I think there may be more than one "right answer" to our guiding question. That is, there may be more than one phenomenon or property picked out by our ordinary ways of thinking and speaking about the "moral" or morality that would make possible more than one (viable, accurate) way of thinking about the relation between intellectual and moral virtues.

our *moral* estimation of him—again according to at least one familiar and intuitive notion of morality. Indeed, while the Smith case may be far-fetched, it is hardly controversial to suggest that intellectual excellence is no guarantee of moral excellence.[19]

Assuming this is an accurate assessment, two additional and correlative points are in order. First, the case is suggestive of a conception of morality according to which "moral" means something like "others-regarding." This conception of the moral was also hinted at in some of the other cases discussed earlier. One of these was an iteration of the Smith case in which he exhibits certain putative character virtues in pursuit of distinctively *artistic* or *aesthetic* ends. Another involved a person who exhibits similar traits in pursuit of a particular *athletic* goal. In each of these cases, we observed, the relevant character excellences notwithstanding, that the person in question is deeply morally defective, and defective, it seems, on account of his negative orientation toward or treatment of other persons. Again, this suggests what we might refer to as an "others-regarding" conception of morality. Second, the iteration of the Smith case just noted indicates a fairly deep distinction between intellectual and moral virtues. For, again, it suggests that one can have intellectual virtues that are not moral virtues. This in turn suggests that intellectual virtues are not a kind or subset of moral virtues and thus that the subset thesis is false.[20]

We will have occasion to revisit the latter conclusion later on; for now, let us consider an even *stronger* conclusion that the version of the Smith case just considered might seem to warrant. This case, together with certain ordinary and plausible ways of thinking about intellectual virtues (including their central bearing on personal inquiry, for instance), might suggest that we should think of intellectual virtues, not merely as epistemically oriented in the relevant sense, but also as strictly *self-oriented* or *egoistic*, that is, as aiming strictly and

[19] This is evident in familiar cases in which an otherwise laudable hunger for scientific knowledge, say, is pursued at the expense of certain persons' (ostensibly moral) rights. For more on this sort of possibility, see Zagzebski (1996: 156), Driver (2000: 132–3), Fricker (2007: 127) and Pouivet (2010: 4–8).

[20] For an in depth discussion of virtue and the self-/others-regarding distinction, see Slote (1992: ch. 8). Slote is critical of an others-regarding conception of morality (chs. 1 and 3), but not, as far as I can see, in ways that present a problem for the view I am defending here. Slote argues (convincingly, in my judgment) that an others-regarding conception of morality leaves out a range of important normative considerations. But the view I am defending is consistent with this claim, both (a) because it is consistent with the possibility that there are other, distinct but also viable conceptions of morality that might capture some of these other considerations, and (b) because it is consistent with the very plausible thesis that the scope of the normative is considerably broader than the scope of the moral.

necessarily at their possessor's own acquisition of knowledge, understanding, or the like. This claim has the potential to underwrite a very strong version of the independence thesis, for it entails that the categories of intellectual and moral virtue are mutually exclusive.

Such a view of intellectual virtues is not without its proponents.[21] It is, however, too restrictive. For, as a number of other authors have noted, intellectual virtues can, as such, be oriented toward the epistemic good or well-being of *others*—they can be aimed at others' acquisition or share in the epistemic goods.[22] Consider, for instance, a final iteration of the Smith case, in which we learn at t_2 that despite being a wretch toward his wife, kids, and neighbors, Smith has a deep and genuine concern for his students' understanding of biology. He is deeply committed to advancing their epistemic well-being, to increasing their share in the epistemic goods proper to his discipline. Thus Smith's love of knowledge encompasses, not just his own acquisition of knowledge, but also that of his students. Moreover, this motivation compels him to teach and communicate with his students in ways that are careful, precise, patient, and fair-minded.

Surely it is plausible to think of Smith as having various intellectual virtues. Again, his intellectual carefulness, precision, patience, and so on are clearly *epistemically* oriented. His fundamental concern is with the development of his students' *minds*—with their *understanding* or *grasp* of an important body of knowledge. Intuitively, it matters not, relative to whether Smith's traits are intellectual virtues, that his concern is also others-regarding, that his intellectual activity is aimed, not primarily at his own epistemic well-being, but rather at that of his students. As Jason Kawall (2002) remarks:

> [I]f we accept the claim that the epistemic point of view focuses solely on acquiring true beliefs and avoiding falsehoods, why assume that the measure of an epistemic agent is the stock of true beliefs she acquires for herself? Why not hold that a good epistemic agent helps to produce true beliefs in general—in her family, in her friends, in her community, and herself? An epistemic agent's virtues are those traits which help to produce true beliefs (and knowledge), whether in herself or others. (266)

It would appear, then, that a trait's being epistemically oriented in the relevant sense is sufficient for its being an intellectual virtue. Thus we may conclude that

[21] See especially Driver (2003: 115). I discuss her view in more detail below.

[22] We examined some of the others-regarding applications of intellectual virtue in Chapter 6. Other relevant discussions include Montmarquet (1993: 109), Battaly (2006), Roberts and Wood (2007: ch. 11) and especially Kawall (2002).

an egoistic conception of intellectual virtues is too restrictive and that the corresponding strong version of the independence thesis is mistaken.

In addition to showing that intellectual virtues can be others-regarding, the foregoing iteration of the Smith case adds to the plausibility of thinking of the moral or of morality in others-regarding terms. For Smith's intellectual carefulness, precision, and patience seem, not just to be intellectually significant, but to be *morally* significant as well, and morally significant on *account* of their others-regarding orientation. While Smith may still, on the whole, be a fairly morally vicious person, surely he is morally better than he would be if he had no regard at all for his students. Indeed, it does not seem too extreme to think of Smith's orientation toward his students as exhibiting a kind of moral virtue, or to think of Smith himself as being at least minimally morally virtuous on account of this orientation.

We have seen that some intellectual virtues have an others-regarding dimension, which in turn suggests that the traits in question are moral as well as intellectual virtues.[23] It is important to note that this is true, not merely of the particular intellectual virtues we have considered, but apparently of *all* intellectual virtues. For any such trait apparently can be oriented toward, or put in the service of, another person's share in the epistemic goods. This applies even to a virtue like curiosity, which might initially appear to be tied strictly to a first-person or egoistic desire for knowledge. A teacher, for instance, might consistently model curiosity to her students with the hope of getting them interested in the relevant subject matter, increasing their knowledge, or expanding their minds. And she might do this for its own sake—not merely as a way of securing for her students certain other, non-epistemic goods.[24] Likewise for virtues like intellectual honesty and integrity. Again, a teacher or parent might regard her own modeling of the kind of thinking or cognitive processing characteristic of these virtues as a way of furthering her students' or child's epistemic well-being,

[23] I am assuming, therefore, that a trait's having an others-regarding dimension is sufficient for its being a moral virtue (at least in some sense—see the discussion in the next section). This might seem too lenient. It might be thought instead that a trait is a moral virtue only if it is *strictly* others-regarding (that is, if and only if it does not as such have any self-regarding application). However, as the discussion in the previous paragraph suggests, this would entail that there are few if any moral virtues, for most of the traits we regard as moral virtues also have a self-regarding application. For a discussion of how intellectual and moral virtues can coincide in something like the way I am suggesting, see Fricker (2007: 127).

[24] Could this be her *only* motivation for being curious? If so, the extent of her intellectual virtue clearly would be limited; however, I see no reason to think that she would not be intellectually virtuous *at all* or that her curiosity would not really be an intellectual virtue. More on this point below.

and she might be compelled to engage in the relevant activity as a result. Therefore, far from being exclusively self-regarding, it would seem that all intellectual virtues have an others-regarding dimension.[25]

A.5 *Implications*

Suppose, then, that all intellectual virtues are others-regarding in the relevant sense. And suppose we think of moral virtues simply as others-regarding character traits. Does it follow that the subset thesis is correct after all—that intellectual virtues are a type of moral virtue? If so, what are we to make of the earlier suggestion that one can possess intellectual virtues that are *not* moral virtues?

These are important and challenging questions. Let us take them in turn. First, are intellectual virtues a subset of moral virtues on the present, others-regarding conception of morality? Yes and no. They are in the sense that all intellectual virtues apparently can, as such, be oriented toward the (epistemic) well-being of others. Further, we can say that any intellectual virtue possessed "in its fullness," that is, any token of an intellectual virtue V that embodies the full range of motivational states proper to V, is also a moral virtue. That said, intellectual virtues are *not* a proper subset of moral virtues in the sense that every token or instance of an intellectual virtue is also a token or instance of a moral virtue, or that every person who possesses an intellectual virtue also possesses a moral virtue. Again, this is because, to possess an intellectual virtue V, one need not possess the full or complete range of motivational states proper to V, including any others-regarding motives. To suggest otherwise is tantamount to claiming that one possesses a given intellectual virtue V only if one embodies the psychological qualities proper to V maximally or perfectly. But such a view is excessively strong and fundamentally at odds with many of our ordinary and well warranted virtue-ascriptions—ascriptions that involve predicating intellectual and other kinds of virtues of persons that we clearly do not think of as embodying the relevant traits maximally well or in their entirety.[26]

[25] This is where I take some issue with Kawall's (2002) otherwise very good treatment of the others-regarding character of intellectual virtues. Kawall marks a self-/others-regarding distinction among intellectual virtues themselves. That is, he seems to think that some intellectual virtues have an others-regarding dimension while others do not.

[26] This obviously requires rejecting a strong unity-of-the-virtues thesis. It is consistent, however, with a range of weaker versions of this thesis, including one according to which a person cannot possess certain members of a given *cluster* of virtues without possessing (at least to some extent) all of the other members belonging to that cluster.

This way of thinking about intellectual and moral virtues also yields a reply to the second question. Specifically, it suggests a way of reconciling the following two claims, both of which we have found to be plausible: (1) every intellectual virtue has an others-regarding motivation and thus qualifies as a moral virtue; (2) a person can possess intellectual virtues without possessing any moral virtues. We saw above that a person can be deeply and genuinely concerned with acquiring knowledge, that this concern can lead to an habitual motivation to act in ways characteristic of various intellectual virtues, and thus that the person can be said to possess these intellectual virtues, notwithstanding the fact that she is not nearly as concerned (or concerned at all) with *others'* acquisition of knowledge and thus fails to possess any moral virtues.[27] It should now be clear why this is entirely consistent with the further claim that all intellectual virtues have an others-regarding dimension or application. For, as we have just seen, the latter claim means merely that the traits in question *can*, as such, be applied in an others-regarding way; or, alternatively, that a person who possesses the relevant intellectual virtues completely or in their fullness will also be concerned, not just with her own share in the epistemic goods, but also with the share of others.

We have seen that there is a sense in which intellectual virtues are a proper subset of moral virtues and a sense in which they are not. What, then, are we to make of the independence thesis? Specifically, how deep is the distinction between moral and intellectual virtues?

Here again the proper response is an ambivalent one. On the one hand, intellectual and moral virtues are fundamentally similar, not merely because both are admirable traits of character, but also because some particular instances or tokens of intellectual virtue are also instances or tokens of moral virtue, and because any intellectual virtue possessed completely or in its fullness is also a moral virtue.

On the other hand, we have arrived at a distinction between intellectual virtues and moral virtues according to which the relevant conceptions of the moral and the intellectual are in some sense *asymmetrical*. Our conception of morality has turned out to be rather formal. Moral virtues are not character traits aimed at "distinctively moral" ends in the way that intellectual virtues are

[27] Admittedly, to the extent that such a person has easily accessible and relatively uncostly opportunities to be concerned about the epistemic well-being of others, and yet is not concerned, we will rightly question the *extent* of her intellectual virtue. But this does not mean that one can possess an intellectual virtue only if one possesses the relevant others-regarding motives. Again, this is required only for "full virtue" or the complete or perfect possession of a virtue.

character traits aimed at "distinctively epistemic" ends. Possessing a moral virtue is not a matter of aiming at or being motivated by certain kinds or types of goods. Rather, it is a matter (merely) of whether the goods at which one aims are goods for *oneself* or goods for *another*. In this sense, the proper counterpart to the present conception of the moral is that of the *prudential* or *self-regarding*. Our conception of intellectual virtue, by contrast, is substantive. Intellectual virtues are character traits aimed at certain sorts of ends—ends like knowledge, truth, and understanding. Some of the examples considered above suggest that intellectual virtues are, in this respect, more on par with what might be thought of as "athletic" or "aesthetic" character virtues, for they suggest that the latter aim at ends or goods that admit of a reasonably substantive specification.

We have reached the conclusion that intellectual virtues can be understood as character traits aimed at epistemic ends and that moral virtues can be understood, on a certain familiar and intuitive conception of the moral, as character traits that are others-regarding or that are aimed at (one aspect or another of) the well-being of another. It worth reiterating, however, that the present conception of the moral may be but one of multiple viable conceptions. Again, I am open to the possibility of a more substantive conception of the moral that would allow for a more symmetrical distinction between intellectual and moral virtues. But this distinction would not conflict with the distinction defended here. Rather, it would amount to an alternative but also plausible way of thinking about the nature and scope of the moral, and thus an alternative but also plausible way of thinking about the distinction between intellectual and moral virtues.

A.6 *Driver on intellectual and moral virtue*

As a final way of approaching our subject matter, let us look briefly at one other account of the relationship between intellectual and moral virtues. Julia Driver's "Moral and Epistemic Virtue" (2003) is one of very few recent attempts to specify the relationship between intellectual and moral virtues in any depth; and it is admirably sensitive to many of the fairly subtle considerations and distinctions we have been forced to grapple with here.[28] Nonetheless, Driver arrives at a rather different, albeit not unrelated, account of the distinction in question.

[28] Pouivet (2010) is another such attempt.

One difference between Driver's account of this distinction and the account developed here is that instead of focusing on the intentional or teleological relations between the relevant character traits and ends, it focuses on the corresponding *causal* relations. That is, Driver thinks that intellectual and moral virtues are the kinds of virtues they are on account of the sorts of goods they tend systematically to produce. Thus she defends a "consequentialist" account of the distinction between intellectual and moral virtues. While not insignificant, this difference need not occupy us here.[29]

A more important difference between Driver's account and my own concerns our respective understandings of the ends or goods proper to each kind of virtue. Again, on my account, intellectual virtues can be distinguished from other kinds of virtues on account of a certain *substantive* criterion (viz. the *kind* of ends at which they aim), while moral virtues can be distinguished on the basis of a relatively *formal* criterion (viz. whether the ends, whatever their intrinsic character, pertain to oneself or to another). Driver's distinction employs both of the these criteria; however, instead of viewing one kind of criterion as relevant to one kind of virtue and the other kind of criterion as relevant to the other kind of virtue, she views both kinds of criteria as relevant to each kind of virtue. Specifically, she argues that intellectual virtues are character traits that reliably produce *epistemic goods for oneself* and that moral virtues are character traits that reliably contribute to the *flourishing or well-being of others*.

As this suggests, Driver defends a strong version of the independence thesis and unqualifiedly rejects the subset thesis. On her view, the categories of intellectual and moral virtue are mutually exclusive. Though I cannot, in the space available here, give her discussion the full attention it deserves, I think we are sufficiently well-positioned to recognize some of its shortcomings. Concerning her account of intellectual virtue, we have seen that it is a mistake to think of intellectual virtues as necessarily self-regarding or egoistic. Again, it is sufficient that the traits in question be epistemically oriented, that they exhibit an intrinsic concern with a share in the epistemic goods; it matters not, relative to the status of intellectual virtue, whether the share is one's own or that of another. As to her account of moral virtue, Driver does very little to explicate her conception of human flourishing. But what she does say indicates that she does not think of human flourishing as partly constituted by a

[29] While Driver (2003: 105) offers some reasons for preferring an "externalist" to an "internalist" account of the distinction in question, these reasons do not, as far as I can tell, threaten the internalist account developed here.

possession of epistemic goods.[30] This, we have seen, is a mistake. Again, surely part of what it is to live well or to be well off has a human being is to enjoy a share in epistemic goods like true belief, knowledge, and understanding. Accordingly, while I think Driver rightly associates distinctively epistemic goods with intellectual virtue, and rightly thinks of moral virtues as necessarily others-regarding, I think she is mistaken to treat intellectual virtues as necessarily egoistic and human flourishing as void of an inherently epistemic dimension.

[30] While at points (e.g. pp. 105–6) she seems to recognize this as a possibility, I see no way avoiding the conclusion that in the final analysis she rejects it. See especially pp. 114–15.

References

Adams, Robert. 1999. *Finite and Infinite Goods* (Oxford: Oxford University Press).

——. 2006. *A Theory of Virtue* (Oxford: Oxford University Press).

Adler, Jonathan. 2004. "Reconciling Open-Mindedness and Belief," *Theory and Research in Education* 2: 127–42.

Alston, William. 1988. "The Deontological Conception of Epistemic Justification," *Philosophical Perspectives* 2: 257–99.

——. 1993. "Epistemic Desiderata," *Philosophy and Phenomenological Research* 53: 527–51.

——. 2005. *Beyond "Justification": Dimensions of Epistemic Justification* (Ithaca: Cornell University Press).

Annas, Julia. 2003. "The Structure of Virtue," in DePaul and Zagzebski (eds.): 15–33.

Anscombe, Elizabeth. 1958. "Modern Moral Philosophy," *Philosophy* 33: 1–19.

Aristotle. 2000. *Nicomachean Ethics*, trans. Roger Crisp (Cambridge: Cambridge University Press).

Axtell, Guy. 1997. "Recent Work on Virtue Epistemology," *American Philosophical Quarterly* 34: 1–26.

——. 1998. "Epistemic Virtue-Talk: The Reemergence of American Axiology," *The Journal of Speculative Philosophy* 10: 172–98.

——, ed. 2000. *Knowledge, Belief, and Character* (Lanham, MD: Rowman and Littlefield).

——. 2007. "Two for the Show: Anti-luck and Virtue Epistemologies in Consonance," *Synthese* 158: 363–83.

——. 2008. "Expanding Epistemology: A Responsibilist Approach," *Philosophical Papers* 37: 51–87.

——. 2010. "Epistemic Virtue," in Jonathan Dancy and Ernest Sosa (eds.), *A Companion to Epistemology* (Malden, MA: Blackwell): 116–17.

Baehr, Jason. 2004. "Virtue Epistemology," in James Feiser (ed.), *Internet Encyclopedia of Philosophy*, <http://www.iep.utm.edu/v/VirtueEp.htm>.

——. 2006a. "Character in Epistemology," *Philosophical Studies* 128: 479–514.

——. 2006b. "Character, Reliability, and Virtue Epistemology," *The Philosophical Quarterly* 56: 193–212.

Baehr, Jason. 2007. "On the Reliability of Moral and Intellectual Virtues," *Metaphilosophy* 38: 457–71.

——. 2008. "Four Varieties of Character-Based Virtue Epistemology," *Southern Journal of Philosophy* 46: 469–502.

——. 2009. "Evidentialism, Vice, and Virtue," *Philosophy and Phenomenological Research* 78: 545–67.

——. 2010. "Epistemic Malevolence," *Metaphilosophy* 41: 189–213.

——. Manuscript. "The Cognitive Demands of Intellectual Virtue," unpublished.

Battaly, Heather. 2006. "Teaching Intellectual Virtues," *Teaching Philosophy* 29: 191–222.

——. 2008. "Virtue Epistemology," *Philosophy Compass* 3: 639–63.

——. 2010. "Epistemic Self-Indulgence," *Metaphilosophy* 41: 214–34.

——. Forthcoming 2011. "Is Empathy a Virtue?" in Peter Goldie and Amy Coplan (eds.) *Empathy: Philosophical and Psychological Essays* (Oxford: Oxford University Press).

Biskupic, Joan. 2005. *Sandra Day O'Connor: How the First Woman on the Supreme Court Became Its Most Influential Justice* (New York: HarperCollins).

BonJour, Laurence. 1985. *The Structure of Empirical Knowledge* (Cambridge, MA: Harvard University Press).

——. 1992. "Externalism/Internalism," in Ernest Sosa and Jonathan Dancy (eds.), *A Companion to Epistemology* (Oxford: Blackwell): 132–6.

——. 1998. *In Defense of Pure Reason* (Cambridge: Cambridge University Press).

——. 2002. *Epistemology: Classic Problems and Contemporary Responses* (Lanham, MD: Rowman and Littlefield).

BonJour, Laurence, and Ernest Sosa. 2003. *Epistemic Justification: Internalism vs. Externalism, Foundations vs. Virtues* (Malden, MA: Blackwell).

Brandt, Richard. 1992. *Morality, Utilitarianism, and Rights* (Cambridge: Cambridge University Press).

Broadie, Sarah. 1991. *Ethics with Aristotle* (New York: Oxford University Press).

Chisholm, Roderick. 1989. *Theory of Knowledge*, 3rd edn. (Englewood Cliffs, NJ: Prentice-Hall, Inc.).

Code, Lorraine. 1984. "Toward a 'Responsibilist' Epistemology," *Philosophy and Phenomenological Research* 65: 29–50.

——. 1987. *Epistemic Responsibility* (Andover, NH: University Press of New England).

Conee, Earl, and Richard Feldman. 2001. "Internalism Defended," *American Philosophical Quarterly* 38: 1–18.

——. 2004. *Evidentialism: Essay in Epistemology* (Oxford: Oxford University Press).

Copp, David, and David Sobel. 2004. "Morality and Virtue: An Assessment of Some Recent Work in Virtue Ethics," *Ethics* 114: 514–54.

DePaul, Michael, and Linda Zagzebski, eds. 2003. *Intellectual Virtue: Perspectives from Ethics and Epistemology* (Oxford: Oxford University Press).

Descartes, René. 1968. *Discourse on Method and the Meditations*, trans. F. E. Sutcliffe (London: Penguin Books).
——. 1998. *Discourse on Method*, trans. Arnold Cress, 3rd edn. (Indianapolis: Hackett).
Doris, John. 1998. "Persons, Situations, and Virtue Ethics," *Nous* 32: 504–30.
——. 2002. *Lack of Character* (Cambridge: Cambridge University Press).
Douglass, Frederick. 2001. *Narrative of the Life of Frederick Douglass, an American Slave* (New Haven: Yale University Press).
Driver, Julia. 2000. "Moral and Epistemic Virtue," in Axtell (ed.): 123–34.
——. 2001. *Uneasy Virtue* (Cambridge: Cambridge University Press).
——. 2003. "The Conflation of Moral and Epistemic Virtue," *Metaphilosophy* 34: 367–83.
Edwards, Bob. 2004. *Edward R. Murrow and the Birth of Broadcast Journalism* (Hoboken, NJ: John Wiley and Sons).
Fairweather, Abrol. 2001. "Epistemic Motivation," in Fairweather and Zagzebski (eds.): 63–81.
Fairweather, Abrol, and Linda Zagzebski, eds. 2001. *Virtue Epistemology: Essays on Epistemic Virtue and Responsibility* (New York: Oxford University Press).
Feldman, Richard. 2005. "Justification is Internal," in Sosa and Steup (eds.): 270–84.
Foley, Richard. 1987. *The Theory of Epistemic Rationality* (Cambridge, MA: Harvard University Press).
——. 1993. *Working without a Net* (Oxford: Oxford University Press).
Foot, Philippa. 2002. *Virtues and Vices* (Oxford: Oxford University Press).
——. 2003. *Natural Goodness* (Oxford: Oxford University Press).
Frankfurt, Harry. 1988. *The Importance of What We Care About: Philosophical Essays* (Cambridge: Cambridge University Press).
Fricker, Miranda, 2007. *Epistemic Injustice: Power and the Ethics of Knowing* (Oxford: Oxford University Press).
Geach, Peter. 1977. *The Virtues* (Cambridge: Cambridge University Press).
Gettier, Edmund. 1963. "Is Justified True Belief Knowledge?" *Analysis* 23: 121–3.
Ginet, Carl. 2001. "Deciding to Believe," in Steup (ed.): 63–76.
Goldman, Alvin. 1981. "What Is Justified Belief?" in George Pappas (ed.), *Justification and Knowledge* (Boston: Reidel): 1–25.
——. 1992. *Liaisons: Philosophy Meets the Cognitive and Social Sciences* (Cambridge, MA: MIT Press).
——. 1998. "Reliabilism," in Edward Craig (ed.), *Routledge Encyclopedia of Philosophy*, <http://www.rep.routledge.com/article/PO44SECT1>.
——. 2001. "Internalism Exposed," in Steup (ed.): 115–33.
Greco, John. 1995. "A Second Paradox Concerning Responsibility and Luck," *Metaphilosophy* 26: 81–96.
——. 2000a. *Putting Skeptics in Their Place* (Cambridge: Cambridge University Press).

——. 2000b. "Two Kinds of Intellectual Virtue," *Philosophy and Phenomenological Research* 60: 179–84.

Greco, John. 2002. "Virtues in Epistemology," in Paul Moser (ed.), *Oxford Handbook of Epistemology* (New York: Oxford University Press): 287–315.

——. 2003. "Knowledge as Credit for True Belief," in DePaul and Zagzebski (eds.): 111–34.

——. 2005. "Justification Is Not Internal," in Sosa and Steup (eds.): 257–69.

——. 2010. *Achieving Knowledge* (Cambridge: Cambridge University Press).

Greco, John, and John Turri. 2009. "Virtue Epistemology," in Edward Zalta (ed.), *Stanford Encyclopedia of Philosophy*, <http://plato.stanford.edu/entries/epistemology-virtue/>.

Griffin, Emilie. 1982. *Turning: Reflections on the Experience of Conversion* (New York: Doubleday).

Grimm, Stephen. 2010. "Understanding," in Sven Bernecker and Duncan Pritchard (eds.), *Routledge Companion to Epistemology* (London: Routledge): 84–94.

Haack, Susan. 2000. *Manifesto of a Passionate Moderate* (Chicago: Chicago University Press).

Haddock, Adrian, Alan Millar, and Duncan Pritchard, eds. 2009. *Epistemic Value* (Oxford: Oxford University Press).

Hare, William. 1979. *Open-mindedness and Education* (Montreal: McGill-Queens University Press).

——. 1985. *In Defence of Open-Mindedness* (Montreal: McGill-Queens University Press).

Hargittai and Hargittai. 2004. *Candid Science IV, Conversations with Famous Physicists* (London: Imperial College Press).

Harman, Gilbert. 1999. "Moral Philosophy Meets Social Psychology: Virtue Ethics and the Fundamental Attribution Error," *Proceedings of the Aristotelian Society* 99: 315–31.

——. 2000. "The Nonexistence of Character Traits," *Proceedings of the Aristotelian Society* 100: 223–6.

Hookway, Christopher. 2000. "Regulating Inquiry: Virtue, Doubt, and Sentiment," in Axtell (ed.): 149–60.

——. 2001. "Epistemic *Akrasia* and Epistemic Virtue," in Fairweather and Zagzebski (eds.): 178–99.

——. 2003. "How to Be a Virtue Epistemologist," in DePaul and Zagzebski (eds.): 149–60.

Hume, David. 1977. *An Enquiry Concerning Human Understanding*, ed. Eric Steinberg (Indianapolis: Hackett).

Hurka, Thomas. 2001. *Virtue, Vice, and Value* (Oxford: Oxford University Press).

Hursthouse, Rosalind. 1995. "Applying Virtue Ethics," in Rosalind Hursthouse, Gavin Lawrence, and Warren Quinn (eds.), *Virtues and Reasons: Philippa Foot and Moral Theory* (Oxford: Oxford University Press): 57–76.

——. 1999. *On Virtue Ethics* (Oxford: Oxford University Press).

Isaacson, Walter. 2007. *Einstein: His Life and Universe* (New York: Simon and Schuster).

Kamtekar, Rachana. 2004. "Situationism and Virtue Ethics on the Content of Our Character," *Ethics* 114: 458–91.

Kant, Immanuel. 1993. *Grounding for the Metaphysics of Morals*, 3rd edn., trans. James Ellington (Indianapolis: Hackett).

Kawall, Jason. 2002. "Other-Regarding Intellectual Virtues," *Ratio* 15: 257–75.

Kornblith, Hilary. 1983. "Justified Belief and Epistemically Responsible Action," *Philosophical Review* 92: 33–48.

Kvanvig, Jonathan. 1992. *The Intellectual Virtues and the Life of the Mind* (Lanham, MD: Rowman and Littlefield).

Locke, John. 1996. *An Enquiry Concerning Human Understanding*, ed. Kenneth Winkler (Indianapolis: Hackett).

Louden, Robert. 1997. "On Some Vices of Virtue Ethics," in Statman (ed.): 180–93.

McDowell, John. 1979. "Virtue and Reason," *The Monist* 62: 331–50.

Merritt, Maria. 2000. "Virtue Ethics and Situationist Personality Psychology," *Ethical Theory and Moral Practice* 3: 365–83.

Mill, John Stuart. 1978. *On Liberty*, ed. Elizabeth Rapappport (Indianapolis: Hackett).

Miller, Christian. 2003. "Social Psychology and Virtue Ethics," *Journal of Ethics* 7: 365–92.

Miller, William Lee. 2002. *Lincoln's Virtues: An Ethical Biography* (New York: Knopf).

Montmarquet, James. 1993. *Epistemic Virtue and Doxastic Responsibility* (Lanham, MD: Rowman and Littlefield).

——. 2000. "An 'Internalist' Conception of Epistemic Virtue," in Axtell (ed.): 135–47.

Nagel, Thomas. 1979. *Mortal Questions* (New York: Oxford University Press).

Napier, Stephen. 2009. *Virtue Epistemology: Motivation and Knowledge* (New York: Continuum).

Nozick, Robert. 1981. *Philosophical Explanations* (Cambridge, MA: Harvard University Press).

Peterson, Christopher, and Martin Seligman. 2004. *Character Strengths and Virtues: A Handbook and Classification* (Oxford: Oxford University Press).

Plantinga, Alvin. 1993a. *Warrant: The Current Debate* (New York: Oxford University Press).

——. 1993b. *Warrant and Proper Function* (New York: Oxford University Press).

Plato. 1997. *The Complete Works of Plato*, ed. John M. Cooper (Indianapolis: Hackett).

Pouivet, Roger. 2010. "Moral and Epistemic Virtues: A Thomistic and Analytical Perspective," *Forum Philosophicum* 15: 1–15.

Pritchard, Duncan. 2007. "Recent Work on Epistemic Value," *American Philosophical Quarterly* 44: 85–110.

Pritchard, Duncan, Alan Millar, and Adrian Haddock. 2010. *The Nature and Value of Knowledge: Three Investigations* (Oxford: Oxford University Press).

Riggs, Wayne. 2002. "Reliability and the Value of Knowledge," *Philosophy and Phenomenological Research* 64: 79–96.

——. 2010. "Open-mindedness," *Metaphilosophy* 41: 172–88.

Roberts, Robert C. 1984. "Will Power and the Virtues," *The Philosophical Review* 93: 227–47.

Roberts, Robert C., and W. Jay Wood. 2004. "Proper Function, Emotions, and Virtues of the Intellect," *Faith and Philosophy* 21: 3–24.

——. 2007. *Intellectual Virtues: An Essay in Regulative Epistemology* (Oxford: Oxford University Press).

Rorty, Amelie. 1988. *Mind in Action: Essays in the Philosophy of Mind* (Boston: Beacon Press).

Sabini, John, and Maury Silver. 2005. "Lack of Character? Situationism Critiqued," *Ethics* 115: 535–62.

Schmitt, Frederick, and Reeza Lahroodi. 2008. "The Epistemic Value of Curiosity," *Educational Theory* 58: 125–48.

Singer, Peter. 2001. *Animal Liberation* (New York: HarperCollins).

Slote, Michael. 1992. *From Morality to Virtue* (New York: Oxford University Press).

——. 2001. *Morals from Motives* (New York: Oxford University Press).

Snow, C. P. 1958 [1934]. *The Search* (London: Penguin Books).

Snow, Nancy. 2009. *Virtue as Social Intelligence: An Empirically Grounded Theory of Virtue* (London: Routledge).

Solomon, David. 2003. "Virtue Ethics: Radical or Routine?" in DePaul and Zagzebski (eds.): 57–80.

Sosa, Ernest. 1980. "The Raft and the Pyramid: Coherence versus Foundations in the Theory of Knowledge," *Midwest Studies in Philosophy* 5: 3–25.

——. 1991. *Knowledge in Perspective* (Cambridge: Cambridge University Press).

——. 2007. *A Virtue Epistemology: Apt Belief and Reflective Knowledge* (Oxford: Oxford University Press).

Sosa, Ernest, and Matthias Steup, eds. 2005. *Contemporary Debates in Epistemology* (Malden, MA: Blackwell).

Sreenivasan, Gopal. 2002. "Errors about Errors: Virtue Theory and Trait Attribution," *Mind* 111: 47–68.

Statman, Daniel, ed. 1997. *Virtue Ethics. A Critical Reader.* (Washington, DC: Georgetown University Press).

Steup, Matthias. 1995. *An Introduction to Epistemology* (Englewood Cliffs, NJ: Prentice Hall).

——, ed. 2001. *Knowledge, Truth, and Duty* (Oxford: Oxford University Press).

Stocker, Michael. 1997. "Emotional Identification, Closeness, and Size: Some Contributions to Virtue Ethics," in Statman (ed.): 118–27.

Swank, Casey. 2000. "Epistemic Vice," in Axtell (ed.): 195–204.

Swinburne, Richard. 2001. *Epistemic Justification* (Oxford: Oxford University Press).

Wallace, James. 1978. *Virtues and Vices* (Ithaca, NY: Cornell).

White, Richard. 2008. *Radical Virtues: Moral Wisdom and the Ethics of Contemporary Life* (Lanham, MD: Rowman and Littlefield).

Williams, Bernard. 1981. *Moral Luck* (Cambridge: Cambridge University Press).

Wolf, Susan. 1982. "Moral Saints," *Journal of Philosophy* 79: 419–39.

Wood, W. Jay. 1998. *Epistemology: Becoming Intellectually Virtuous* (Downer's Grove, IL: InterVarsity Press).

Wright, Sarah. 2009. "The Proper Structure of Intellectual Virtues," *Southern Journal of Philosophy* 47: 91–112.

Zagzebski, Linda. 1994. "The Inescapability of Gettier Problems," *The Philosophical Quarterly* 44: 65–73.

——. 1996. *Virtues of the Mind* (Cambridge: Cambridge University Press).

——. 1998. "Virtue Epistemology," in Edward Craig (ed.), *Routledge Encyclopedia of Philosophy* (London: Routledge): 617–21.

——. 1999. "What Is Knowledge?" in John Greco and Ernest Sosa (eds.), *The Blackwell Guide to Epistemology* (Oxford: Blackwell): 92–116.

——. 2001. "Recovering Understanding," in Steup (ed.): 235–56.

——. 2004. *Divine Motivation Theory* (Cambridge: Cambridge University Press).

——. 2008. *Epistemology* (Belmont, CA: Wadsworth).

Index

Made in the USA
Las Vegas, NV
02 May 2022

48312420R00142